Battlegr

The French on the Somme

Battleground Series

Stamford Bridge & Hastings by Peter Marren
Wars of the Roses - Wakefield/ Towton by Philip A. Haigh
Wars of the Roses - Barnet by David Clark
Wars of the Roses - Tewkesbury by Steven Goodchild
Wars of the Roses - The Battles of St Albans by Peter Burley, Michael Elliott & Harvey Wilson
English Civil War - Naseby by Martin Marix Evans, Peter Burton and Michael Westaway
English Civil War - Marston Moor by David Clark
War of the Spanish Succession - Blenheim 1704 by James Falkner
War of the Spanish Succession - Ramillies 1706 by James Falkner
Napoleonic - Hougoumont by Julian Paget and Derek Saunders
Napoleonic - Waterloo by Andrew Uffindell and Michael Corum
Zulu War - Isandlwana by Ian Knight and Ian Castle
Zulu War - Rorkes Drift by Ian Knight and Ian Castle
Boer War - The Relief of Ladysmith by Lewis Childs
Boer War - The Siege of Ladysmith by Lewis Childs
Boer War - Kimberley by Lewis Childs

Mons by Jack Horsfall and Nigel Cave
Néry by Patrick Tackle
Retreat of I Corps 1914 by Jerry Murland
Aisne 1914 by Jerry Murland
Aisne 1918 by David Blanchard
Le Cateau by Nigel Cave and Jack Shelden
Walking the Salient by Paul Reed
Ypres - 1914 Messines by Nigel Cave and Jack Sheldon
Ypres - 1914 Menin Road by Nigel Cave and Jack Sheldon
Ypres - 1914 Langemarck by Jack Sheldon and Nigel Cave
Ypres - Sanctuary Wood and Hooge by Nigel Cave
Ypres - Hill 60 by Nigel Cave
Ypres - Messines Ridge by Peter Oldham
Ypres - Polygon Wood by Nigel Cave
Ypres - Passchendaele by Nigel Cave
Ypres - Airfields and Airmen by Mike O'Connor
Ypres - St Julien by Graham Keech
Ypres - Boesinghe by Stephen McGreal
Walking the Somme by Paul Reed
Somme - Gommecourt by Nigel Cave
Somme - Serre by Jack Horsfall & Nigel Cave
Somme - Beaumont Hamel by Nigel Cave
Somme - Thiepval by Michael Stedman
Somme - La Boisselle by Michael Stedman
Somme - Fricourt by Michael Stedman
Somme - Carnoy-Montauban by Graham Maddocks
Somme - Pozières by Graham Keech
Somme - Courcelette by Paul Reed
Somme - Boom Ravine by Trevor Pidgeon
Somme - Mametz Wood by Michael Renshaw
Somme - Delville Wood by Nigel Cave
Somme - Advance to Victory (North) 1918 by Michael Stedman
Somme - Flers by Trevor Pidgeon
Somme - Bazentin Ridge by Edward Hancock
Somme - Combles by Paul Reed
Somme - Beaucourt by Michael Renshaw
Somme - Redan Ridge by Michael Renshaw
Somme - Hamel by Peter Pedersen
Somme - Villers-Bretonneux by Peter Pedersen
Somme - Airfields and Airmen by Mike O'Connor
Airfields and Airmen of the Channel Coast by Mike O'Connor
In the Footsteps of the Red Baron by Mike O'Connor
Arras - Airfields and Airmen by Mike O'Connor
Arras - The Battle for Vimy Ridge by Jack Sheldon & Nigel Cave
Arras - Vimy Ridge by Nigel Cave
Arras - Gavrelle by Trevor Tasker and Kyle Tallett
Arras - Oppy Wood by David Bilton
Arras - Bullecourt by Graham Keech
Arras - Monchy le Preux by Colin Fox
Walking Arras by Paul Reed
Hindenburg Line by Peter Oldham
Hindenburg Line - Epehy by Bill Mitchinson
Hindenburg Line - Riqueval by Bill Mitchinson
Hindenburg Line - Villers-Plouich by Bill Mitchinson
Hindenburg Line - Cambrai Right Hook by Jack Horsfall & Nigel Cave
Hindenburg Line - Cambrai Flesquières by Jack Horsfall & Nigel Cave
Hindenburg Line - Saint Quentin by Helen McPhail and Philip Guest
Hindenburg Line - Bourlon Wood by Jack Horsfall & Nigel Cave

Cambrai - Airfields and Airmen by Mike O'Connor
Aubers Ridge by Edward Hancock
La Bassée - Neuve Chapelle by Geoffrey Bridger
Loos - Hohenzollern Redoubt by Andrew Rawson
Loos - Hill 70 by Andrew Rawson
Fromelles by Peter Pedersen
The Battle of the Lys 1918 by Phil Tomaselli
Accrington Pals Trail by William Turner
Poets at War: Wilfred Owen by Helen McPhail and Philip Guest
Poets at War: Edmund Blunden by Helen McPhail and Philip Guest
Poets at War: Graves & Sassoon by Helen McPhail and Philip Guest
Gallipoli by Nigel Steel
Gallipoli - Gully Ravine by Stephen Chambers
Gallipoli - Anzac Landing by Stephen Chambers
Gallipoli - Suvla August Offensive by Stephen Chambers
Gallipoli - Landings at Helles by Huw & Jill Rodge
Walking the Gallipoli by Stephen Chambers
Walking the Italian Front by Francis Mackay
Italy - Asiago by Francis Mackay
Verdun: Fort Douamont by Christina Holstein
Verdun: Fort Vaux by Christina Holstein
Walking Verdun by Christina Holstein
Verdun: The Left Bank by Christina Holstein
Zeebrugge & Ostend Raids 1918 by Stephen McGreal

Germans at Beaumont Hamel by Jack Sheldon
Germans at Thiepval by Jack Sheldon

SECOND WORLD WAR

Dunkirk by Patrick Wilson
Calais by Jon Cooksey
Boulogne by Jon Cooksey
Saint-Nazaire by James Dorrian
Walking D-Day by Paul Reed
Atlantic Wall - Pas de Calais by Paul Williams
Atlantic Wall - Normandy by Paul Williams
Normandy - Pegasus Bridge by Carl Shilleto
Normandy - Merville Battery by Carl Shilleto
Normandy - Utah Beach by Carl Shilleto
Normandy - Omaha Beach by Tim Kilvert-Jones
Normandy - Gold Beach by Christopher Dunphie & Garry Johnson
Normandy - Gold Beach Jig by Tim Saunders
Normandy - Juno Beach by Tim Saunders
Normandy - Sword Beach by Tim Kilvert-Jones
Normandy - Operation Bluecoat by Ian Daglish
Normandy - Operation Goodwood by Ian Daglish
Normandy - Epsom by Tim Saunders
Normandy - Hill 112 by Tim Saunders
Normandy - Mont Pinçon by Eric Hunt
Normandy - Cherbourg by Andrew Rawson
Normandy - Commandos & Rangers on D-Day by Tim Saunders
Das Reich – Drive to Normandy by Philip Vickers
Oradour by Philip Beck
Market Garden - Nijmegen by Tim Saunders
Market Garden - Hell's Highway by Tim Saunders
Market Garden - Arnhem, Oosterbeek by Frank Steer
Market Garden - Arnhem, The Bridge by Frank Steer
Market Garden - Arnhem by Tim Saunders
Rhine Crossing – US 9th Army & 17th US Airborne by Andrew Rawson
British Rhine Crossing – Operation Varsity by Tim Saunders
British Rhine Crossing – Operation Plunder by Tim Saunders
Battle of the Bulge – St Vith by Michael Tolhurst
Battle of the Bulge – Bastogne by Michael Tolhurst
Channel Islands by George Forty
Walcheren by Andrew Rawson
Remagen Bridge by Andrew Rawson
Cassino by Ian Blackwell
Anzio by Ian Blackwell
Dieppe by Tim Saunders
Fort Eben Emael by Tim Saunders
Crete – The Airborne Invasion by Tim Saunders
Malta by Paul Williams
Bruneval Raid by Paul Oldfield
Cockleshell Raid by Paul Oldfield

Battleground

The French on the Somme

*August 1914–30 June 1916:
From Serre to the River Somme*

David O'Mara

Series Editor
Nigel Cave

Pen & Sword
MILITARY

First published in Great Britain in 2018 by
Pen & Sword Military
an imprint of
Pen & Sword Books Ltd,
47 Church Street
Barnsley,
South Yorkshire, S70 2AS

Copyright © David O'Mara, 2018

ISBN 978 152672 240 9

The right of David O'Mara to be identified as Author
of this work has been asserted by him in accordance with the
Copyright, Designs and Patents Act 1988.

A CIP catalogue record for this book is
available from the British Library.

All rights reserved. No part of this book may be reproduced or
transmitted in any form or by any means, electronic or mechanical
including photocopying, recording or by any information storage and
retrieval system, without permission from the Publisher in writing.

Typeset in Times New Roman by Chic Graphics

Printed and bound in England by
CPI Group (UK) Ltd., Croydon, CR0 4YY

Pen & Sword Books Ltd incorporates the imprints of
Pen & Sword Archaeology, Atlas, Aviation, Battleground, Discovery,
Family History, History, Maritime, Military, Naval, Politics,
Railways, Select, Social History, Transport, True Crime,
Claymore Press, Frontline Books, Leo Cooper, Praetorian Press,
Remember When, Seaforth Publishing and Wharncliffe.

For a complete list of Pen & Sword titles please contact
PEN & SWORD BOOKS LIMITED
47 Church Street, Barnsley, South Yorkshire, S70 2AS, England
E-mail: enquiries@pen-and-sword.co.uk
Website: www.pen-and-sword.co.uk

Contents

Introduction vi
Introduction by Series Editor..ix
List of Maps xi
Prelude xiii
Car Tour of the 1871 Bapaume Battlefield...........................xxi

Chapter 1:   Pre-war and the 120e régiment d'infanterie at
                  Péronne 1

Chapter 2:   The German Invasion and the Northern Actions
                  of August and September 1914 8

Tour 1:   A Car Tour of the Northern Somme Actions of
                  August and September 1914 48

Chapter 3:   Final Adjustments and the Stabilisation of the
                  Line, September-October 1914 82

Chapter 4:   Hébuterne to the River Ancre 1914-15 95

Tour 2:   Hébuterne to the Ancre 1914-15 – Walking and
                  Driving Tours 116

Chapter 5:   The Ancre to the Somme 1914-15 138

Tour 3:   The Ancre to the Somme 1914-15 – Walking and
                  Driving Tour 159

Epilogue: 1916 and the Return of the French Army to the
                  Northern Sector 179

Appendices:
   1. Advice to Tourers..184
   2. Organisation of The Metropolitan Infantry 1914-16 190
   3. Organisation of the *corps du génie* 1914-16 196
   4. French Army Rank (*grade*) Structures 1914-18 200
   5. French War Graves on the Somme 202
   6. French Army Abbreviations 1914-18 208
   7. French Orders of Battle, Somme 1914-15...............................214

Acknowledgements 220
Sources and Bibliography..222
Index 228

Introduction

Out of the whole series of five books about the French Army on the Somme that I am currently working on, I must admit that this was one of the two that I was looking forward to the most. For far too many years, the great majority of books on the Somme in general, both in English and French, have paid scant attention to the events prior to the 1916 battle, devoting just a few sentences – or a couple of paragraphs at the most, summing up the events in the area over the first twelve months of the war… and that is if or when they get any mention at all.

A common omission can be found in books where the introduction includes a passage such as '…war first arrived on the Somme in September 1914…'. This is actually quite common and one that (even though it seems to forget completely the sacrifice of the thousands of *piou-pious* who were killed or wounded on the Somme battlefields of August 1914 in an action that delayed the rapidly advancing German Armies, thereby buying valuable 'breathing space' for the retreating French [and British] Armies) can be forgiven, seeing as the actions during September fighting were the ones that started the formation of the Somme battlefield as we think about it today. One serious problem with the historical understanding of the past few decades, however, is the frequency that one encounters adjectives such as 'idyllic', 'peaceful', 'quiet' and 'tranquil' to describe the pre-1916 Somme battlefield. Again, this can give a false impression of the area during the period before the British took over the line. Though there actually were short periods and locations that could probably have been described as such, those periods were certainly very short and the locations very few during the first ten or eleven months of the war (and I am quite sure that the British soldiers who inherited locations such as the Redan Ridge and the 'Glory Hole' would be hesitant in describing their sectors as 'idyllic' or 'quiet'!). One of my hopes is that this book will assist in the illustration of this point. As you might suspect by now, researching and writing this book (and the first volume in this series on *The French on the Somme – The Somme 1916: Touring the French Sector*) has actually proven to be quite therapeutic for me!

The geographical area covered in this particular book will be very familiar to many readers, many of whom will have visited most of the locations at least once. For just this reason (and also because it is about the French Army's occupation in the period before the British arrived!)

the British Army and the July-November 1916 events in these locations gets very little mention within the pages of this book. These details are easily available elsewhere, with many of the locations having individually dedicated books within other volumes of Pen and Sword's *Battleground Europe* series, for example. This book is intended to allow the visitor to revisit these familiar places and see them in a totally different light. It is not an alternate history, it is an extended history of these locations and a history that is necessary to know if the events that followed, and the battlefield itself, are to be fully understood.

On a personal note, I wish that I had had this book thirty odd years ago. I still remember as a twelve or thirteen year old on a family holiday in the early 1980s finding two French 8mm Lebel bullets (manufacture date of August 1913 if anyone is interested!) on the path leading up to Devonshire Cemetery and, with a head full of information about William Noel Hodgson, the 9/Devons on 1 July 1916 and the 1916 actions before Mametz and Fricourt from the (then) current guide and history books, wondering why I had just found two French bullets on a 'British' battlefield. Fast forward a few years and, while stepping into a ditch to get out of a squalling rainstorm on the open plain between Authuille Wood and the Thiepval Memorial in 1991, another Lebel round was found. I was far more knowledgable by that point, but it took quite a bit of work to find the information about exactly why it was there. Thus a book such as this would have been very handy for me back then.

The twenty-seven years that have passed since that day have seen hundreds, if not thousands, of books on the Great War published (or republished) but, so far as I know, nothing up to now has been specifically focussed upon the French Army's occupation during the early days on the Somme and which has led to the complete story of this famous and (dare I say it?) 'popular' battlefield never being readily available. For just that reason, my thanks must go to Nigel Cave for giving me the opportunity actually to try to do something about rectifying that matter!

A quick 'note on numerics'.

As opposed to the British (and German) Army styles of formation nomenclature, the French Army of the Great War period used Arabic numerals to denote all formations up to the 'Army' level (for example: *1e compagnie, 2e bataillon, 3e régiment, 4e brigade, 5e division, 6e corps, VII armée*). As can be seen by the example, it was only the 'Army' that was denoted in Roman numerals. (One other use of Roman numerals was in denoting a recruiting district or military region for a particular corps such as the *4e corps d'armée* hailing from the *IV corps* 'area', the *11e corps d'armée* hailing from the *XI corps* 'area', etc.)

Though it goes against the grain a little with me, it has been recommended that I adopt the 'British' style of nomenclature when mentioning such formations in order to ease the understanding of the reader who is probably more familiar with such styles. Therefore, within the pages of this book, a formation such as the *11e corps d'armée* is recorded as the *XI corps d'armée* and the *V armée* is recorded as the *Fifth Army*, etc.

Admittedly, when looking at a page that includes an Anglicised style of formation listing, I find myself getting a little confused as to what nationality a particular formation actually is. For this reason, within the pages of this book, all French formations have been *italicised* and are listed with their full title…if it is not *italicised*, then it is not French. If for no other reason, it assists me and will help to preserve my own sanity.

'What's in a name'?
It may be noticed that, in this book, the commonly accepted nick-name for the French soldier – the *poilu* – does not get a single mention in the narrative. This is intentional as, being a term popularised by the press from the spring of 1915, this is not how the French soldier was referred to during the period of the majority of actions covered here. The terms *piou-piou* – for a new, young soldier – or *pitou* were more commonly encountered at the time, with the veteran front line soldier being more likely to refer to himself as a *briscard*, a *grognard* (more archaic and becoming rarer as 1914 progressed) or, from late 1914 to early 1915, a *biffin*.

Biffin:	Rag picker (a reference to the appearance of the French front line soldier of 1914-15)
Briscard	Veteran
Grognard	Grumbler
Poilu	Hairy (as in 'tough' or 'macho')
Piou-piou	A small child (newly conscripted young soldiers)
Pitou	Similar to the above – little one

With terms of endearment such as *piou-piou* and *pitou* being in vogue for references to the soldiers of 1914, it is not difficult to understand why, especially after the battles of that year, the term *poilu* grew in popularity as 1915 progressed!

Introduction by Series Editor

This year marks the fiftieth anniversary of my first trip to the Somme battlefields, essentially a one, full day affair in the summer of 1968. I suppose that I have visited the area well over a hundred times since and have read the contents of several bookshelves about it, the books devoted entirely or in large part to the Somme and overwhelmingly to the efforts of the BEF in 1916. When the *Battleground Europe* series commenced, getting on for thirty years ago, I made the conscious decision to concentrate titles mainly on areas directly related to the 1st July 1916. In large measure this was driven by commercial decisions based on where people go and where the greatest interest lay.

At an early stage I was aware of some French involvement in the area – the French cemetery at Serre (which was in such a depressingly poor state of maintenance until some ten years ago) probably being the most notable sign of the French army's presence on the battlefield. Over time I 'found' more signs – the French burials in Ovillers British Cemetery, the few individual memorials by the roadside or in woods like Bois Francais, some of the remaining craters in the Glory Hole; I was vaguely aware of the fighting on the Somme in 1914 during the 'opening moves' (but the memory of which was swamped by even more significant fighting elsewhere, notably at Ypres); I learnt quite a bit about the fighting at Serre in June 1915. For many years the interest almost had a border – venturing up to Gommecourt but there was almost an invisible line from Carnoy to Gueudecourt (and in the early days I only went to the latter because my grandfather – who served in the 7th Leicesters – wrote about it in his diary), with even areas of great British interest, such as Morval, falling on the 'next time, maybe' list. As for venturing down to the banks of the Somme and, even more adventurously, across the river and the southern part of the battlefield, these were excursions that were prompted by an interest in the battlefields of the spring and summer of 1918.

To be fair, this state of affairs was largely dictated by the available sources. In a pre-internet world one had to work hard to lay hands on French source material. The French official history, to put it mildly, is dauntingly long, unattractively presented and could be considered as one of the world's great cures for insomnia. French produced guide books to the battlefield were, effectively, restricted to one – ie the Michelin guide. This has its uses but is getting on for a hundred years old, full of (then) useful tips such as the fact that a given road was impassable. French regimental histories were out of reach unless you could get to the reading room in the IWM. To be honest, except notably for the sterling efforts of *Souvenir Français*, the French seemed to have no interest in the Somme until the *Historial* was established in the 1980s.

However, within a few years of having my own car, I knew that the French had been on the Somme in numbers, that there were significant actions at places such as Serre, Redan Ridge, Ovillers, the Glory Hole and Point 110: but any sort of detail was very limited. My interest remained almost exclusively BEF (but, over time, to an increasing extent German army) – centred; the French efforts were acknowledged but in a rather cerebral, academic way – significant, they were there, they have to be considered, the contribution was considerable – but …

The problem was: who was there who could write authoritatively about the French? Who could write about the French army who understood its ethos and its structures? Who had a rounded view of its activity on the Somme? For this series, who could relate all of this accurately to the ground? Who could place the French contribution on the Somme and yet also have an understanding of the German army and, as it arrived on the scene, the BEF?

Having found the ideal author, Dave O'Mara, through the Great War Forum, the next issue was to persuade the British visitor that the French side of the Somme campaigns were integral to understanding the BEF's activities there: the British did not arrive to a sector where nothing had happened; nor did they fight the Somme alone. Thus the decision was made to start the process off with an overview *Battleground* book on the French contribution to the Somme Offensive of 1916 and then to develop the theme with four others – two devoted to events prior to 1 July 1916 (with the River Somme providing a convenient boundary) and two to a more detailed look at the Offensive itself.

It is my earnest hope that these accessible books will encourage more anglophone visitors to broaden their touring: not only to appreciate the enormous efforts of the French but also become aware of the impact of her army on the ground and how this impinged on the activity of the BEF when it came here from the summer of 1915 onwards.

Nigel Cave
Ratcliffe College, May 2018.

List of Maps

Movements of the German 1. *Armee* and the French *Armée du Nord* in Picardy, November 1870 to January 1871 xvii
French and German troop dispositions, 2 January 1871 xx
Locations of Artillery Batteries, 2 and 3 January 1871 xxi
Battle of Bapaume Tour Route xxiv
V Army Situation during the afternoon of 27 August 1914 10
The Action at Moislains, 28 August 1914 19
The *338e, 263e* and *278e régiments d'infanterie* at Sailly-Saillisel and Le Transloy, 28 August 1914 21
The 'Race to the Sea'. (*British Official History*) 27
Situation on the evening of 27 August 1914 29
The attacks of 26–29 September 1914 31
The 26th (and 28th) Reserve Divisions on the Albert-Bapaume Road, 27–28 September 1914 37
Tour 1: Tour of the Northern Somme Actions of August and September 1914: Route Overview 48
Tour 1: Tour of the Northern Somme Actions of August and September 1914: Points 1 to 6 49
Tour 1: Tour of the Northern Somme Actions of August and September 1914: Points 7 to 9 55
Tour 1: Tour of the Northern Somme Actions of August and September 1914: Points 9 to 14 59
Tour 1: Tour of the Northern Somme Actions of August and September 1914: points 14 to 24 65
Tour 1: Tour of the Northern Somme Actions of August and September 1914: Points 24 to 28 77
French situation, 30 September 1914 83
Attack of the 1. Garde-Infanterie-Division, 3 October 1914 87
Situation between Beaumont Hamel and Thiepval, 6 October 1914 ...91
French situation, 8 October 1914 95
Touvent (Toutvent) Farm trench map extract, 7 June 1915 100
Second Army Operations at Toutvent, 7–13 June 1915 103
Toutvent detail, illustrating first day gains near the farm 105
Tour 2: Hébuterne to the Ancre 1914–15 117
Cote 143 and the Serre road, June 1915 127
La Boisselle, November 1914 to March 1915 141

26. Reserve-Division front, October 1914-March 1915 and the
attacks of 17 and 24 December 1914 142
Ovillers and La Boisselle December 1914 to January 1915 147
Mine craters at La Boisselle, March 1915 151
The La Boisselle crater field, June 1916...153
Trench map of the 'Tambour' crater field, May 1915.......................154
Trench map of the Carnoy crater field, May 1916.............................155
French and German trenches from Fargny on the River Somme
to the south of Maricourt Wood, April 1915 157
Tour 3: The Ancre to the Somme 1914–15. Walking and Driving
Tour: Points 1 to 7 159
Tour 3: The Ancre to the Somme 1914-15. Walking and Driving
Tour: Points 8 to 19 167
Cote 110 to the Mametz crater field, 1916..172
Cote 110 and the crater field 173
Cote 110, March 1915..175
Regimental order of *XX corps d'armée,* 1 July 1916........................183

* * *

Dedication

This book is dedicated to the memory of my mum and sister, Joyce and Janice O'Mara who, I think, would, have both been extremely proud to have seen this in print. Also, to my brother-in-law, Ian Lavin, who would probably have thought that it was 'alright'!
'*...Ce n'est qu'un au revoir...*'

Prelude

The German Invasion of 1870 and the Battle of Bapaume 1871

Otto von Bismarck, Prussia's Minister President since 1862, skilfully manipulated the political opportunities that arose through the rise of Prussia and the decline (and the potential threat) of the French Empire. He managed to arrange the scenario so that it would appear that it was France who would be the aggressor in any future conflict with the rapidly strengthening Prussian state. Thus, Prussia and her North German Confederation allies were joined by the southern German states in a coalition unified against France. To the dismay of France, Austria-Hungary and Denmark (who had both suffered defeats at the hands of Prussia within the previous six years) remained strictly neutral; as did Russia. The latter had been the recipient of Prussian assistance in various internal affairs since 1863 and had, in 1868, made an agreement to send 300,000 troops into Galicia should Austria declare war on Prussia. Italy remained aloof: the government was pro-French, but public opinion was bitterly opposed to this view due to the presence of a French garrison in Rome. France, not many years previously the leading power in continental Europe, was now dangerously isolated.

Following the French declaration of war on 19 July 1870, it was decided to act fast and strike first before German mobilisation could be completed and her forces deployed. On 31 July, a move was made by the newly formed *Armée du Rhin* to the Saar, with the intention of crossing the German border and capturing Saarbrücken, which had been identified by reconnaissance as being only lightly held by the Prussian 16. Division. On 2 August, the 72,046 soldiers from *II* and *III corps d'armée*, under the command of *général de division* Charles Auguste Frossard and *Maréchal* François Achille Bazaine respectively, of the *Armée du Rhin* crossed the German border. In the first skirmishes of the war, in which eighty-six Frenchmen and eighty-three Prussians were casualties, Füsilier-Regiment Nr. 40 (32. Infanterie-Brigade, 16. Division) was driven from Saarbrücken in what was hailed as a great victory in some French reports. However, unbeknown to the French at that time, three German armies had massed to the south east, north and north east, with

Kronprinz Friedrich Wilhelm's 120,000 strong Third Army located a mere thirty kilometres from Saarbrücken.

Upon learning of the Prussian Third Army's location, it was decided to withdraw the French 'Victors of Saarbrücken' on 4 August and move into defensive positions along the Franco-German border between Forbach and Spicheren. On that same day, however, German forces advanced and the first set-piece battle of the war took place at Wissembourg, when *général* Abel Douay's greatly outnumbered *2e division d'infanterie* of *I corps d'armée* was surprised and, after an extremely tenacious fight, during which *général* Douay himself was killed in action, defeated by the Prussian V and XI Armeekorps and elements of the Bavarian II.Korps (Third Army).

Following the victory at Wissembourg, the First Army was in action at Spicheren and the Third Army clashed with the main body of the *Armée du Rhin* at Wörth on 6 August, with both battles proving to be decisive, if costly, victories for the Germans, forcing the *Armée du Rhin* to withdraw towards the defences of Metz in order to regroup.

At around the same time, the French had reassessed the situation and orders were issued for the entire army to actually fall back on Châlons-sur-Marne, thereby placing the entire army between the advancing Germans and Paris. However, in the aftermath of the Battle of Wörth, part of the army was retreating in a different direction to the other, increasing the gap between the two elements. With the army split in such a way, it became necessary to use the two concentration points in the hope that, once concentrated at Metz, the *Armée du Rhin* could continue its retreat, through Verdun, to Châlons and, with the influx of new recruits called up since the start of the war, form a new army, the *Armée de Châlons*.

Twice in the following days, however, the retreat path of the *Armée du Rhin* was blocked. An indecisive action at Mars-le-Tour on 16 August and a defeat at Gravelotte two days later cost the army around 30,000 men and forced a retreat into the defences of Metz where, between 19 August and 27 October 1870, the entire army was held up and then besieged. During the siege and its associated actions such as the Battle of Noisseville, 38,000 men from the *Armée du Rhin* died and 142,000 went into captivity following the capitulation of Metz. Other than a few parts of the Army located at Bitche and at Strasbourg, the *Armée du Rhin* now ceased to exist.

While Metz was still under siege, the *Armée de Châlons*, under the personal command of Napoleon III, had marched north eastwards towards the Belgian border before turning direction and sweeping southwards in an attempt to reach and relieve Bazaine's beleaguered *Armée du Rhin*. However, the Prussians, under the command of Field Marshal Count

Helmuth von Moltke, took advantage of this move to perform a pincer manoeuvre around the French forces. He left the Prussian First and Second Armies besieging Metz (except for three corps who were detached from these to form the Fourth Army; known as the 'Army of the Meuse' under the Crown Prince of Saxony). With this new Fourth Army and the Third Army, Moltke marched northwards and caught up with the French at Beaumont on 30 August, where a costly defeat was inflicted upon *V corps d'armée* by the Prussian IV, XI and I Bavarian Armeekorps. The *Armée de Châlons* was now forced to fall back on Sedan – intending to rest and resupply under the comparative protection of the fortress before moving on.

The *Armée de Châlons* deployed the *I corps d'armée* to check the German advance on 1 September but, unable to retreat due to exhaustion and unable to put up much of a fight due to being desperately short of ammunition, was immediately isolated by the converging German armies. Moltke divided his forces into three groups: one to detain the French where they were; another to race forward and catch them if they retreated; and a third (the smallest force) to hold the river bank. The *Army of Châlons*, unable to move, was trapped between the German forces and their own defensive boundary, the hills and fortress to their rear. Forced to either capitulate or stand and fight, a breakout was at first attempted during the early hours; but this move had already been anticipated and was located at the same place that the Prussians had decided to launch an attack of their own. Desperate fighting continued for the remainder of the day as the French tenaciously defended positions and attempted attacks in a forlorn hope of a break out. However, intense artillery bombardments and Prussian, Saxon and Bavarian assaults from all directions pushed the *Armée de Châlons* back into the Bois de la Garenne, where they were surrounded. Three desperate attacks on the nearby village of Floing, where the Prussian XI Corps was concentrated, were carried out by the French cavalry under the command of *général de division* Jean Auguste Margueritte in order to attempt to force an escape route, but these amounted to nothing more than adding to the casualty list. Margueritte himself was mortally wounded whilst personally leading the first charge – he would succumb to his injuries in Beuraing, in Belgium, five days later.

Realising that all was lost, Napoleon III called off all further French attacks during the evening of 1 September and the following day raised the white flag and surrendered himself and the entire *Armée de Châlons* to Moltke. After suffering nearly 18,000 killed and wounded during the battle, a further 104,000 French soldiers marched into captivity on 2 September.

With the capture of Napoleon, the Prussians were left without an opposing government willing to make a quick peace. Two days after the news hit Paris, the French Second Empire collapsed in a bloodless uprising and the Third Republic was born. A provisional government, known as the *Gouvernement de la défense nationale* and headed by *général* Trochu, was set up and, on 6 September 1870, after a declaration by Jules Favre that France would not 'yield an inch of its territory nor a stone of its fortresses', renewed the declaration of war and began a drive for recruits from all over France to form a new republican army.

Following this declaration, orders were issued to the German armies to march on Paris where, relatively unopposed, they began to besiege the city on 19 September. On 7 October, the Minister of the Interior for the new government, Léon Gambetta, escaped from Paris via hot air balloon (the *Armand-Barbès*) and, after arriving at Tours, became the government's Minister of the Interior and of War. One of his first tasks was the organisation and raising of several 'new' regional armies and he was personally instrumental in the raising of one of these himself – the *Armée de la Loire*. This would see action into 1871 and, following reorganisation after defeats at Luigny and Orléans in December 1870, was split into two armies – the (second) *Armée de la Loire* and the *Armée de l'Est*. Two other armies were also formed around the same time – the relatively small *Armée des Vosges*, under the command of Giuseppe Garibaldi and comprising many foreign volunteers (especially Italians), and the *Armée du Nord*.

The *Armée du Nord*

After the Deputy Commissioner for Nord-Pas de Calais and Picardy, Achille Testelin, granted powers to the former commander of the Arras fortified zone, *général* Jean-Joseph Farre, to raise an army in the north of France, it was found that the units manning the defences of the area were in such disarray that it would take weeks to reorganise them. However, following the appointment of *général de division* Charles-Denis Bourbaki as commander of the northern military region on 22 October, rapid progress was made and the *Armée du Nord* was finally created on 18 November 1870, with Bourbaki as its commander. Bourbaki's tenure was extremely brief, however, as on the following day he was transferred to the *Armée de la Loire* to assist in the formation of the *Armée de l'Est*, intended to relieve the siege of Belfort; Farre temporarily replaced him in the role until he, in turn, was replaced by *général de division* Louis Faidherbe on 5 December.

Only partially ready to enter the field on 24 November 1870, the *Armée du Nord* first moved into action following the threat on Amiens

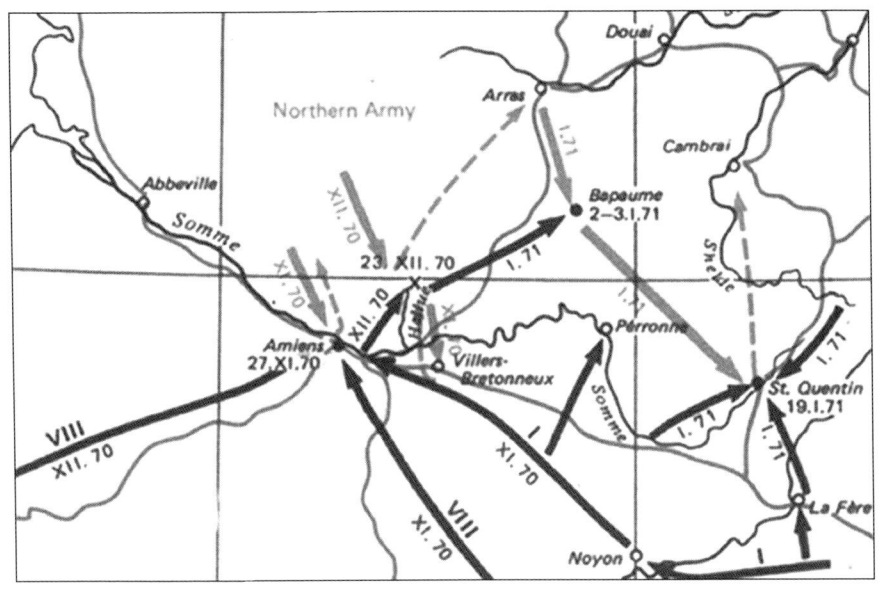

Movements of the German *1. Armee* and the French *Armée du Nord* in Picardy, November 1870 to January 1871.

by General Hans Edwin von Manteuffel's First Army and suffered nearly 2,400 casualties around Dury, Boves, Gentelles and Villers-Bretonneux on 27 November during the Battle of Amiens. Though defeated in this first engagement, an organised withdrawal back to the fortified stronghold of Arras was conducted, thereby depriving the Germans of a conclusive victory and allowing the *Armée du Nord* to regroup and strengthen. The lightly defended town of Amiens fell the following day and Manteuffel began preparations for a move on Péronne in order to capture and hold the Somme river line as a precaution to prevent any attempted relief on Paris from the north.

Into December, the *Armée du Nord* sat in the relative safety of the fortified zone north of Bapaume and Doullens undergoing training, re-equipping and receiving reinforcements. Within a fortnight the army had doubled in size and prepared to re-enter the field under its new commander (Faidherbe).

The commander of the *Armée du Nord*, and the 'Hero of Bapaume', *général* Louis Léon César Faidherbe 1818-1889. He, and his *Armée du Nord*, are also commemorated for their actions during the Battle of the Hallue in December 1870 by a memorial column – the *colonne Faidherbe* – at Pont-Noyelles, Somme.

Part of the Army moved on St Quentin and another captured Ham on 9 December (but evacuated it on the 18th), while the remainder concentrated on the area to the west of Amiens and into Normandy following the fall of Rouen on 4 December. On 17 December Faidherbe established his headquarters at Corbie and placed his army across the Somme to attempt to prevent the Germans from performing the expected advance on Péronne; but, three days later, a strong German patrol skirmished at Querrieu and forced a slight withdrawal of the French units in the area. This patrol was followed by a general attack on 23 December and, after the indecisive Battle of the Hallue (Pont Noyelles), a French retreat ensued on 24 December towards Bapaume. Only after reconnaisance patrols reported that the majority of French forces had departed did the German advance begin on 25 December, reaching Péronne – and beginning the siege on the town – on 27 December. On the same day the Germans entered Bapaume and the *Armée du Nord* took up positions around Fampoux, Vitry and Corbehem, with support positions at Arras and Douai.

Following on from the start of the bombardment of Péronne on 28 December, Faidherbe decided to attempt to break through the siege lines and save the town. He was afraid that should the town fall the German defensive position along the Somme would be complete and thus block the route of any advance, preventing any relief of the siege of Paris from the north.

On 31 December, the *Armée du Nord* began to move, once again, southwards. Faidherbe's plans met with the disapproval of his commanders, assembled at Beaurains on 1 January 1871:

'Gentlemen, you may well be correct, but to leave Péronne without any attempting of rescue when I have, under my command, at least 30,000 men and 90 pieces of artillery, certainly incurs dishonour. I prefer to be beaten in the line of duty than disgraced by a charge of pusillanimity. We leave in the morning to advance on the enemy. You will, tonight, receive the marching orders.'

The Battle of Bapaume

Under a grey sky, and in freezing conditions, the *Armée du Nord* closed upon Bapaume from the north and north west on 2 January. During the morning, *division Derroja* (*XXII corps d'armée*), under the command of *général de division* Alphonse-Théodore Lecointe, which formed the right flank of the advance, moved through Bucquoy and Puisieux. This forced the withdrawal of the German 3rd Cavalry Division, along with three

The Battle of Bapaume 1871: the attack of *division Derroja* on Thilloy, 3 January 1871.

infantry companies, before his troops swung left and took Achiet-le-Petit without firing a shot. In the centre, *division du Bessol* (same corps) arrived, unopposed, at Ablainzevelle at mid-day and, to their left, *division Payen* (*XXIII corps d'armée*) advanced via Boisleux-au-Mont to Ervillers, where a brigade, under *colonel* Hippolyte Michelet, was detached to Behagnies. Confidently advancing in three columns on Behagnies, Michelet's central column was surprised by a withering fire from the Prussian defenders of the village when the first houses were reached and was forced to withdraw in some disarray. After regrouping, a more cautious advance was made, by-passing Behagnies and taking Sapignies before moving into Behagnies from the south. Hit by grapeshot from Prussian artillery and charged by cavalry, Michelet's brigade was pushed out of Behagnies by early afternoon and returned to Ervillers – leaving 250 of their number as prisoners of war in Behagnies. Michelet's badly hit brigade was replaced in Ervillers by that of *colonel* Delagrange. A further division – a *Garde nationale mobile* division, *division Robin* (*XXIII corps d'armée*) – failed to arrive on time as a consequence of getting lost around Croisilles during the move south.

At 5pm on 2 January the advance stopped for the night behind Biefvillers-lès-Bapaume and Grévillers. Faidherbe set up his headquarters

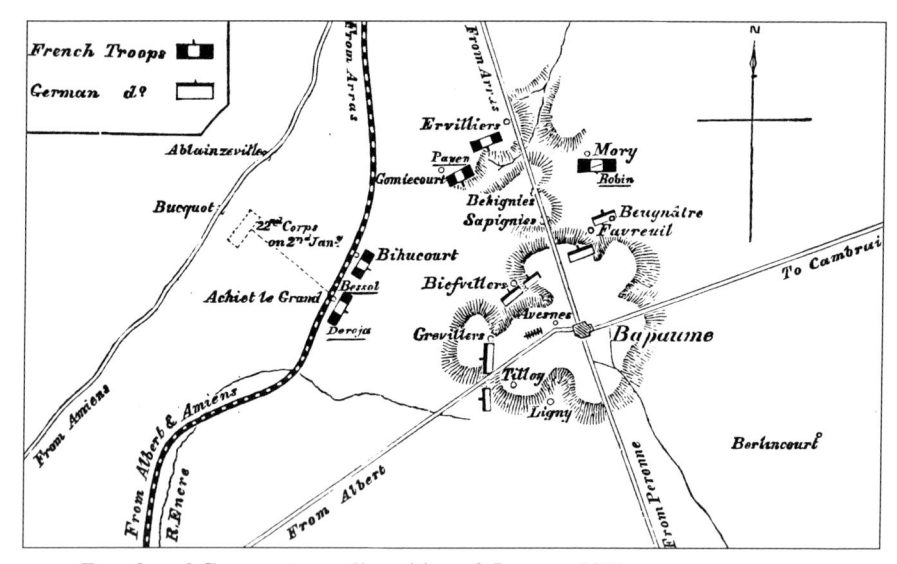

French and German troop dispositions, 2 January 1871.

at Achiet-le-Grand while the German defenders, under the command of General August Karl Friedrich Christian von Goeben, began to prepare their defences.

With the Prussian 15. Infanterie-division gathered in Bapaume, von Goeben began to set up defences along the line between Grévillers, Biefvillers-lès-Bapaume, Favreuil and Beugnâtre at 7pm. An infantry battalion, four cavalry squadrons and an artillery battery moved into Pys and further troops took over Combles and Bertincourt to form a reserve. Furthermore, von Goeben ordered General Christof von Barnekow to release three infantry battalions and four artillery batteries of the 16. Infanterie-division from the siege of Péronne and make them available as support at Sailly-Saillisel. These troops arrived in position by 9am the following morning.

On the bitterly cold (-18°c) morning of 3 January 1871, Faidherbe issued his orders for the attack to begin. *XXIII corps d'armée* was to advance south on Bapaume, with *division Payen* advancing directly down the Arras-Bapaume road from Ervillers and through Béhagnies and Sapignies (both abandoned by the Germans during the night); *division Robin* was to advance through Mory to Beugnâtre before turning to attempt to take Favreuil. In the *XXII corps d'armée* area, *division du Bessol* was to advance from Bihucourt to directly assault Biefvillers-lès-Bapaume and *division Derroja* was to move from Achiet-le-Petit to attack Grévillers.

The attack began during the morning as *division Payen* took Béhagnies and Sapignies without firing a single shot before advancing on the strongly held village of Favreuil, which was under bombardment on two sides. *Division Robin*, to the east of here and on the extreme left wing of the attack, moved on Beugnâtre but failed to enter the village and, instead, offered flank protection to *Payen's* division. Very stubbornly held, considerable resistance was encountered from the German held villages, especially at Biefvillers-lès-Bapaume, which held out against several frontal assaults by *division du Bessol* and only fell after it was outflanked by *du Bessol* on the left with the assistance of *division Derroja* on the right after *Derroja* had captured Grévillers.

By now, Biefvillers-lès-Bapaume and the road leading to Avesnes was littered with dead and wounded Prussians as *division du Bessol* continued the advance on this latter village and, under heavy fire from German artillery accumulated on the Bapaume-Albert road, moved its artillery forward to give support. After a short while the French artillery managed

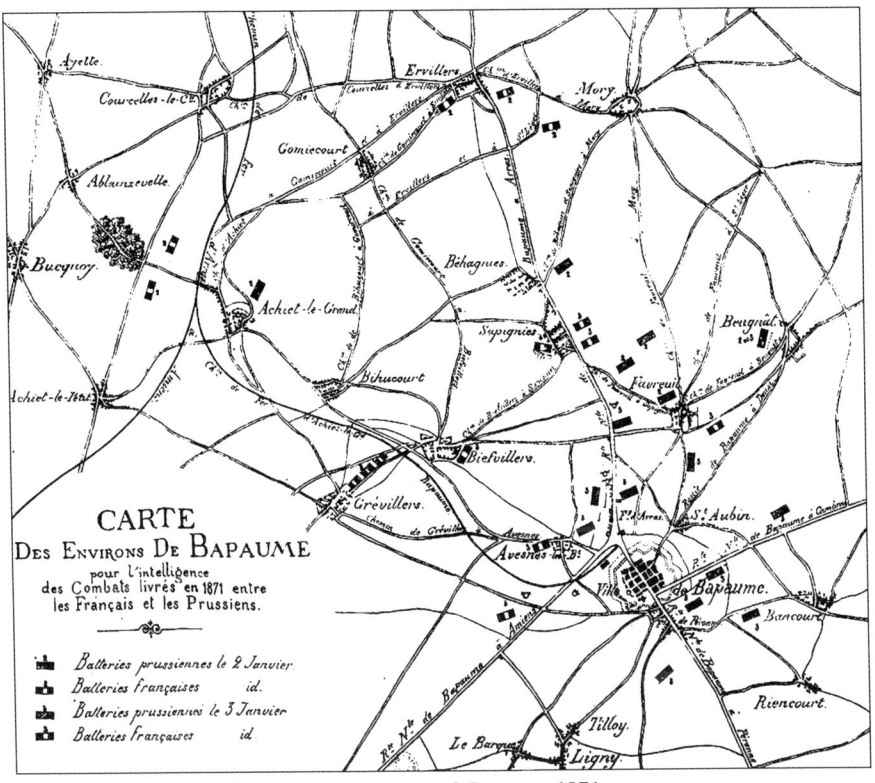

Locations of Artillery Batteries, 2 and 3 January 1871.

to suppress these batteries and a general advance was made on Bapaume, with Avesnes being taken in a single rush from two directions by *divisions Derroja* and *du Bessol* and a column from *du Bessol* assaulting (without success) the Faubourg d'Arras in Bapaume itself.

In 1847 most of Bapaume's ancient ramparts had been dismantled and the ditches filled in; however, a very large and irregular esplanade presented a serious obstacle to the French attackers, who were exposed to fire from the walls and loopholed houses. Artillery would be needed to destroy the positions where the German defenders were positioned, but Faidherbe could not bring himself to order this destruction of a French town, particularly as he was not convinced of the necessity of actually taking Bapaume. He preferred to attempt to flank the town. As the town was approached from the north and west, it was reported that the Germans had moved into the twin villages of Ligny and Thilloy on the French right wing and that a column, with artillery, was advancing up the Albert road. This necessitated immediate action and a brigade of *division Derroja*, under the command of *colonel* Pittié, was sent south east from Grévillers to capture Thilloy, which fell (and was held) only after a fierce house to house fight. Similarly, on the left flank, Favreuil fell to *division Payen*, who moved on to St Aubin before being pushed back beyond Favreuil as reinforcements from the Prussian Hohenzollernsches Füsilier Regiment Nr. 40 (16. Division), sent up from Péronne, arrived and launched a furious counter-attack.

During the afternoon, *division Robin* was replaced by two battalions from *division Payen* for a further attack on the wing. Supported by artillery located on the Arras road and bolstered by a battalion of *voltigeurs mobilisés*, the German barricades and positions on the flank were all overcome, sending the defenders into full retreat. Favreuil was recaptured and several German counter attacks on both flanks were successfully repulsed into the evening. By nightfall, the French had been successful along the whole line. Skirmishing continued at Ligny into the night but, by the early hours of the next morning, the German withdrawal from the whole area had begun.

Faidherbe wished to billet his troops in the newly captured villages for a few days to rest and recover but, with them so choked with dead and wounded and the fact that they were so near to the huge German army at Amiens that a German counter-attack could be imminent, this was not possible and he decided to move his troops on, without rest, at 4am on 4 January. The Battle of Bapaume – a rare tactical victory for the French – was over. Losses within the *Armée du Nord* amounted to 183 killed, 1,136 wounded and over 800 missing, with *division Payen* the worst hit. German casualties amounted to just over 1,100.

Aftermath

Although a pause in the bombardment of Péronne occurred at around the same time as the Battle of Bapaume, the failure of Faidherbe to press the attack allowed the siege to continue. In fact, General von Barnekow was within just two hours of calling off the siege to assist von Goeben when the advance stalled. The town capitulated on 10 January 1871. The *Armée du Nord* gradually marched to the anticipated safety of St Quentin in order to regroup, rearm and prepare for further moves in an attempt to relieve Paris. It was not unmolested – small actions took place during its march, such as the *affaire de Pozières*, during which, amongst other buildings in the area, the Gribauval farmhouse at what would become known as the *Îlot* at La Boisselle received extensive damage, the *combat de Masniéres* on 15 January and the *combat de Vermand* on 18 January. However, the defeat of the *Armée de la Loire* at Le Mans on 11 – 12 January and defeats for the *Armée de l'Est*, forcing it away from Paris and towards the Swiss border (they had also failed in their mission to relieve Belfort), made the relief of Paris by Faidherbe seem an extremely unlikely event.

To snuff out even the slimmest of chances, von Goeben's First Army shadowed the *Armée du Nord* to St Quentin where, at 8am on 19 January (a day after King Wilhelm I of Prussia was proclaimed as Kaiser Wilhelm I of a unified Germany in the Hall of Mirrors at Versailles), it launched an assault on the south and west of the town. The French were decisively beaten: 3,500 Frenchmen were killed or wounded and 9,000 went into captivity. The remainder scattered, making their way northwards, where the survivors were billeted in Cambrai, Douai, Valenciennes, Arras and Lille. Rapidly reorganised, the Army received reinforcements of several thousand newly trained *mobilots* and, by the end of January, it was almost up to the same strength that it was prior to St Quentin. However, with Paris still under siege and the population starving, an armistice was arranged that came into effect at midnight on 27/28 January, with a suspension of hostilities that was to be in force until the 19th, but then extended to 26th February, during which period neither side could restart hostilities. The war had, effectively, ended and the *Armée du Nord*, which saw no further action after St Quentin, served on as fortress garrison units until its disbandment on 7 March 1871.

Car Tour
of the 1871 Bapaume Battlefield

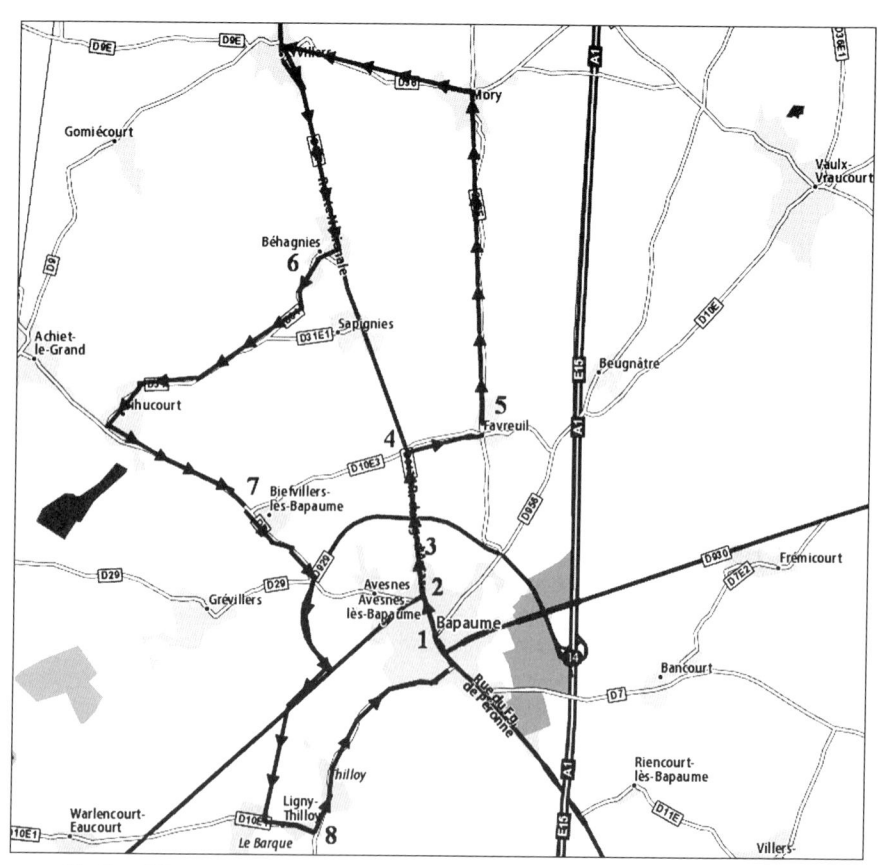

Battle of Bapaume Tour Route.

Begin the tour on the square in front of the town hall in the centre of of **Bapaume**. Here, you will see the **statue of *général de division* Louis Faidherbe (1)** – the commander of the *Armée du Nord* – standing on its original, shrapnel scarred, pedestal. Sculpted by Louis Noël, it was originally dedicated on 27 September 1891 but was removed by the German Army on 29 September 1916 to melt down for war *matériel*. The (1916-18) battle damaged pedestal remained empty for thirteen years until the statue was recast, using the original plans, by Louis Noël's son in law, Jules Déchin, and replaced on the pedestal on 18 August 1929. The statue was moved a few metres from its original location following the redevelopment of the town square in 1997. Note, also, the memorial on the town hall wall to politicians Albert Taillandier and Raoul Briquet, who were both killed by the detonation of a booby trap mine left by the withdrawing German army in the Mairie on 25 March 1917. The town hall also contains a couple of well-known paintings by Charles Édouard Armand-Dumaresq and Charles Desavary depicting the battle at Bapaume.

The remains of the original statue commemorating Faidherbe and the Battle of Bapaume as it appeared in 1917.

*Leave Bapaume via the rue d'Arras (signposted Arras and Cambrai) which leads, after 430 metres, to the **Faubourg d'Arras**.*

The road junction here (direction Amiens – near the Carrefour supermarket) was the location of the **action of the column from *division du Bessol*** (**2**) that almost broke through the German lines into the town.

Continue on the Arras road for a further 430 metres. On the right can be seen **Bapaume's town cemetery** (**3**).

In the left hand side of the cemetery, and about half way in, is a **monument and cross** commemorating the Battle of Bapaume, the base of which contains a listing of the regiments and battalions of the *Armée du Nord*. The monument was erected over a mass grave containing the remains of 186 soldiers who fell in the battle. Towards the back wall of the cemetery there is the, unusually well maintained, **grave of Leutnant Siegmund**

The monument in Bapaume cemetery erected over the grave of 186 unnamed fallen from the Battle of Bapaume as it appeared in the 1910s.

Rebuilt following its partial destruction during the Great War, the monument as it appears today.

Oden of Rheinische Feldartillerie-Regiment Nr. 8 (8. Artillerie-Brigade, VIII.Armee-Korps). Born in Kassel in 1847, he was killed in action near Bapaume just three days short of his twenty-fourth birthday on 3 January 1871.

Continue on the Arras road (D917), driving straight ahead at the roundabout, for 1.1 kilometres. At the crossroads with the Biefvillers/ Favreuil road, stop.

On the left hand side of the road, you cannot fail to notice the **major 1870-71 Memorial dedicated to the fallen of the Battle of Bapaume (4)**. In the same plot there is a memorial stone (erected by the French) to Philipp Oskar Becker, from Leipzig, of the Husaren-Regiment König Wilhelm I (1. Rheinisches) Nr.7 part of 15. Kavallerie-Brigade, 15. Division, who was killed in action here on 3 January 1871. The monument is located on the actual front line of 3 January (running along the Biefvillers – Favreuil road to your front) and offers superb views of the 1871 battlefield and the attacks of *divisions du Bessol* and *Payen*.

A Hessian artilleryman serving in a Prussian regiment, the individual grave of 23 year old Leutnant Oden in Bapaume cemetery.

The main monument commemorating the Battle of Bapaume, which possibly also marks the location of a post-battle burial pit.

Turn right at the crossroads (direction Favreuil) and travel the 900 metres to that village, following the German front line that ran along this road. To your left, towards the road upon which you are travelling, attacked the Marine Infantry from Division Payen. In **Favreuil** *– heavily shelled and fought over twice on 3 January – take the first road to the left (the D36E4, rue de Mory) for 300 metres. Turn right onto the rue du Cimetière*

Early battlefield tourism? German officers pose for a photograph at the 1870-71 monument in 1915.

(directly towards the village church) and continue on this road, to the left of the church, for 400 metres.

At the end of the road is the village **communal cemetery (5)**. There is in it a monument dedicated to the memory of the soldiers who died on 3 January 1871. Under the monument lie the remains of nine German and twenty-eight French soldiers who died on 3 January 1871.

Return the way you came, back to the D36E4 (rue de Mory) and turn right towards Mory. To the left of this road, on 3 January 1871, advanced division Payen and, to the right, division Robin. In the centre of Mory (after 3.65 kilometres), turn left towards Ervillers, which is reached after a further 2.4 kilometres. In Ervillers (the concentration area of division Payen), turn left onto the D917 (direction Bapaume) and continue southwards – following the exact direction of assault of Michelet's column on 2 January and that of division Payen, as a whole, on 3 January – for 2.1 kilometres. At this point, turn right onto the D31 to visit Béhagnies. Follow the D31 for 400 metres into the centre of Béhagnies and stop at the church.

Here, at the scene of vicious skirmishing on the 2 January 1871, is the **village war memorial (6)**. Commemorating the fallen from the village who died in the two world wars, the memorial was built on top of an **1871 mass grave** and marks the final resting place of sixty-seven French soldiers and three Prussians who died here on 2-3 January 1871. A commemorative plaque detailing this was recently (2003) fixed to the memorial.

Continue along the D31 for 3.37 kilometres to Bihucourt and turn left onto the D7 – following the route of the attack of division du Bessol – to reach Biefvillers-lès-Bapaume after a further 1.9 kilometres.

Part of the main German defensive line north and north west of Bapaume, Biefvillers-lès-Bapaume was heavily fought over on the morning of 3 January 1871, eventually being captured by the *division du Bessol* at bayonet point after much house to house fighting.

The village war memorial at Béhagnies that marks the mass grave of seventy soldiers from the 1871 battle.

Before entering the village, turn left onto the D10E3 (rue de Favreuil), signposted 'Biefvillers-lès-Bapaume – centre'. After eighty metres (just past the buildings and hedgerow on the left), there is a stone calvary on the left that doubles as the **village war memorial (7)**.

This memorial dates from 1894, though it had to be replaced after 1918 and (obviously) the 1914-18 names were a later addition, and was renovated in 1992. Commemorating the Battle of Bapaume, it was placed on the site of an old quarry which, following the battle in 1871, was used as a **mass grave** and contains the remains of 290 French (and German) dead from the following units (although only French units are listed): *Fusiliers Marins; 2e, 18e et 20e bataillons de chasseurs à pied; 33e, 48e, 65e, 75e et 91e régiments de ligne; 44e régiment de mobiles (Garde); 91e régiment de mobiles (Pas-de-Calais); 12e et 15e régiments d'artillerie.*

Return to the D7 and follow this road in the direction of Bapaume. Travel straight on (third exit) at the new roundabout, 500 metres beyond which was the German second defensive line of 3 January. Contnue for 2.35 kilometres in the direction of the attack of du Bessol after the German forward line at Biefvillers had been breached. Once the road junction (near the supermarket we passed at the beginning of this tour) is reached, turn sharp right onto the D929 (rue d'Albert), signposted Ligny-Thilloy.

Continue down the D929 for 2.1 kilometres before turning left at a rather odd road junction towards Ligny-Thilloy. Take the right hand road (the C2, signposted Ligny-Thilloy/Hameau de la Baue) and travel a kilometre to the village. As you travel along this road, to your right was the German flank defensive line at the start of the battle and, to your left, the main battle ground in this area (between the two visible villages) during the afternoon and into the evening of 3 January.

At the crossroads in Ligny-Thilloy, turn left onto the D10E1 (rue de Miraumont) for 850 metres. At the junction with the calvary, turn right onto the D10 (signposted Flers/Longueval). On your left, after 320 metres, is the **village cemetery (8)** that contains a memorial dedicated to the 'Brave French soldiers who died gloriously on the field of battle, 2-3 January 1871'.

The 1871 mass grave and village war memorial at Biefvillers-lès-Bapaume.

Turn around at this cemetery and return back up the D10. Travelling towards Bapaume, the small village of Thilloy, where the final skirmishes of the Battle of Bapaume took place well into the night of 3/4 January 1871, is reached after 700 metres. A further two kilometres on the road leads into the Faubourg de Péronne suburb of southern Bapaume; a left turn onto the D917 will bring you, after 400 metres, to the **statue of général de division** **Louis Faidherbe** and the start (and end) point of this tour.

End of Tour

GPS Waypoints, Battle of Bapaume Tour

1 – 50° 6'13.28"N, 2°50'58.67"E
2 – 50° 6'26.59"N, 2°50'50.83"E
3 – 50° 6'41.41"N, 2°50'49.03"E
4 – 50° 7'18.34"N, 2°50'39.64"E
5 – 50° 7'35.58"N, 2°51'43.50"E
6 – 50° 8'28.39"N, 2°49'47.54"E
7 – 50° 6'57.37"N, 2°49'12.36"E
8 – 50° 4'51.77"N, 2°49'50.33"E

Chapter One

Pre-war and the *120e régiment d'infanterie* at Péronne

Once the payment of reparations imposed by the Treaty of Frankfurt was completed, leading to the final withdrawal of German troops from French soil in north eastern France in 1873, it was hoped that a return to normality could begin. The world wide financial 'Long Depression' that began in 1873 did not have as much of an effect in France as elsewhere as, due to government measures intended to raise funds for the reparation repayments, a system of deliberate deflation was already in operation. However, in 1882, the Union Générale bank failed, which prompted the French to withdraw three million pounds from the Bank of England, triggering a collapse in French stock prices and launching the country into an almost decade long depression. This 'Paris Bourse Crash of 1882' became France's worst economic crisis since the ending of the Napoleonic Wars in 1815.

With the Somme and southern Pas-de-Calais being a mainly agricultural area, however, the effects outside of the major towns were minimal. The rebuilding of Péronne – where over 600 buildings had been destroyed or seriously damaged during the siege – was completed within a few years. A railway and station on the main Paris – Cambrai line was constructed, a bicycle factory opened and the river port of Péronne became a hub of activity for the transport of flour, agricultural products and phosphates – quarried locally in quarries that would become major defensive positions during the Battle of the Somme in 1916. As a sign of its prosperity during a nationally challenging time, the population of Péronne increased by almost a fifth between the conclusion of the Franco-German War and the birth of the new century. Bapaume on the other hand, though it had similarly benefited from the construction of branch line connecting the town to Achiet-le-Grand (on the main Paris-Lille railway) during the months following the end of the war in 1871, was more reliant on the local market and saw no major growth during this period.

Militarily, seemingly unaffected by the economic crises (though, later, rocked by political scandal), huge sums of money were allocated to the reform of the French army and to the building of border defences such as Séré de Riviere's *barrière de fer*. A gradual militarisation of the population, based on the German system, was introduced in July 1872. Under a selective ballot, twenty year old recruits were required to serve for five years in the active army followed by a further four, five and six years in the reserve, the territorial and territorial reserve respectively (a total of twenty years). A change in July 1889 saw the active army commitment drop to three years but reserve and territorial service increase, so that the total commitment amounted to twenty five years; a further reshuffle of reserve service occured in July 1892. On 21 March 1905, the ballot system of conscription was abandoned and every nineteen year old Frenchman became eligible for national service from his twentieth birthday. The active army commitment was also dropped to two years, but with eleven in the reserve, six in the territorials and a further six in the territorial reserve. A final change was implemented on 7 August 1913 as a consequence of fears regarding the potential size of the army should mobilisation be necessary. It involved an increase in full time service back to three years, achieved immediately by the early mobilisation of the *classe* of 1913, a drop in reserve service to ten years but with an increase to eleven years service in each of the territorials and territorial reserve, making a total commitment to military service of twenty-eight years.

The mobilisation *classe* of each soldier usually (though not always) corresponded to the year in which he celebrated his twentieth birthday. In other words, the *classe* of 1909 would, in the main, have been born in 1889, the *classe* of 1914, in 1894, etc. Following registration at his local *mairie,* the recruit was usually called into full time service locally during the autumn intake following his twentieth birthday. There were a number of reasons why service could be deferred to a later time, including a failure to make the grade medically (this would be followed by a periodic re-assessment in the years following), being engaged in higher education, being employed in a job in which military service could prove detrimental, or an older sibling being still in service. Medical failure in which it would seem that an improvement would be unlikely could lead to a lesser service in the *service auxiliaire*, which provided ancilliary services to the military. Annually, approximately 250,000 young men, representing about 33% of any given *classe* year, were conscripted into full time military service during their correct intake. A further 18% entered service at other times due to voluntary enlistment or deferred service. Due to this system, a very rapid mobilisation of an *Armée active* of approximately 1.7 million trained soldiers from all walks of life could be achieved at any given time.

Each infantry regiment was allocated a home garrison and recruited almost exclusively from the districts around the vicinity of this garrison

The mobilisation of the Class of 1912 at *Caserne Foy*, Péronne. In percentage terms, this particular class year would be the hardest hit during the Great War years, with nearly one out of every three listed as a casualty.

('technical' units such as artillery and engineers were slightly more varied) and, because of the nature of the French conscription, whole groups of young men from any given area would enlist into the same regiments at these local depot towns at the same time. Groups of classmates, workers in the same factories and farm hands from the same fields would, if they were of the same or similar age, have served together during their compulsory service, with their older (and younger) siblings, friends and colleagues serving alongside them during their reserve and territorial service. At the outbreak of war in 1914, they would have been mobilised together and, in the case of many thousands, died together in the early blood lettings of August 1914.

For the majority of young men resident in the area covered by this book, the particular garrison was Péronne. Its barracks, named in honour of a locally born Napoleonic era general, *général* Maximilien Sébastien Foy, born at Ham, Somme in 1775, was home to the *120e régiment d'infanterie* and shared a depot with the *16e régiment d'infanterie territoriale* at the château de Péronne.

Originally formed as part of Napoleon's *Grande Armée* in the Peninsular War, the *120e régiment d'infanterie de Ligne*, as it was then designated, was created in 1808. Fighting in Spain from 1808 to 1813, the regiment gained the battle honours 'Rio Seco 1808', 'Santander 1809'

The *120e régiment d'infanterie* parading in Péronne prior to embarking on the annual exercises of 1912.

and 'Arapiles 1812'; it also took part in actions at Burgos (1808), Vitoria (1813) and Pamplona (1813)) before being pushed into France. It then fought at Bidassoa, Bayonne and Orthez in 1813, earning the battle honour 'Toulouse 1814' in its final battle.

Dissolved following the conclusion of the War of the Sixth Coalition in 1814, the *120e* did not exist again until the proclamation of the Third Republic following the fall of the French Empire after Sedan in 1870. During the reorganisation of the armies of the new republic, the remains of several units were amalgamated to form the 'scratch' *20e* and the *35e régiments de marche* within the besieged walls of Paris. On 30 October 1870, the *35e régiment de marche* became the *135e régiment d'infanterie de ligne* and then, just two days later, incorporated the *20e régiment de marche* into its ranks, being renamed to the *120e régiment d'infanterie de ligne* and attached to *XIV corps d'armée* in the process. Transferred to *XXIII corps d'armée, 2e Armée de Paris* on 7 November and then, finally, to *I corps d'armée, 2e Armée de Paris* on 5 December 1870, the regiment, in its various guises, took part in the attempted breakout actions at Le Bourget (October 1870), Villiers (December 1870 – during which, the intriguingly named *capitaine* Conor O'Kelly, in command of *1ᵉ compagnie* of the *1ᵉ bataillon*, was hospitalised, La Malmaison and Buzenval (January 1871).

Placed into abeyance on 1 April 1871, the regiment was reactivated on 4 April 1872 and, on 5 October, moved its depot to Péronne under the command of the regimental second in command, *lieutenant-colonel* Armand O'Neill (who would remain here in this role until he was promoted to *colonel* and given command of the *12e régiment d'infanterie de ligne* in 1877). At this point, the main body of the regiment was based at Sedan but, from 1876, the battalions began to rotate through barracks at Sedan, Montmédy and Péronne with major exercises taking place throughout the 1870s and 1880s in the areas of Péronne, Chaulnes and Nesles. In 1882, in line with the rest of the army, the regimental title was adjusted slightly and the 'line' designation was dropped. From now on, the regimental title was simply *120e régiment d'infanterie* and, in 1883, Péronne became the main recruitment depot for the whole regiment with something like 85% of the annual intake being from the areas over which the Battles of the Somme would later be fought.

The regiment would remain at Péronne (but with a battalion located at St Denis) until October 1913, when it moved to Stenay, on the Meuse. The depot, however, remained and it was at Péronne that the reservists of the regiment mobilised in August 1914, with some of them incorporated into the newly formed reserve regiment – the *320e régiment d'infanterie*.

As part of the *4e division d'infanterie*, the *120e régiment d'infanterie* was in action as early as 10 August 1914 between Mangiennes and Pillon before being moved into Belgium, to play a role in the offensive actions

The *120e régiment d'infanterie* during exercises between Péronne and Chaulnes circa 1910. In the fields where these war games were conducted, real battles would take place within the next few years.

of the Battle of the Ardennes (part of the Battles of the Frontiers), north west of Virton. On 22 August, the regiment suffered some 896 casualties (573 of which were confirmed as killed or missing), including twenty-one officers killed in action during attacks towards Bellefontaine before taking part in the Allied retreat of 1914 and the Battle of the Marne that turned the tide.

Following the Marne, the *120e* occupied various sectors of the Argonne and was engaged in several offensives into 1915 (sustaining a further 1,400 casualties between the end of September 1914 and January 1915) before engaging in the lengthy First Battle of Champagne where, in two months, another 1,700 casualties were endured. A 'quieter' period followed in the Wöevre sector from April 1915, but the regiment was, once again, thrust into major offensive action during the Second Battle of Champagne in September and October; a further 700 men were added to the casualty list.

A period of rest and the occupation of a quiet sector followed in early 1916, along with the arrival of a sizable number of much needed reinforcements – just in time for a stint in the Souville and Douaumont sectors at Verdun and the loss of another 700 soldiers during April. June saw an occupation of the Oise sector but, between August and October, the regiment went 'home' when it served in the Belloy and Estrées sectors during the Battle of the Somme. By this point of the war, however, the 'local' aspect of the regiment had long gone and, after taking nearly 6,000 casualties since the mobilisation of August 1914, there were not many men left in the *120e* to whom the fields and villages around where they were now serving was familiar territory. By now, like the majority of other French infantry regiments by this stage, the *120e* was simply just another regiment made up mainly of conscripts from all over France; a great many of the local boys lay in the soil of Belgium, the Champagne and the Meuse, with others recovering from injuries or invalided to locations throughout France. Most were unable to return home – if their homes were still standing – as their towns or villages were in the war zone or behind German lines.

In 1917, the *120e* fought in the Nivelle Offensive in the vicinity of Berry au Bac in April (following which, in late May and early June, small scale mutinous activities took place within the ranks) before, again, serving at Verdun and St Mihiel between July and February 1918. The regiment took part in the bloody actions of the Second Battle of Verdun between August and September 1917. 1918 saw action during the retreat to the Ourq, the Second Battle of the Marne and in the Champagne, before advancing through Lorraine where, near Bois Blâmont, the *120e régiment d'infanterie*'s war ended.

During the war, the regiment gained three more battle honours – 'La Marne 1914', 'Verdun 1916' and 'Champagne 1915-18' – and was awarded the *Croix de guerre* with two palms. Thirty-two officers and soldiers also received individual awards of the *Légion d'honneur* for actions during the war and 446 *medailles militaire* were awarded. Although specific figures are unavailable, between them the *120e* and *320e régiment d'infanterie* suffered approximately 14,000 casualties during the Great War.

In 1923 the regiment was, yet again, disbanded and its honours and traditions passed to the *155e régiment d'infanterie* and then, following the dissolution of that regiment too, to the *94e régiment d'infanterie*. However, with the onset of another war, the *120e* was reformed on 8 September 1939 and, as part of the *71e division d'infanterie*, was attached as a reinforcement to the *136e régiment d'infanterie de forteresse* manning the Maginot Line at Mouzon in the *secteur fortifié de Montmédy*. In April 1940, it transferred as part of a reserve division to the vicinity of Machault in the Ardennes and was hit badly during the breakthrough at Sedan, forcing a retreat towards Verdun. On 31 May 1940, the *71e division d'infanterie* ceased to exist and its units were restructured, becoming the *59e division légère d'infanterie*. Within this new division the remains of the *120e régiment d'infanterie* were amalgamated with the remnants of the *205e* and *246e régiments d'infanterie* to form a new *83e régiment d'infanterie*. Born in war 132 years previously, the *120e régiment d'infanterie* – the regiment of Péronne for forty of its seventy-five years of active service – was no more. Memorials to its Great War service can be found on the entrance of the château de Péronne and on the road to Verdun just outside Stenay.

The memorial to the *regiments de Péronne* on the wall of their regimental depot, Péronne Château – now home to the *Historial de la Grande Guerre* museum.

Chapter Two

The German Invasion of 1914 and the actions on the northern Somme

Following on from the general mobilisation of French forces on 1 August 1914 and the actual declaration of war on 3 August, several small scale skirmishes took place at various locations along the Franco-German border. In fact, the first French and German casualties of the war had actually occurred just east of Joncherey, near the Swiss border, on 2 August, the day before the formal declaration of war and several hours after the first shots were exchanged. The casualties were the result of skirmishes between French *douaniers* and German infantry, some six miles to the north, when, as one of eleven border incursions of that day, a German cavalry patrol of the Jäger Regt-zu-Pferd Nr. 5 clashed with an outpost manned by the *6ᵉ companie*, *2ᵉ bataillon* of the *44ᵉ régiment d'infanterie* that left two dead, one wounded and three prisoners. *Caporal* Jules-André Peugeot and Leutnant Albert Otto Walter Mayer have the dubious distinction of being the first combat deaths on the Western Front and the first combat deaths of the whole war for France and Germany respectively. [As an interesting footnote: one of the possibilities for the last French combat death of the war was Auguste-Joseph Renault, *6ᵉ companie*, *2ᵉ bataillon* of the *411ᵉ régiment d'infanterie*, who was killed in action at Robechies at about 10.57am on 11 November 1918. It is at least strange that both the first and last shared their names with major French car manufacturers.]

Actions in these areas were fully expected and, indeed, the major part of the French plans for action in the case of war – Plan XVII (the final draft of which was issued in May 1914) – stated that it was *chef d'État-Major des Armées' (général* Joseph Joffre) intention to advance, with all available forces, into an attack on the German armies. This was to develop into two main operations: one, on the right between the wooded area of the Vosges and the Moselle below Toul; and the other, on the left, north of a line between Verdun and Metz, with the two operations being closely connected by forces operating on the Hauts de Meuse and in the Woëvre. What was not expected was the German Aufmarsch II deployment plan, which concentrated a considerable number of troops on the Belgo-German border, intended to launch an offensive into Belgium and forcing a decisive battle with the French army beyond the fortified Franco-German border. With the Somme not featuring in any of the French war plans, as it was totally inconceivable to the French high command that war would ever reach the region, it was a very lightly defended area in August 1914.

After the Germans began the invasion of Belgium on 4 August 1914, their successes soon made it apparant that the Somme country would soon become an unexpected – and (relatively) lightly defended – entry point into France. Consequently, Joffre made an alteration to the French plans by diverting troops that were originally intended for the French offensive in Alsace and Lorraine that had been, tentatively, begun on 5 August before gathering pace a couple of days later, and ordered a *Fifth Army* advance into mid and southern Belgium on 14 August in an attempt to counter this threat.

With both sides suffering massive casualties throughout the Battles of the Frontiers in the Ardennes, Lorraine and Alsace – leaving the *First* to the *Fourth Armées* heavily engaged on the 120 mile wide battlefield between Sarrebourg and Bouillon – the *Fifth Army* advanced, unmolested, into central Belgium and concentrated on a twenty-five mile front that was centred on Charleroi. Linked with the British Expeditionary Force on their left flank, they were thrust into battle with the German Second and Third Armies on 21 August while the BEF came up against the First Army at Mons two days later.

Northern actions and the '*bataille de Péronne*', 27-28 August 1914
The allies were forced into a general retreat after the Battles of Charleroi and Mons; with the evacuation of Lille on 24 August, it soon became apparent that Amiens was possibly under threat from the German First Army as it pursued the BEF and the French *Fifth Army* back into France. Several thinly held defensive lines were hastily formed to the north of the Somme but only six divisions (plus 25,000 troops from the evacuated Lille garrison) could be spared to hold the seventy mile line from Douai to Béthune and from Aire to the sea.

On 25 August, the German II Korps advanced westwards to the vicinity of Cambrai, where, after being stopped temporarily in a holding action by French territorial divisions, consisting of 'elderly' – but, in many cases, experienced – soldiers aged between 35 and 41, they continued to advance the following day. (The Brritish were engaged in the Battle of Le Cateau on the 26th.) The unattached territorial divisions of the *groupe d'Amade* were ordered to move south west to Combles and Péronne to become part of the *VIe Armée* but continued to retreat westwards, covered by their *84e division d'infanterie territoriale*, who followed closely behind from Cambrai, through Bourlon and towards Moeuvres in a move that, though potentially strengthening the situation to the north, left Péronne dangerously exposed.

After a brief cavalry action between the *3e division de cavalerie* and the German III Korps at Roisel that resulted in the town being left open for IV Korps to completely capture it the following day, German cavalry patrols approached and entered Péronne on 27 August 1914. On this same day, to the north, the *61e* and *62e divisions d'infanterie* of *groupe d'Ebener*, divisions made up of reservists aged between 24 and 34 that were originally intended to be part of the Paris garrison but were ordered forward to the area south and east of Arras began to move to the vicinity of Bapaume. They were amongst the six divisions holding the line to the English Channel.

Approaching from a roughly south easterly direction to the south of Bapaume during the early hours of 27 August, the leading elements of the *61e division d'infanterie*, following several small skirmishes with roving patrols of Uhlans during the advance to Bapaume, were intending to congregate between Beulencourt and the railway line south of Ginchy before extending towards Combles. The *62e division d'infanterie*, after

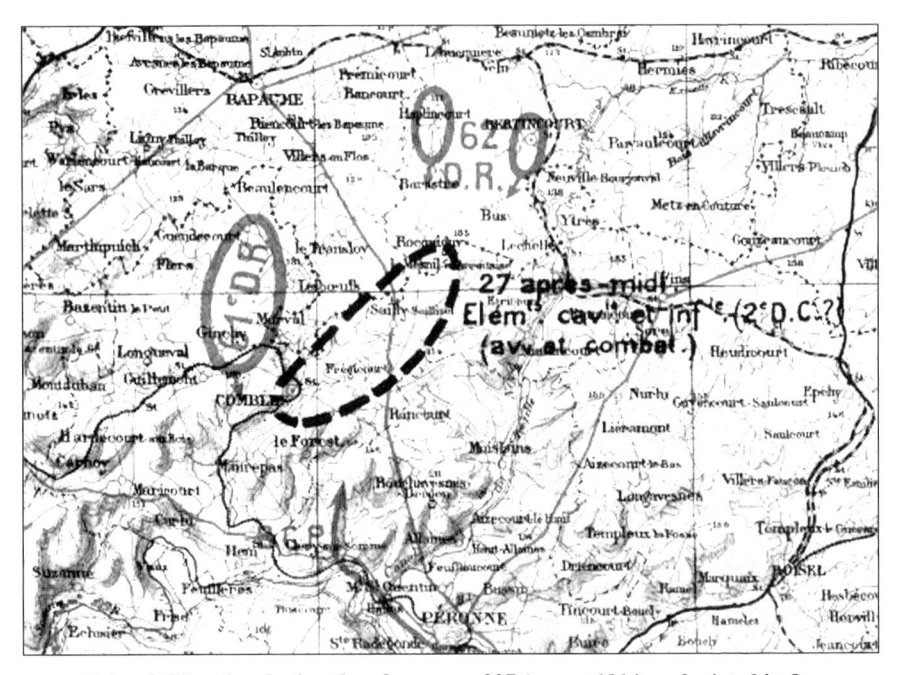

V Armée **Situation during the afternoon of 27 August 1914, as depicted in** *Les Armées Françaises dans la Grande Guerre.*

Though taken on a training exercise, this image illustrates the massed rank assaults that resulted in such high casualties throughout the late summer and early autumn of 1914.

moving overnight from the area of Arleux to the east of Arras and forming up in two formations at Haplincourt and Bertincourt, intended to advance southwards through Barastre and Bus and head towards the main Bapaume-Péronne road at Sailly-Saillisel. In the south, a provisional *division de cavalerie* under the command of *général* Cornulier-Luciniere (made up from surviving, functional, elements of *général* Sordet's *I corps de cavalerie*) moved westwards along the northern bank of the River Somme from the western outskirts of Péronne to Cléry-sur-Somme. There they headed north towards Le Forest, intending, but ultimately failing, to join with the *62e division d'infanterie* in the vicinity of Sailly-Saillisel and assisting in blocking any German advance through this area.

The area of the *61e division d'infanterie*:
With the exact whereabouts of the advancing Germans unknown to the French, the *61e division d'infanterie* moved into their sector to the west of the *62e division d'infanterie* and south of Bapaume. Their left flank, guarded by the *264e régiment d'infanterie* holding the road between Ginchy and Longueval, would remain unmolested as yet but, to their immediate east, the *265e régiment d'infanterie* opened fire on an Uhlan patrol near Ginchy before launching an attack on Combles.

Led by the *5ᵉ bataillon*, the attack was conducted, according to the regimental history, 'as if on an exercise' as the dead and wounded fell

11

under German rifle and artillery fire in the open fields between Ginchy and Bois des Bouleaux, protecting the north western approach to Combles. Though badly wounded himself, *sergent-major* Lalauze continued to encourage his men and direct the assault for as long as his voice could be heard, thus gaining himself the first award of the *medaille militaire* for the regiment during the war. C*hef-de-bataillon* Marcel Commailleau, at the head of the three leading companies (the *17e, 18e and 19e*) with drawn sword and pistol in hand, led his men through and around the woodland and into the outskirts of Combles itself – the first of three actions over the coming days for which he would eventually be awarded the *Légion d'honneur*. At this point Commailleau called a pause in the assault, pulled back slightly, and waited for supporting artillery to bombard the village before relaunching the attack. Only light resistance was encountered due to the artillery and, with darkness approaching, Combles soon fell into the hands of the *265e régiment d'infanterie* after a two hour long battle. A fruitless search for Germans amongst the houses and streets, aided by some of the inhabitants who had remained, continued until 11pm. Orders were then received to return towards Ginchy because of events elsewhere on the battlefield. A restless night was spent in the village and the nearby sugar refinery at Waterlot Farm.

To the north of the *265e*, the *316e régiment d'infanterie* who, now attached to the *Groupe d'Amade,* moved southwards independently of the other regiments of the *61e division d'infanterie* in their march towards the forming up point at Ginchy. Throughout the day they could hear the gunfire coming from the actions taking place in the villages near to their location. At nightfall on 27 August it was decided to stop at Flers and Lesboeufs rather than risk stumbling into enemy columns in the dark. From the still burning ruins of neighbouring Morval, French soldiers from the *262e régiment d'infanterie*, fresh from the action there during the day, moved towards Lesboeufs and German troops came into contact with the *316e* in the fields to the south of the village, triggering a very confused action towards Combles in the near darkness. By 10pm everything was quiet and the men of the *316e* who were not already there were ordered to proceed to Flers and await further orders. A very uncomfortable, but short, night was then spent in the densely crowded streets of Flers.

The *262e régiment d'infanterie* had left Arras at midnight on 26/27 August with orders to proceed to Lesboeufs and Morval. Ten hours into the march, enemy detachments were reported in front of and to the left of the column, pursuing elements of the *28e régiment d'infanterie territoriale* of the *84e division d'infanterie territoriale*, who had been retreating since their rearguard actions at Cambrai. At 11am, the regiment was ordered to move into Beugnâtre as brigade reserve in preparation for an attack, along with the other two regiments of *122e brigade d'infanterie* (*219e régiment d'infanterie* and the *318e régiment d'infanterie*), at Beugny (which in fact was deserted) and Frémicourt. However, by 1.30pm the action was over without the *262e* becoming actively involved and the march continued.

After passing through Beaulencourt, the *6e bataillon* left the column via a dirt road just before it reached Le Transloy while the remainder pushed south towards Sailly-Saillisel, where it was intended to billet for the night along with battalions from the *318e régiment d'infanterie* and *219e régiment d'infanterie*. At 4.30pm, the vanguard of the *5e bataillon* entered the village from the north but, soon after a warning from the parish priest that many of the buildings housed German ambushers, came under heavy machine gun and rifle fire. In immediate response, *chef de bataillon* Clément Baju gave orders for an assault and the companies, led by some exceptional officers, threw themselves upon the enemy. One company, led by (according to the regimental history) the 'wonderful' *lieutenant* Alexandre Souabaut, even attacked to the accompaniment of Breton folk songs.

Pushing through Sailly-Saillisel, its southern edge was eventually captured and, despite heavy enemy fire, a foothold was obtained in the chateau gardens. However, a massive German counter-attack (during which the Germans outnumbered the French in a ratio of six to one) pushed into the western side of the village and a fierce hand to hand melee

The rue de Péronne at Sailly-Saillisel before the war, illustrating the close proximity of the houses that would be fought through – house to house – several times throughout the first eight weeks of the war.

ensued in which all resemblance of order within the French units collapsed and the command was given to withdraw. The brigade commander, the regimental commander, the battalion commander, all of the captains and a dozen lieutenants were all killed. Non-commissioned officers took over the roles of the dead officers and a gradual, fighting withdrawal was conducted back to Le Transloy, where the final stragglers arrived at 7:30pm. The three surviving officers then rallied the remains of the *5e bataillon* and withdrew, out of the action to Bapaume.

The aftermath of the action at Sailly-Saillisel on 27 August was later described in a letter dated 2 December 1917 by the parish priest, l'Abbé ME Finot, who had earlier tried to warn the advancing *5e bataillon* of the danger:

> 'Unfortunately, I could not personally take care of the dead. The German *médecin-major* had left 550 wounded completely in my charge without bread, without meat, without doctors and without drugs. For three days I had to find them something to eat and to find some linen – in a word all that was necessary for these poor wretches. The arrival, after three days, of two French doctors (immediately taken prisoner) and of some ladies of the Red Cross relieved me for ten days. I did not know where to give help. I was not allowed to visit the wounded, as that had just been reserved for the German major. In addition, I had to respond at all times to the multiple injunctions of the leaders to stop the disorder as much as possible. Ah! the sad days! We had more to suffer because the first Germans were really ferocious. They also died of hunger and thirst. They had taken three days to come from Brussels to Sailly, according to the major who slept at my house. I had recommended to the people of my parish that they bury the dead and bring me their medals (identity discs). They did it during the first days; but after that the bodies were so decomposed that they did not dare do it. They were also terrorised by the Germans, who made them walk at revolver point. There were, in this battle, about 4,000 French and Germans killed....'

While the *5e bataillon* was in action at Sailly-Saillisel, the *6e bataillon, 262e régiment d'infanterie*, who had left the column near Le Transloy about half an hour before the fighting started, came under rifle fire from the wheat fields to the east of Morval. A company was despatched, with fixed bayonets, into the field ; but there was no further incident until they came under heavy artillery fire, forcing them to advance in small groups towards Morval. Managing to enter the village with very little loss, the

Germans were driven out at bayonet point and, with the village in flames to their rear, continued skirmishing up the road towards Lesboeufs, where an artillery battery and a battalion of the *316e régiment d'infanterie* assisted in driving the Germans back. To ease the congestion in the villages of area, the night was spent in bivouacs along a line of trees west of Flers.

The second regiment of the *122e brigade d'infanterie*, the *219e régiment d'infanterie,* arrived at Beugnâtre at 9am on 27 August, where the brigade commander, *colonel* Schmitz, was made aware of the proximity of German troops in the villages of Beugny and Frémicourt. He decided to halt the southwards march in order to eliminate this threat.

Attacking from the north west with two battalions of the *219e* and, on their right, two battalions of the *318e régiment d'infanterie*, the village was found to be deserted when entered. However, upon the French occupation of it, German guns located at Delsaux Farm, half a mile to the south, immediately began a bombardment on the village. With no retaliatory fire from the French guns, a full frontal and successful, assault on these guns was needed. At 1.30pm, *lieutenant-colonel* Stuhl, the regimental commander, realised that there was no contact with the companies to the right of his position and, finding himself alone with the *5e bataillon* plus the *22e compagnie* of the *6e bataillon* and a battalion of the *318e régiment d'infanterie,* decided to withdraw to Bapaume after receiving an erroneous message from a cyclist that the remainder of *122e brigade d'infanterie* had returned there. Upon reaching Bapaume, he learned that they were actually some two to three hours away in the direction of Rancourt and Sailly-Saillisel and, after a short meal break (his men had not eaten since the previous day), set off to join up with the remainder of his brigade. At 5.45pm, a cyclist informed the small column that the *122e brigade d'infanterie* was in action at Sailly-Saillisel and so a diversion was made towards Lesboeufs and Morval with the intention of approaching Sailly-Saillisel from the west and hitting the German counter-attackers there from behind. However, during this manoeuvre it was learned of the northwards retirement and so Stuhl decided to billet his men in Martinpuich, where they arrived at 11pm.

Stuhl was unaware that *colonel* Schmitz had given the order to break off the attack on Beugny and Frémicourt and continue the march towards Combles at 1pm. On Stuhl's flank at Beugny, *chef de bataillon* Germain, the commander of *6e Bataillon*, had received this order and left the battle to continue the march with his *21e, 23*, and *24e companies* forming the head of the brigade's column. Upon arrival at Sailly-Saillisel, Germain learned of German troop movements to the south of the village in the direction of Combles and was ordered to proceed through the village as

A typical scene in villages such as Sailly-Saillisel following close contact actions in the streets at the end of August 1914.

quickly as possible in order to engage these units. With fighting taking place to their rear and sides as they fought to progress down the main street, the *6e bataillon* managed to get as far as the château before they were stopped and subjected to a heavy artillery bombardment. Two companies were located in the château itself and the third in the grounds behind as they desperately fought against the German counter-attacks until the order was finally received, after several hours, to withdraw to the north.

Withdrawing to Le Transloy, *chef de bataillon* Germain learned of the disappearance of *colonel* Schmitz during the battle, along with that of the senior officers of the *262e* and *318e régiments d'infanterie* and, after realising that he was the most senior surviving officer, assumed command of *122e brigade d'infanterie*, who he ordered back to Arras.

The final regiment of the *122e brigade d'infanterie*, the *318e régiment d'infanterie*, was the easternmost regiment in the *61e division d'infanterie* column on 27 August, with the *5e bataillon* holding the flank. Located at Vaulx-Vraucourt at 10am, the battalion commander, *chef de bataillon* Collardet, was tasked with supplying flank protection during the attack on Beugny. After a short exchange of fire with a German cavalry patrol

16

near Bois de Maricourt, the evacuated village was entered, athough this was not without loss. *Lieutenant* Brousmiche's *20e compagnie* was hit quite badly and suffered significant casualties during the German bombardment before moving on to Bancourt at 4pm, where barricades were erected in case of German counter attack. The night passed quietly. While the *5e bataillon* was at Beugny, the regimental staff and the *6e bataillon* continued on their southwards journey, marching with the *122e brigade d'infanterie* by Le Transloy and on to Sailly-Saillisel. As with the other units, the battalion was suddenly greeted with effective fire from the village buildings, hedgerows and a concealed trench. Launching themselves forward with fixed bayonets, a desperate fight ensued for the next few hours, the horror being added to by the German artillery. Yet again, another regimental commander, *colonel* Boblet, was wounded and knocked out of action, as were most of the other senior officers. In some disarray and with a mixture of different units fighting as one, the survivors of the *318e régiment d'infanterie* withdrew to Le Transloy with the remains of their brigade.

The area of the *62e division d'infanterie*:
Slightly to the east of the *61e division*, but about four miles behind, the *62e division d'infanterie* advanced in the same general direction and were uninvolved in the majority of events of 27 August other than for the occasional skirmish.

The leading elements of the division, from the *278e régiment d'infanterie*, witnessed German shells falling on the village of Beugny from their vantage point above Bullecourt during the early afternoon of the 27th before continuing their advance. By-passing Beugny to the west at 2.45pm they arrived at at Villers-au-Flos later in the afternoon, where they billetted for the night. Beugny itself was occupied by the *338e régiment d'infanterie*, where the sporadic shellfire only ceased at nightfall. To their immediate east, the *263e régiment d'infanterie* had come into contact with the Germans between Beugny and Lebucquière and assisted in pushing the Germans out of the latter – reinforced by a company from the *338e* and two machine gun sections, who directed their fire towards German positions in Bois de Vélu. Other elements of the regiment spread out along the railway line and between the villages of Lebucquière and Haplincourt before concentrating and, with the exception of the *17e compagnie*, a platoon from the *22e compagnie* and the two machine gun sections in Lebucquière, spent the night in Haplincourt.

The vanguard unit of the *124e brigade d'infanterie*, the *308e régiment d'infanterie*, harrassed by German cavalry patrols upon approaching the

Cambrai to Bapaume road, was stopped by artillery and rifle fire at 12.30pm just north of Lebucquière. With the assistance of a battalion from the *307e régiment d'infanterie* (and from the *263e régiment d'infanterie* attacking from the west), Lebucquière was captured and the advance continued to Bertincourt where, with the *307e régiment d'infanterie* and the *250e régiment d'infanterie,* who had also been in skirmishes with German cavalry patrols along the Cambrai to Bapaume road to the north of Beaumetz, billets were found for the night.

In the early morning mist of 28 August the *62e division d'infanterie* began to move towards Péronne once again. The division's command did not know of the withdrawal of the majority of the units of the *61e division d'infanterie* to their west by the early hours of the morning, as well as the proximity of the German II Corps approaching Péronne and the western River Somme from the north east. They also did not know that Marwitz's Cavalry Corps was shadowing them from the direction of Beaumetz les Cambrai, all resulting in the heavily outnumbered division marching, all unawares, on a collision course with the Germans in the vicinities of Rocquigny, Le Transloy, Cote 128, Morval, Sailly-Saillisel and the approach to Moislains.

Advancing southwards from Bertincourt, *124e brigade d'infanterie*, with the *5e bataillon* of the *307e régiment d'infanterie* at the head of the column, moved towards Moislains. Expecting to find it unoccupied, patrols from the *20e régiment de dragons* were surprised by the (equally surprised) German troops holding positions to the north and north west of Moislains when they appeared out of the mist. They hurriedly reported their findings back to the column, which had already begun to approach the village.

With the *308e régiment d'infanterie* approaching via Bus, Mesnil-en-Arrouaise and then down the road to the immediate west of Bois de Vaux, the *307e régiment d'infanterie* advancing, via Manancourt, before sweeping westwards and down the same road and the *250e régiment d'infanterie* following up in the rear to the north of the wood, *124e brigade* advanced upon Moislains through the rapidly clearing morning fog. To their immediate rear a battery of 75s from the *34e régiment d'artillerie de campagne* set up in the field to the south of La Gouvernement Farm, between Bois St Pierre Vaast and Boix des Vaux, intending to give covering fire for the infantry. Upon reaching the open land to the south of Bois des Vaux at about 9am, the well entrenched German defenders – established not just in front of the village, but also along the Moislains-Manancourt road to the north east and along the track from Moislains to Bois Germain in the north west – opened fire with devastating effect on the leading elements of the *307e* and *308e régiments*

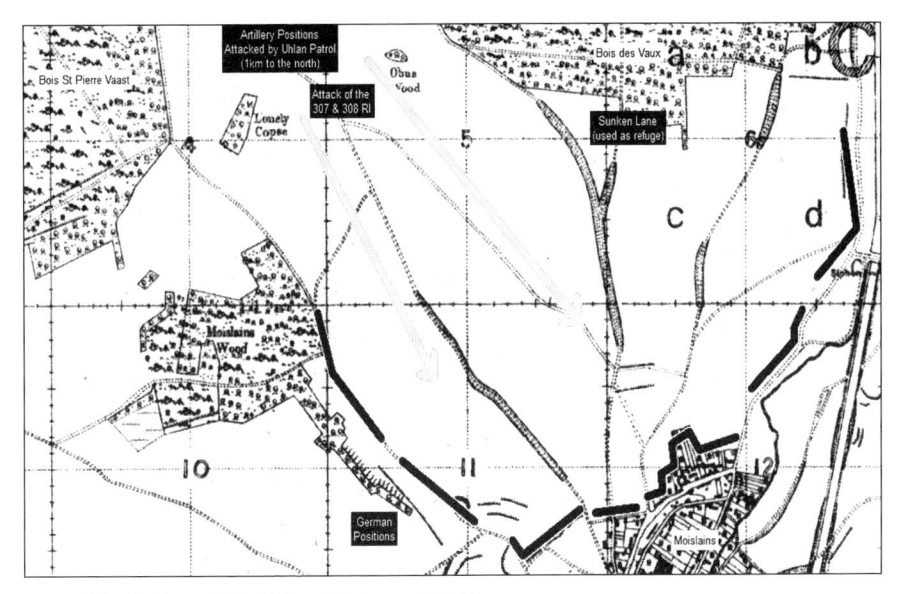

The Action at Moislains, 28 August 1914.

d'infanterie. To their rear, an Uhlan patrol, after riding through Manancourt and between Bois St Martin and the northern section of Bois des Vaux, charged the guns of the *34e régiment d'artillerie de campagne* from the side, rendering them ineffective as support and forcing a withdrawal of the surviving guns back to the gun lines near Mesnil-en-Arrouaise.

Caught in the cross fire from three German positions on a very exposed plateau, the survivors of the *307e* and *308e régiments d'infanterie* were forced to make the most of the shelter of the slightly lower lying roads to the south of Bois des Vaux. Four companies attempted an assault directly on Moislains in order to try and break the centre of the German defences, but these were destroyed within seconds – one company of the *307e régiment d'infanterie* being reduced to just two men – and a German counter-attack from the flanks forced a general retreat from the area towards Rocquigny, where a defensive line was established. French artillery at Mesnil-en-Arrouaise covered the retreat. The German units following close behind suffered such high casualties as they entered the 'killing ground' between Bois St Pierre Vaast and Bois des Vaux that they halted the pursuit and allowed the French to withdraw. Casualties were massive within the two regiments involved ; the *307e régiment d'infanterie* lost 1,246 officers and men killed, wounded and missing, and the *308e régiment d'infanterie* 748. Including those who

French soldiers killed whilst seeking scant cover from withering German rifle fire in a scene similar to that at Moislains, August 1914.

were captured, the two regiments suffered losses totalling over 2,000 during this hour long action, including several battalion and company commanders.

During the action at Moislains, the third regiment of the brigade, *250e régiment d'infanterie,* was deployed defensively towards Sailly-Saillisel, where it only saw limited action in support of *123e brigade d'infanterie* and along the Sailly – Bus line. There, during the afternoon, the *5e bataillon* was ordered to hold the line against any and all enemy attacks for at least two hours to enable the safe withdrawal of the units enagaged in action earlier that day.

In the *123e brigade d'infanterie* area, *lieutenant-colonel* Robert of the *338e régiment d'infanterie* received orders during the early hours of 28 August to reach Cote 123 and the Bapaume-Pèronne road to the north of Sailly-Saillisel. The *278e régiment d'infanterie* was to march on Morval and Combles via Le Transloy, and the *263e régiment d'infanterie* was ordered to serve as left wing flank protection for the division and head due south towards Sailly.

Setting off from the Beugny/Haplincourt area at 3:30am on 28 August, *123e brigade* advanced in a south and south westerly direction to Rocquigny, where they split: the *263e régiment d'infanterie* proceeded down the *voie des carimas,* leading directly to the northern entry of

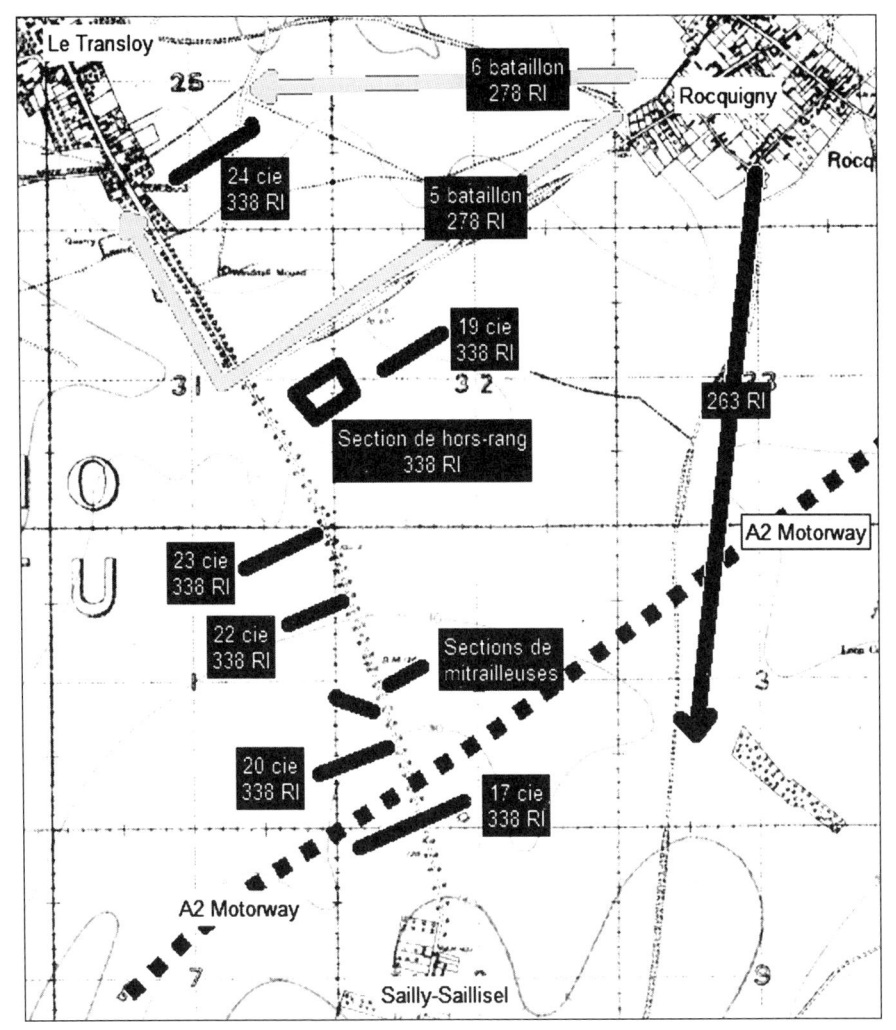

The *338e*, *263e* and *278e* regiments *d'infanterie* at Sailly-Saillisel and Le Transloy, 28 August 1914.

Saillisel; the remainder moved west, along the *chemin de l'abbaye*, towards the Bapaume – Péronne road. The *5e bataillon* of the *278e régiment d'infanterie* (with the *6ᵉ bataillon* advancing through the fields to the north) and the *4ᵉ* and *5ᵉ bataillons* of the *338e régiment d'infanterie* advanced unmolested to the road. There they split to head north and south respectively until about 8.45am when, after the morning fog cleared, *338e régiment d'infanterie* came under fire from German positions on the heights above the northern end of Sailly-Saillisel. The *278e régiment d'infanterie*, after advancing through Le Transloy, came under heavy fire

21

in the area of the western exit of that village from German positions located to the north of the mill at Morval.

The leading companies of the *338e régiment d'infanterie* (*17ᵉ* and *20ᵉ compagnies*, under the command of *capitaines* Nigot and Gaborit), deployed on either side of the Péronne road, made good progress through the sugar beet fields but were forced to ground about 400 yards north of the outskirts of Sailly-Saillisel. The *17ᵉ compagnie* returned fire and advanced towards the German positions but were met with a hail of rifle, machine gun and artillery fire that effectively destroyed the company and was followed by a German infantry counter attack. *Capitaine* Nigot was instantly killed by a bullet to the forehead, whilst *sous-lieutenant* Delaunay of *3ᵉ section* and fifteen (out of seventeen) *sergents* fell alongside approximately 200 men. Many others, including two other section commanders (*sous-lieutenant* Therade of *1ᵉʳsection* and *adjudant* Roy of *4ᵉ section*) were taken prisoner. One soldier from the *17ᵉ compagnie* who was captured on that day later wrote of the events:

> 'We were lying in a field of beet and fired for a long time through the fog towards Sailly-Saillisel. The *sergents* had ordered us to shoot without stopping but, as they were easily identified by the stripes arranged on their forearms, they were an easy prey for our opponents and we were soon on our own. The scene was terrible; the dead, all around me, became more and more numerous and the wounded moaned or implored for a loved one whom they might never see again.
>
> During the late morning, we saw Germans skirmishers advance upon us like a human tide, quite obviously happy with the turn of events. When they arrived in my area, one of them hit me hard in the kidneys with the butt of his rifle and then tried to break my rifle on a metal grill that was nearby. I was then taken prisoner along with a dozen comrades and led behind a hillock, where we were finally safe from bullets.
>
> An hour later we were returned to the national road a hundred yards distant. Here, I saw that many men, in a bid to escape the fire, had hidden behind the sheaves in the fields and in the ditches of the road where the German machine guns had taken them in enfilade, killing a lot. The Germans had brought the body of *capitaine* Nigot (from which they had removed his decorations) to the side of the road along with the bodies of some NCOs and even soldiers in order to show them to us prisoners and attempt to demoralise us even further if needed. We were then taken to the

The result of grouped advances against a defensively established enemy across open terrain. Note the hay stacks in the distance; at Sailly-Saillisel, such cover was all that was available to some.

church of Sailly-Saillisel, where we stayed for three days before being moved to Cambrai and then on to Germany.'

Out of 250 men, less than a dozen from the *17ᵉ compagnie* managed to withdraw to safety after the action.

The *20ᵉ compagnie*, positioned a couple of a hundred yards behind the *17ᵉ* and bolstered by two machine gun sections, were also forced to ground by the same withering fire but, due to the positioning of the *17ᵉ compagnie*, were unable to return fire as they, too were destroyed by the German guns and counter attack. *Sergent-major* Lespignal and *adjudant* Demerville, in command of the *2ᵉ* and *3ᵉ* sections, were wounded and captured, *sous-lieutenant* Bonodeau of the *4ᵉ* section was killed and about a hundred non-commissioned officers, corporals and men also died, with the vast majority of survivors taken prisoner. About ten men escaped unscathed and *capitaine* Gaborit, himself badly wounded in the onslaught, was later seen leaning against a tree sobbing and muttering forlornly: '… Look at my company… it has been annhialated…'

In order to outflank the Germans at Sailly, *lieutenant-colonel* Robert ordered the *22ᵉ compagnie* (*capitaine* Drapier) and the *23ᵉ compagnie* (*capitaine* Crouchet) to cross the fields towards Morval ; but they fell victim to machine guns located in a small copse, Bois Transloy, after advancing only a short distance from the main road. *Capitaine* Crouchet and the commanders of *2ᵉ*, *3ᵉ* and *4ᵉ sections* (*adjudant* Brunery, *adjudant-chef* Blanchard and *sous-lieutenant* Rabache) were all killed within minutes of crossing the road.

In the meantime, the German counter-attack from Sailly-Saillisel continued up the road through the *20ᵉ compagnie* position and towards the area of the regimental headquarters near Cote 123. Realising the danger, *lieutenant-colonel* Robert issued the order *'sauve que peut'* and several soldiers – mainly snipers and a handful of other volunteers under the command of a few officers and non-commissioned officers – managed to hinder the German advance long enough for the majority of survivors to gain distance from their pursuers and join *lieutenant-colonel* Robert, with the *19ᵉ compagnie* (*capitaine* Flamini), parts of the *24ᵉ compagnie* (*capitaine* Imbert-Laboiseille) and the *2ᵉ section de mitrailleuses* (*lieutenant* Merzaux), in attempting to organise a final resistance line between Cote 129 and the southern part of the village of Le Transloy. However, after coming under severe fire from artillery and rifle fire from the approaching Germans and suffering further high casualties, including the loss of *lieutenant* Merzaux and *capitaine* Imbert-Laboiseille, the position became untenable and, during the afternoon, a general retreat – which soon descended into a rout as the Germans approached – was ordered in the direction of Villers-au-Flos.

While the *338e régiment d'infanterie* was in action north of Sailly-Saillisel, the *5ᵉ bataillon* of the *278e régiment d'infanterie* eventually managed to silence the German gunners located at Morval Mill with overwhelming rifle fire. They then proceeded to advance in that direction until they came under machine gun fire on the left flank, possibly from the same gunners who had caused havoc to the *22ᵉ* and *23ᵉ compagnies* of the *338e régiment d'infanterie*. Taking heavy casualties whilst in the exposed fields, which included the battalion commander, who was twice wounded, a retirement to the north was ordered. Over 200 men were now out action.

The *6e bataillon*, who had advanced across the fields between Rocquigny and Le Transloy, left a company to support the divisional artillery before moving to the north of Le Transloy and taking up positions on a ridge about half a mile to the north east of the village. There a second company was made available to the artillery. Taking no real part in the action, this battalion came under light fire from two sides at about 11.30am and withdrew northwards without being pursued. During the evening both battalions met up at Achicourt and an orderly withdrawal was conducted from there.

By 4pm on 28 August, after realising that further advance would be impossible and that, due to the events and withdrawals of the day, the northern flank of the *62e division* was exposed and in severe danger, the

263e régiment d'infanterie was moved. It had advanced towards Sailly-Saillisel with the sole intention of engaging and slowing the German pursuit, but was now ordered to the ridges north of Barastre to assist, along with elements of the *338e régiment*, in repelling any German attack in this area. Under heavy fire, the regiment was forced to withdraw in stages before receiving orders to abandon the positions and fall back to Arras. Their actions and their fierce resistance throughout the evening allowed other retreating troops of the *62e division* to escape without having to engage an enemy far superior in strength; but the cost was high. Sixteen officers and 1,299 non-commissioned officers and men became casualties during their two days of action, of whom 450 were dead.

With the *61e division d'infanterie* retreating through Longueval and Albert in the direction of Amiens and the *62e division d'infanterie* falling back on Arras, the battle in this area was now over. Having delayed the advance of II Armee Korps and IV Reserve Korps by approximately twenty-four hours, precious breathing space had been gained for the retreating allied armies; this would be of benefit in the coming weeks. The cost, however, had been massive and the German advance continued; by 29 August, IV Reserve Korps had reached the line between Albert, Proyart and Chaulnes and, by 30 August, had reached Amiens; II Armee Korps's direction took them south of the River Somme.

For a short while, with the passing of the armies and the battle areas moving to the west and south east of the area, a certain sense of normalcy returned to the Somme battlefield, albeit with the light presence of German occupation, whilst their columns passed nearby en route to other

Infantrymen from IV Reserve Korps entering Amiens on 30 August 1914.

The *cimetière des Charentais* battlefield cemetery at Moislains as it appeared in 1914. Located in the sunken lane where so many sought cover from the German bullets, the outline of the original lane can still be seen.

actions some miles distant. Farmers returned to their fields and villagers and townsfolk attempted repairs on their dwellings and property. The thousands of dead were also afforded burials, usually en masse, but occasional individual burials also occurred in the local churchyards and village cemeteries if space permitted. A number of small and, usually, temporary military cemeteries also cropped up, such as the *cimetière des Charentais*, located on the spot where soldiers from the *307e* and *308e régiments d'infanterie* had sought refuge from the horrendous German cross fire at Moislains on 28 August. Later, when the Germans returned to this area in force, the cemetery was enlarged, landscaped and officially dedicated by them. This tranquil respite, however, would only be for a very short time.

The 'Race to the Sea' and the northern actions of the *bataille d'Albert*, September 1914

Held by the Germans for just under a fortnight, the German garrison at Amiens withdrew from the city on 11 September 1914, following reversals suffered at the Battle of the Marne and the general retreat of the German line back to the area of the Champagne and the River Aisne. After the Battle of the Aisne, the war there descended into the stalemate of what became trench warfare. Both sides now began to attempt to outflank the other to the north of this established line, resulting in the series of actions that would later (slightly misleadingly) become known as the 'race to the sea'. The failure by either side to achieve this objective

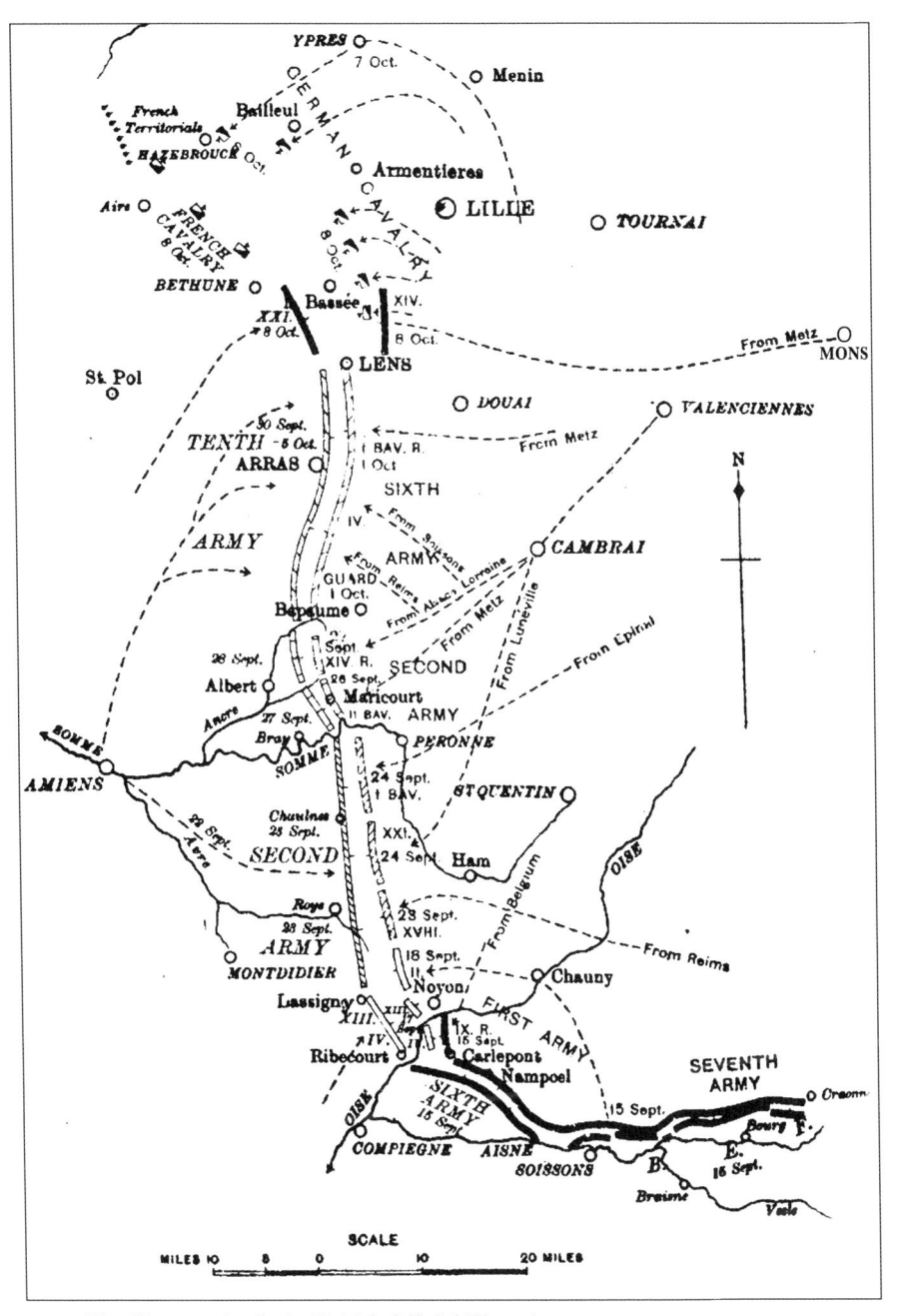

The 'Race to the Sea'. (*British Official History*)

finally resulted in the establishment of the semi static and firmly entrenched front line that is so familiar today to everyone with even the most basic knowledge of the Great War.

With major, but inconclusive, actions during this period taking place to the south of the River Somme between 17 and 24 September 1914, which resulted only in costly stalemate between the German XVIII and XXI Armee Korps and the French *XIV* and *IV corps d'armée*, the I. Königlich Bayerisches Armee-Korps were rushed from Namur and arrived in the area east of Péronne on 23 September. A few of its units saw some limited action south west of Péronne against the *28e, 27e* and *11e divisions d'infanterie* who, after a few sharp actions on 24 September, were thinly, but stubbornly, dug in and holding the line between Chaulnes and Frise on the southern bank of the Somme river. The following day, they moved slightly north and took over the area between Bantouzelle and Péronne as the II. Königlich Bayerisches Armee-Korps began to arrive from Thionville and manoeuvred into position to their north. By the morning of 26 September, II. Kgl.Bay.A.K. were in position immediately south east of Bapaume and I. Kgl.Bay.A.K. were located on the Amiens – St Quentin road south of Péronne; with the XIV. Reserve-Korps already in transit from Sarrebourg and ordered to move into the line at Bapaume to the immediate north of II. Kgl. Bay.A.K.

Meanwhile, though the area of Péronne and the immediate north had been lightly held by the *1e* and *5e divisions de cavalerie* and elements of *corps de cavalerie Bridoux* (later, Buisson) since 15 September, the imminent arrival of a whole Bavarian Army corps forced a slight withdrawal and necessitated speedy reinforcement of the area. By 25 September, the *11e division d'infanterie*, the *81e, 82e, 84e* and *88e divisions d'infanterie territoriale* and the *1e, 5e* and *10e divisions de cavalerie* had all assembled in the area between the north of Bapaume and the River Somme. To the south of the river the military situation had become relatively static, with both armies in the process of establishing their trench lines. To the north of the river, however, and just four weeks after it had last passed through, the war had returned.

The *11e division d'infanterie*, sitting astride the River Somme, attempted a move on Péronne along the southern bank on 25 September; but this was thwarted by increasingly heavy German artillery fire and lack of support from the south. Combined with a large scale German counter-attack, which resulted in the capture of Feuilléres and the bridge spanning the Somme to Monacu, this meant that any further attempted outflanking manoeuvre would have to take place to the north. The initiative was taken by the *1e* and *5e divisions de cavalerie*. During the morning of 25 September they advanced from the area of the Albert-

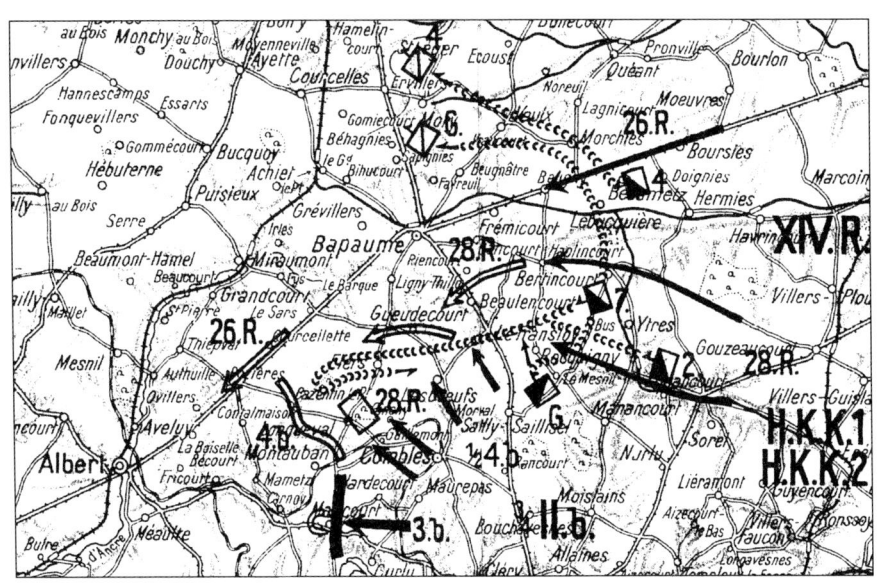

Situation on the evening of 27 August 1914. (*Der Weltkrieg 1914 bis 1918*).

Bapaume road towards the Péronne-Bapaume road in the hope of being able to cross it and then wheel round to the rear of Péronne, attacking the German troops flooding across the Somme crossings to the south of the town. They were, however, stopped before they even reached the road and, with the units of *11e division d'infanterie* that were located north of the river beginning to advance in conjunction with their comrades on the south bank, called off the attack. They began, along with the *10e division de cavalerie*, who had been operating with the *11e division* south of the

One of the Somme crossings at Feuilléres – firmly in German hands at the time of this photograph.

river, to withdraw northwards to the rear of Bapaume to assist the four territorial divisons that were positioned in and around the town.

Under heavy machine gun and artillery fire, the *11e division d'infanterie* advanced through Maricourt and to the north of Curlu towards Péronne before being forced further northwards by the intensity of the fire to their front and south near Hem, through Le Forest and Maurepas, towards Combles. In the same vicinity, the *45e régiment d'infanterie*, accompanying two *compagnies* of Zouaves as part of the infantry element temporarily attached to Sordet's *corps de cavalerie*, moved through Mametz, Carnoy and the Carnoy ravine to the Château de Maricourt. From there, at noon, the *1er bataillon* was despatched to attempt to capture and hold the Somme crossings at Hem in order to facilitate the movement of the cavalry (specifically the *10e division de cavalerie* who were, at that time, crossing the river at various points) and two brigades were sent directly towards Péronne. However, with the I. Königlich Bayerisches Armee-Korps having already reached Feuilléres, to the south of the river, an intense fight for the bridge spanning the Somme ensued. As a result, the *1er bataillon*, along with the brigades moving on Péronne, failed in their objectives, other than in forcing the few Bavarian units that had crossed the river at Hem and Monacu to evacuate their positions; the French remained in position overnight and so prevented any German encroachment to the north.

During the morning of 26 September, the *2e bataillon* of the *45e régiment d'infanterie* pushed towards Cléry in another, failed, attempt on Péronne and soon afterwards received orders to fall back, along with the *1er bataillon* at Hem, to join the *3e bataillon* at Maricourt and there set up defensive positions.

By now, the whole of the II. Königlich Bayerisches Armee-Korps had arrived north of the river and, at 5pm, the 3. Königlich Bayerische Division, having gradually pushed back parts of the *11e division d'infanterie* throughout the day, advanced through Bouchavesnes, Le Forest and Hardecourt and attacked Maricourt from the direction of Combles. They were stopped here by the *45e régiment d'infanterie*, reinforced by the *69e régiment d'infanterie* of the *11e division* (located in entrenchments and barricades to their west and holding the line from the north of Carnoy to Mametz), in their firmly and newly entrenched positions to the north, north east and east of Maricourt and were forced to dig in opposite – thereby beginning to establish a part of the line that would, give or take a few hundred metres, remain practically unchanged here until 1916.

The 4. Königlich Bayerische Division, to their north, advanced in conjunction with the 3. Kgl. Bay. Division, and stumbled into their first

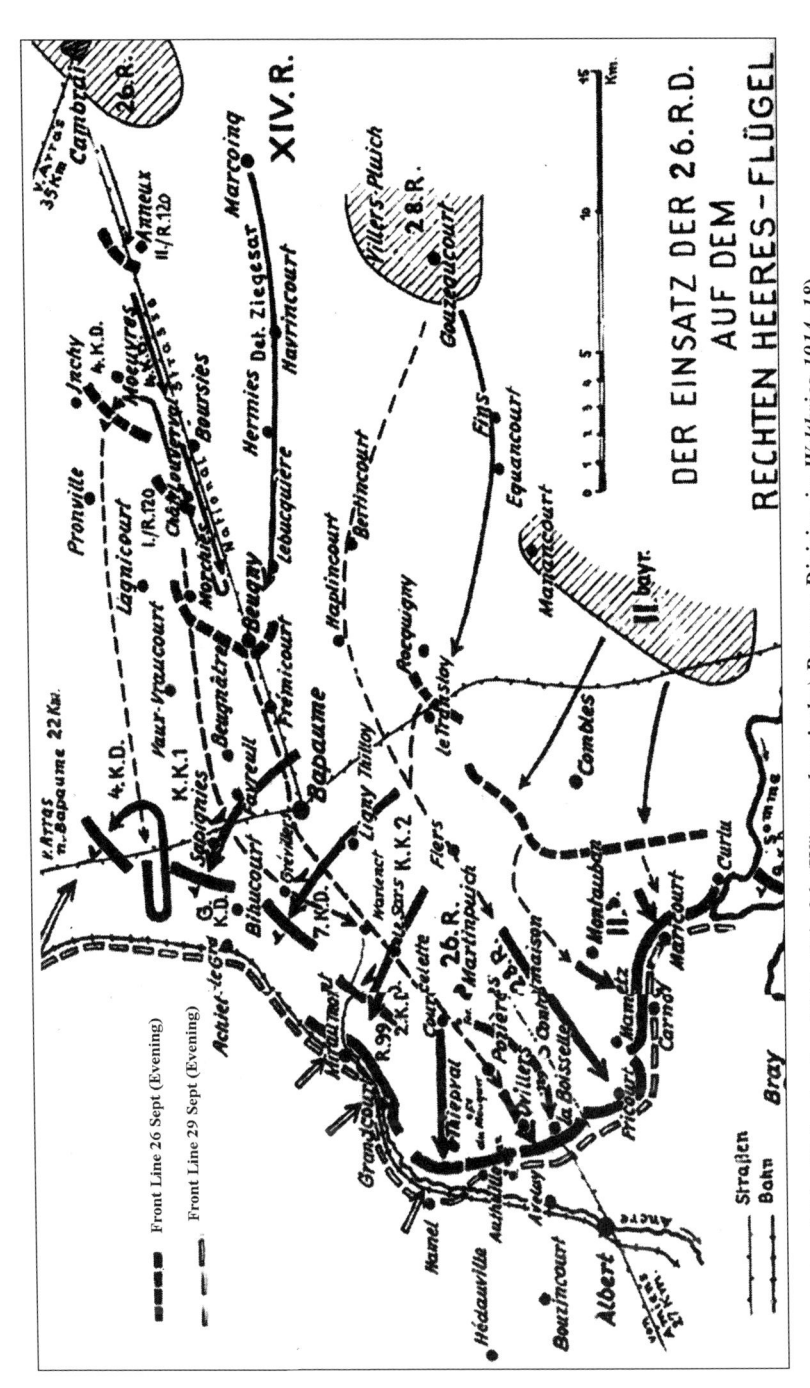

The attacks of 26 – 29 September 1914. (Die 26. (Württembergische) Reserve-Division im Weltkrieg 1914–18)

engagement of the battle at Villers-au-Flos. Lightly defended by the *27e régiment d'infanterie territoriale*, who evacuated this outpost village at a cost of eleven wounded and three missing before withdrawing a short distance to the more strongly held positions at Beaulencourt, the French defence was intended as nothing more than a delaying action to allow the *83ᵉ* and 26ᵉ *régiments d'infanterie territoriale* to take up potentially stronger positions at Beaulencourt and along the road between Le Transloy and Sailly-Saillisel. This was an attempt to bar any further advance in this sector and also to assist in protecting the southern flank of a, temporarily successsful, French attack mounted against XIV. Reserve-Korps further north along the Bapaume-Cambrai road. With further defences being set up by the *82ᵉ division d'infanterie territoriale* around Flers (*18ᵉ régiment d'infanterie territoriale*), between Ginchy and Lesboeufs (*22ᵉ régiment d'infanterie territoriale*) and at Longueval (*21ᵉ régiment d'infanterie territoriale*) to defend the south, it was hoped that this central sector of the battlefield, presenting the formidable obstacle that it potentially did, could hold firm and drive the main battle north to the area between Bapaume and Arras. At this stage, immediately prior to the arrival of the bulk of the German Sixth Army en route from the area east of Metz, the French, for now, still held some numerical superiority.

The *26ᵉ régiment d'infanterie territoriale* of *167ᵉ brigade d'infanterie* deployed four companies of the *1ᵉʳ bataillon* towards Sailly-Saillisel during the morning, leaving two companies of the *2ᵉ bataillon* holding the area south of Le Transloy. Encountering entrenched German positions at Sailly, several fruitless assaults were conducted that resulted in the survivors of these companies being pinned down in open countryside and, just like their predecessors from the *62e division d'infanterie* at this same location exactly a month earlier, were forced to make best use of the generally open ground for cover.

At 1pm, the commanding officer of the *1ᵉʳ bataillon*, *commandant* Brunet, was warned that his left flank was under threat from German infantry approaching from the direction of Rocquigny and that the units covering this area could not hope to be able to contain them. Consequently, he ordered a cautious withdrawal from Sailly and by 6pm all of the survivors of the *26ᵉ régiment d'infanterie territoriale* had managed to regroup between Le Transloy and Beaulencourt. This area was, thus far, successfully held by the *83ᵉ régiment d'infanterie territoriale* of the *88ᵉ division d'infanterie territoriale*. However, they withdrew from these positions during the night and fell back as far as Serre where, thanks to a reinforcement of 1,300 officers and men, the two battalions were reformed the next day.

Within the *88ᵉ division d'infanterie territoriale*'s area, from the north of that of the *84ᵉ* as far as the mid-way point between Bapaume and Arras and now strongly reinforced by the *81ᵉ division d'infanterie territoriale* and the three divisions of *corps de cavalerie Buisson* (soon to become the *1er corps de cavalerie)*, the *83ᵉ régiment d'infanterie territoriale* managed to hold the road between Le Transloy and Beaulencourt against sporadic attacks throughout the night of 26/27 September. Successfully covering the retreat of the *84ᵉ division d'infanterie territoriale* and offering southern flank protection for the withdrawal of their own *84ᵉ régiment d'infanterie territoriale* (who had been in action throughout the 26th in a bitter fight against XIV. Reserve-Korps at Beugny) as they fell back, past Bapaume and along the north/west bank of the Ancre, to Beaumont-Hamel, the *83ᵉ régiment d'infanterie territoriale* was ordered to abandon their positions on 27 September and fall back towards Cote 137 on the plateau above Beaumont-Hamel in order to cover the slopes of Hamel and Beaucourt. The reserve regiment of the division, the *82ᵉ régiment d'infanterie territoriale*, played no part in the fighting of 26 September as they were, at that time, several miles behind the action, hastily constructing defensive positions in the rear in the area of Thiepval Château and organising the bridges at Aveluy and Authuille for defence.

Holding the southern flank of a rapidly forming salient in the centre of the battlefield between the Somme river and Bapaume, the *82e division d'infanterie territoriale* saw its first action on 26 September at the windmill immediatly west of Longueval, when cyclists from the *22ᵉ régiment d'infanterie territoriale* exchanged shots with Württemberger horsemen from 26. Kavallerie-Brigade. Soon afterwards, however, the situation here grew more serious as the 28. Reserve-Division launched an attack from the area of Combles and Hardecourt in a north westerly direction directly on Ginchy, Guillemont and Longueval and pushed the *18ᵉ régiment d'infanterie territoriale* back to Flers under heavy fire.

Partly occupying both Ginchy (two companies) and Longueval, the *22ᵉ régiment d'infanterie territoriale* pushed outposts forwards slightly to hold Waterlot Farm and the railway station at Guillemont along with a company from the *21ᵉ régiment d'infanterie territoriale*. Fighting off relentless assaults for the whole day, these positions held, thereby delaying the German advance in this area, easing the withdrawal of the formations to the north and allowing the consolidation of defensive positions to the rear. Under intense fire, entrenchments were dug along the south and south east edges of Delville Wood in order to make the positions more tenable into the night. At 3am on 27 September, with the villages of Lesboeufs, Combles, Ginchy, Guillemont and Longueval all ablaze, the order was received to withdraw beyond the Ancre. Between

The sugar refinery at Waterlot Farm between Guillemont and Longueval as it appeared in the years leading up to the war. Serving as both a place of respite and a defensive position at various times during the August and September 1914 battles, nothing remains of the original buildings today.

them, the regiments of the *82e division d'infanterie territoriale* who had been involved in the actions of 26 September sustained 25% losses.

With the abandonment of positions along the Péronne-Bapaume road and the southern flank of the 'Bapaume salient', by daybreak on 27 September the ground from that road, north of the line between Contalmaison and Montauban, to the area beyond the Ancre was left only lightly defended by roving cavalry patrols and infantry outposts. The route was open for the Germans to the Albert-Bapaume road and an advance towards the town of Albert on this day of tactical withdrawals

Guillemont railway station – tenaciously defended by units from the *21e* and *22ᵉ régiments d'infanterie territoriale* throughout 26 September 1914.

by the French (albeit with small scale offensive actions on the north bank of the Somme intended to protect the south). Orders were received in the XIV. Reserve-Korps concentration area to march on Albert; they were issued to the 26. Reserve-Division by the divisional commander at the 1870-71 War memorial at Bapaume. The 28. Reserve-Division of XIV. Reserve-Korps wheeled in a south westerly direction and therefore no longer in pursuit of most of the French formations that had been engaged the previous day; this allowed them even more time to organise a defence line to the west. However, by the end of the day, it was in complete occupation of Longueval and most of the area between there and Bapaume with, to their front and to the south west, the 4. Königlich Bayerische Division of the II. Königlich Bayerisches Armee-Korps holding the line between Bazentin-le-Petit and Bernafay Wood and 3. Königlich Bayerische Division located on the now static line between there and the Somme river bank just east of Curlu. To the north, the 26. Reserve-Division advanced through Bapaume and moved down the Albert-Bapaume road, through Courcelette and Pozières – defended by just two companies of the *22ᵉ régiment d'infanterie territoriale* – directly towards Albert.

Recognising the threat, the *21ᵉ* and *22ᵉ divisions d'infanterie* were rushed forward by rail and lorry from the Amiens area during 27 September to bolster the *11ᵉ division d'infanterie*, which had tenaciously held both banks of the Somme river line but was now in serious danger of being overwhelmed from the north and, consequently, threatening the French line to the south should the XIV. Reserve-Korps and II. Kgl. Bay. Armee-Korps succeed in breaking through to Albert.

During the night of 27/28 September, the *21ᵉ division d'infanterie* arrived at Albert. At 6am on the morning of 28 September, the *93ᵉ régiment d'infanterie* was sent forward to hold positions either side of the Albert-Bapaume road in front of Ovillers (*3ᵉ bataillon*) and La Boisselle (*2ᵉ bataillon*), to be joined within the hour by the *65ᵉ régiment d'infanterie*, who were deployed to Contalmaison, La Boiselle and Fricourt ; the *64ᵉ* and *137ᵉ régiments d'infanterie* were held close behind in reserve. To their north, the *22ᵉ division d'infanterie* also began to arrive in position at 11am, with the *62ᵉ régiment d'infanterie* moving through Albert to Mesnil and across the river to Authuille and Thiepval. They were ordered, along with the *19ᵉ régiment d'infanterie,* to capture and hold Thiepval. The *116ᵉ* and *118ᵉ régiments d'infanterie* travelled via Baizieux and Bouzincourt to Martinsart and Aveluy, where they were to remain temporarily in reserve.

28 September 1914 began misty with light rain and patches of dense fog in the low lying areas, especially in the vicinity of the Somme river

The town of Albert – a primary target of the German attacks in September 1914 – served as the main rail head and supply point for French troops reinforcing this sector of the Somme during the September battles. Coming under bombardment several times during these actions, the top of the tower of the basilica – a useful targeting reference point – was off-limits to German gunners, as can be seen in this photograph from the late autumn of 1914. (The spire was eventually hit on 15 January 1915, giving birth to the legend of the famous 'Leaning Virgin').

and the Ancre valley. Ordered to approach Albert directly as follow up to a II. Kgl. Bay. Armee-Korps advance, the XIV. Reserve-Korps plans were altered slightly during the morning due to the increase in strength and resistance of French forces in the south and before Albert, preventing as substantial an advance by the Bavarians as had been anticipated. An independent attack was launched by this corps, not just down and either side of the Albert-Bapaume road but also westwards, towards the line of the Ancre.

In the southern sector (II. Kgl. Bay. Armee-Korps), from the north bank of the Somme, east of Curlu, curving around Montauban to just beyond Mametz Wood, the *11e division d'infanterie* gave up precious little territory under increasingly heavy German pressure. This was achieved despite sustaining heavy losses in several ultimately fruitless and small-scale advances in front of the line Maricourt – Carnoy – Mametz the previous day but during which, however, the *69e régiment d'infanterie* managed to seize and hold Montauban. In no small part

36

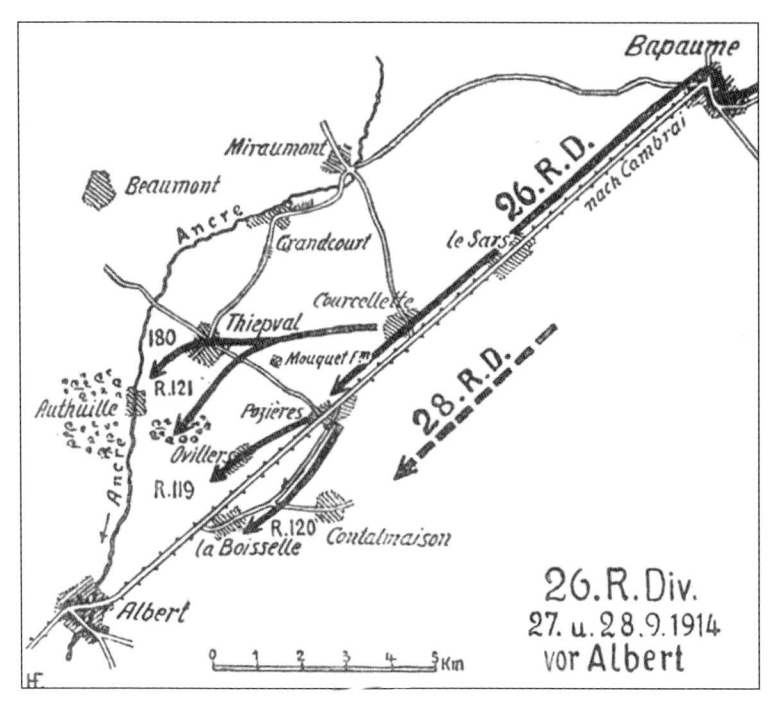

The 26th (and 28th) Reserve Divisions on the Albert-Bapaume Road, 27-28 September 1914. (*Die 26. (Württembergische) Reserve-Division im Weltkrieg 1914–18*).

thanks to the effectiveness of batteries of 75s manned by the gunners of *3e groupe, 8e régiment d'artillerie de campagne* located in the area between Maricourt and Carnoy, the Bavarians only managed minimal gains in this area. Though Montauban, Mametz and the high ground overlooking Maricourt fell despite several counter-attacks and slight progress was made along the north bank of the Somme to just beyond Curlu, *21[e] brigade d'infanterie* managed to halt the advance dead in its tracks in front of Carnoy and Maricourt. Here the defensive positions dug over the previous days held. Caught in the open on the gentle slopes facing the French positions, the Bavarians were forced to dig in and, joining up with the line established north, east and south east of Maricourt, the entrenched front line in this area that would endure for the next two years began to form.

Slightly overlapping the right wing (north and north east) of the II. Kgl. Bay. Armee-Korps, 55. Reserve-Infanterie-Brigade of the 28. Reserve-Division proceeded, under heavy artillery fire, to positions in Bazentin-le-Petit Wood and Mametz Wood with orders to capture the heavily defended village of Contalmaison. Only several hours earlier it had been reinforced by the *65ᵉ* and (elements of) the *137ᵉ régiments d'infanterie*. After some heavy fighting that lasted for much of the morning, Contalmaison finally fell to Badisches Reserve-Infanterie-Regiment Nr. 109 (supported by Württembergisches Reserve-Infanterie-Regiment Nr. 120 of 52. Reserve-Infanterie-Brigade, 26. Reserve-Division) around mid-day. The latter's first battalion, due to strong flanking fire, were forced too far to the right and ended up advancing, along with Reserve-Infanterie-Regiment Nr. 120, towards La Boisselle.

Immediately to the north of Contalmaison, 52. Reserve-Infanterie-Brigade, which had cleared the village of the enemy, was free to advance down the Albert-Bapaume road. With Reserve-Infanterie-Regiment Nr. 120 on the south side, and Reserve-Infanterie-Regiment Nr. 119 on the north, the next, and final, obstacles before Albert were the villages of Ovillers and La Boisselle. These were held by the *3e* and *2e bataillons* of the *93ᵉ régiment d'infanterie* with the *64ᵉ* and *137ᵉ régiments d'infanterie* in close support, along with part of the *82e régiment d'infanterie territoriale*.

Just after midday, Reserve-Infanterie-Regiment Nr. 120 made a relatively unopposed approach to La Boisselle along the road from Contalmaison and down the main road from Pozières until the final hundred or so metres prior to entering the village, when they came under heavy rifle fire. Steadily advancing across the open until the village was reached, it soon became clear that the French were not going to cede control without a fight and hand-to-hand and house-to-house combat ensued, with heavy losses on both sides. By 5pm, however, the village

La Boisselle in more peaceful times. This street would become a scene of vicious hand to hand fighting on 28 September.

was eventually cleared, and the numerically superior French pushed out of the southern and south western sections past the village cemetery and beyond an isolated farmhouse on a slightly elevated piece of ground known to the French as *l'Îlot de la Boisselle* (Granathof or Granatenhof – Shell Farm – to the Germans). Once here, in two lines of entrenchments already previously prepared by the divisional *génie* companies and with the support of the guns of *51e régiment d'artillerie de campagne*, who began a relentless bombardment on La Boisselle, the French held firm.

Following the fall of La Boisselle, Badisches Reserve-Infanterie-Regiment Nr. 109, Reserve-Infanterie-Regiment Nr. 40 and Reserve-Jäger-Bataillon Nr. 8 of 55. Reserve-Infanterie-Brigade joined with Kgl. Bay. 5. Infanterie-Regiment of the 4. Kgl. Bay. Division for an attack on Fricourt. Protected by the terrain during the initial advance from Mametz Wood, the final approach to Fricourt was more open and here the attackers began to suffer heavy casualties from the rifle and machine gun fire coming from the *41e brigade d'infanterie* positions in and around the village and were forced to ground. Later reinforced by the Badisches Reserve-Infanterie-Regiment Nr. 111, the assault continued into the darkness as evening fell; but, with the battlefield lit only by blazing stacks of wheat and the burning houses of the village, it was decided to postpone further attacks. However, the order to halt was not received by all units and elements of Reserve-Infanterie-Regiment Nr. 40, accompanied by Reserve-Jäger-Bataillon Nr. 14, carried on the attack into the night. Losing direction in the dark, they headed for the burning buildings that they assumed to be Fricourt but came under withering fire from the German defenders. In the confusion, they had headed directly towards Mametz, which had fallen earlier in the day and was under the occupation of Bavarian troops who assumed, not unreasonably, that their 'attackers' were French.

Orders were received at 11pm for the attack on Fricourt to recommence. With fixed bayonets, a battalion from Reserve-Infanterie-Regiment Nr. 111, elements of Reserve-Infanterie-Regiment Nr. 40 and Reserve-Jäger-Bataillon Nr. 8 advanced to within 300 metres of Fricourt before their attack was halted by rifle fire as they encountered barbed wire obstacles set up by the French during the day. Stealthily moving through the darkness after the attack, the southern edge of Fricourt was reached and Cote 110 partially occupied before another attack, intended to capture the terrain immediately east of the village. This would provide a new direction from which to launch a subsequent attack to secure Fricourt. This final assault of the night, however, also descended into a chaotic and costly failure in the darkness. Fricourt did not fall to German pressure on this day but, in the mistaken belief that the position was

The rue d'Arras in Fricourt, looking southwards, before the war.

untenable, the village was abandoned during the early hours and the defenders from the *65ᵉ* and *26ᵉ régiments d'infanterie* pulled back to the area of Fricourt station and cemetery.

Whilst the attacks at Contalmaison and La Boisselle were in progress, the Württembergisches Reserve-Infanterie-Regiment Nr. 119 was ordered to switch direction to the north west to assault Ovillers. However, in the face of heavy fire from the *3e bataillon, 93ᵉ régiment d'infanterie* and the *64ᵉ régiment d'infanterie*, holding the area between Ovillers and La Boisselle, German progress was slow and faltered entirely at 1pm when the supply of shells began to run low. The French defences had been bolstered by the machine guns of the *section de mitrailleuses* of the *2e bataillon, 93ᵉ régiment d'infanterie*. These guns were prevented from being effective in their own area due to the close proximity of their own troops; but they could fire across the road from La Boisselle towards the southern part of Ovillers. Following a resupply of the German artillery during the afternoon, heavy gun fire on Ovillers forced the French to evacuate the village and they pulled back to their pre-dug defensive positions on the low hill opposite. Subsequent French shelling of Ovillers forced the Germans to dig in and here, again, the advance was halted.

North of Ovillers, 51. Reserve-Infanterie-Brigade was dispatched to capture Thiepval and the east bank of the Ancre during the morning of 28 September. Heading west from Courcelette, they skirted north of Ferme du Mouquet before moving to occupy the undefended village of

Thiepval. Upon approaching the village 4. Kompanie of Württembergisches Reserve-Infanterie-Regiment Nr. 121 came under rifle (or, more accurately *mousqueton* or *carabine de cavalerie*) fire from some of the buildings and gardens as they stumbled into a patrol from *3e groupe cycliste du 18e bataillon de chasseurs à pied*. After quickly rushing the village, all resistance ended, and several prisoners were taken, the remainder of the patrol taking flight. Several German patrols were sent out from Thiepval, confirming that there was a build up of French troops between Mesnil and Hamel and that they were also defensively dug in near Thiepval Wood, Aveluy Wood and to the west of Ovillers The German command was faced with a static situation developing further south; in order to assist any breakthrough down the Albert-Bapaume road, it became imperative that the heights, woods and river crossings to the north west of Ovillers be taken. At 11am, therefore, the 2. Bataillon of Württembergisches Infanterie-Regiment Nr. 180 replaced the 2. Bataillon of Reserve-Infanterie-Regiment Nr. 121 in Thiepval, freeing the latter to take part in an attack between Thiepval and Ovillers later that day. However, this resulted in only slight gains because of effective French shelling and the failure to capture the villages of Authuille and Aveluy. The capture of these settlements would have enabled an encirclement of Albert from the west bank of the Ancre.

Elements of 2. Kavallerie-Division, ordered to protect the movements of the northern flank of the XIV. Reserve-Korps, advanced from Courcelette to cover the river crossings at Grandcourt and Miraumont. The 2. Bataillon of Reserve-Infanterie-Regiment Nr. 99, along with two

Thiepval church at the turn of the century.

companies from the 3. Bataillon of Infanterie-Regiment Nr. 180, after a short, sharp clash with the *82e* and *83e régiments d'infanterie territoriale*, crossed at Grandcourt before driving the *84e régiment d'infanterie territoriale* temporarily out of Beaucourt completely. They forced the *84e* in their entirety onto the slopes in front of Beaumont-Hamel before having to defend themselves (successfully) against two large counter-attacks after Beaucourt was re-occupied by the French. The river crossing at Miraumont easily fell to the 2. Bataillon of Reserve-Infanterie-Regiment Nr. 99 who, with their third battalion moving to the right of the village, then proceeded towards the fortified farmhouse of Beauregard, north west of the village, to relieve a company of Jäger cyclists that were then in occupation. Soon after the relief was completed, however, French artillery made the position untenable and it was abandoned for the relatively safe location of a nearby sunken road and trenches at the western edge of Miraumont.

During the night of 28/29 September further French reinforcements arrived along the line, along with several artillery batteries from Amiens, which allowed a general strengthening of their situation. Even the *19e division d'infanterie*, en-route to Arras directly from the fighting on the Champagne front, ordered a pause at Albert in order to bolster the west bank defences of the Ancre. The division deployed its troops mainly between Aveluy and Hamel; and dispatched the *71e régiment d'infanterie* as far north as Gommecourt in order to assist in preventing any attempt at a breakthrough there. Although the German attacks towards Albert would continue throughout 29 September, the stengthened French forces meant that they, too, would now be in a better position to launch organised attacks of their own. As had occurred all along the Western Front to the south, situational stalemate was looming.

The early morning of 29 September was, like the previous day, misty and dank in the southern sector of the battlefield. During the early morning darkness, the machine-gun company of Reserve-Infanterie-Regiment Nr. 109 moved to a small copse in front of Fricourt to provide support for the attack on the village that would be the main focus of the day's actions in this sector. At 5.45am, two battalions of Reserve-Infanterie-Regiment Nr. 40, Reserve-Infanterie-Regiment Nr. 109 and Reserve-Jäger-Bataillon Nr. 8, with the 3. Bataillon of Reserve-Infanterie-Regiment Nr. 40 in reserve, made a quick rush towards the northern section of the village, advancing under heavy fire from the *65e* and *26e régiments d'infanterie* located on the heights to the south and west of Fricourt. After storming the first houses in the north of the village at 6am, the Germans discovered that the rest of the village had been abandoned and moved through the streets only to be greeted by an intense artillery bombardment that destroyed many of the buildings and inflicted heavy casualties. Pushing on, two attempts were made on Fricourt railway station, but these were both repulsed with heavy losses. Unknown to the attackers, the station was at that time only very thinly held by part of a section scratched together from various companies of the *65ᵉ régiment d'infanterie*; they were desperately short of ammunition and supplies and had even, according to the regimental history, been forced to dig in using spoons and *quarts*, the army issue aluminium drinking cup. They had been ordered to ensure that every shot hit a target in order to give the illusion that the defences were far stronger than they actually were. German survivors from thèse attacks moved into the houses and gardens at the southern edge of the village and began to dig in.

At 7:30am, *41e brigade d'infanterie* launched their own counter-attack on Fricourt; but this was easily repelled by the machine gunners of Reserve-Infanterie-Regiment Nr. 109, who managed to inflict heavy casualties on the attackers. The French responded by laying down a heavy bombardment on the village for much of the remainder of the day. Three German attacks to the east and north of Fricourt, aiming to remove a salient that had formed around the village, and several French counter-attacks during the afternoon all met with failure, with the final assault achieving the same result at midnight. One location in which there was some progress of the German line, however, was at Cote 110, located south of Fricourt. It was a dominant height, providing commanding views over the battlefield. Reserve-Infanterie-Regiment Nr. 40 and Reserve-Infanterie-Regiment Nr. 111 began an assault on this heavily defended location once news was received that Fricourt was in German hands. Advancing slowly up the northern slope, enduring withering rifle fire and a shrapnel storm from the French artillery ranged on the hill, the attackers lost heavily, especially on the right wing, where the 1ˢᵗ batallion of Reserve-Infanterie-Regiment Nr. 40 was badly mauled. However, by noon, the crest was reached; but well directed artillery fire prevented any further advance and shallow defensive trenches were constructed to defend against the numerous counter-attacks that occurred in the following hours. After a final counter-attack, conducted by the *37e régiment d'infanterie* and the *2e bataillon de chasseurs à pied* at 11:30pm failed in its objectives, the French also began to dig in opposite the German scrapes on the crest of Cote 110.

Partly as a result of the events that had unfolded at Fricourt during the darkness of the early hours of the morning, in the northern sector of the battlefield (where, since the close of the previous day, the French had begun to hold numerical superiority in, both, men and *matériel*), it was the French who struck first. At about 7am, just as the first light of the day

Thiepval Château – the location of 51. Reserve-Infanterie-Brigade headquarters until French artillery made the location untenable on 29 September – as it appeared before the war.

was breaking on 29 September, the newly supplied (and, in some cases, newly arrived) French artillery opened up on the German positions all along this part of the line at about 1am. With numerous batteries located between Hamel, Mesnil, Aveluy and Albert, and with heavier pieces brought up in the rear around Bouzincourt and Hedauville, special attention was paid to the German held Bois d'Authuille, causing heavy casualties amongst those parts of Reserve-Infanterie-Regiment Nr. 121 and Infanterie-Regiment Nr. 180 who were sheltered in it. With some of the positions being held at a right angle to the main German line, French fire could be directed into both flanks and the rear simultaneously, rendering it an untenable location. Consequently, at 10am, the main body of the German troops withdrew from the wood to the high ground to the south east of Thiepval and Cote 150, to the north of the village. A strong attack on this latter position launched by *176e brigade d'infanterie* of the *88e division d'infanterie territoriale* on the 3. bataillon of Infanterie-Regiment Nr. 180 from the direction of Hamel and St Pierre Divion was successfully repulsed. The Germans withdrew to the village itself, leaving a rearguard in the wood to provide cover for the move. The rearguard remained in this impossible position until nightfall, by which time it had been possible to evacuate all the wounded in the wood. Surprisingly, no French attack took place followed the earlier bombardment and only after the Germans had withdrawn did the French, hesitatingly, move in to occupy this wood. Thiepval Château, up to that point used as a headquarters for 51. Reserve-Infanterie-Brigade, was specifically targeted by the French guns when they bombarded Thiepval for several hours and set it ablaze. The headquarters was forced to relocate to Mouquet Farm.

Mouquet Farm in 1914. It was here that 51. Reserve-Infanterie-Brigade headquarters relocated following their forced evacuation of Thiepval Château.

Ovillers and La Boisselle, both densely populated with German troops that were being assembled to continue the push on Albert, were both subjected to similar heavy bombardments that caused large losses. A combination of factors disrupted the German plans: both villages were under prolonged shell fire and the consequent high casualties amongst the reinforcements arriving in these villages; the right flank of Reserve-Infanterie-Regiment Nr. 119 in Ovillers was dangerously exposed because of the withdrawal from Bois d'Authuille; and a lack of fog to provide cover for an advance in this sector. Despite the fact that the German artillery did begin a preliminary bombardment at 7:30am that, at least temporarily, drove the *22e division d'infanterie* defenders beyond the low ridges protecting the eastern approaches to Albert, a major attack was cancelled at 9am and orders were received to dig in and prepare defences. It had now become painfully clear that Albert would not be captured and that, for the present at least, Ovillers and La Boisselle would be joined up with Thiepval to the north and Fricourt, Mametz and the high ground north of Carnoy and Maricourt (before sweeping southwards to the Somme) to the south to form the front line in the area for some time yet.

The line along the Ancre north of Thiepval was less stable. All but two of the river crossings were controlled by either French infantry from the *82e* and *88e divisions d'infanterie territoriale* or, at the very least, by French artillery as far as Miraumont, with massed batteries located in the area of Beaumont-Hamel, Serre and Puisieux. Orders received by Reserve-Infanterie-Regiment Nr. 99 to capture the hills north of

The thickly walled – and much disputed – Beauregard Farm in 1913. Note the dove cote from which it was possible to attain commanding views over the Ancre.

Grandcourt and Miraumont were unable to be carried out due to three separate – and failed – attempts by the *82e division d'infanterie territoriale* to force the river crossings during the morning. Further French attacks occurred throughout the afternoon and all available German reserves were redirected to the southern and eastern heights of the Ancre to hold the line there, with a reserve line set up between Courcelette and Le Sars in the event of a French break through. However, artillery – both French and German – proved instrumental in the prevention of any advance in either direction during the day and, other than the repeated loss of Beauregard Farm (a company from *21e régiment d'infanterie territoriale* had re-occupied the evacuated farm but were themselves shelled out of the position during the early hours of 29 September, suffering numerous casualties), which would be a disputed position for some days to come, the situation along the Ancre at the end of 29 September would be pretty much the same as it was at the beginning of the day.

In many official accounts, the *bataille d'Albert* ended on 29 September 1914, with other battles of the 'Race to the Sea' taking place further to the north – beginning with the First Battle of Arras immediately north of the Somme within twenty-four hours of the 'conclusion' of the Albert battle and (technically) culminating in the inundations of the

Belgian polders and the Battle of the Yser at the end of October 1914 and of First Ypres in late November. Both sides endeavoured but ultimately failed to outflank one another and strike a decisive blow. Though the French had been knocked onto the back foot during the eary encounters of the battle, their ability to utilise the available railways and transport systems and other communications behind the combat zones enabled them to quickly transport reinforcements, artillery, ammunition and supplies to where they were needed the most (moving up to 200 trains and thousands of motor vehicles per day to the front lines), allowing a very quick recovery rate which, in turn, bought them that most precious of all commodities in a defensive battle – time. This, in turn, allowed a more cautious use of tactics; an immediate and decisive victory was no longer as crucial to the French as it was to the Germans and the preservation of the defensive capability of the French Army could be a major objective.

The front line now ran south down the railway line from Achiet-le-Grand to the Ancre crossing at Miraumont, before traversing the high ground south of Grandcourt to Thiepval and then on past Ovillers, La Boisselle, Fricourt, Mametz, Carnoy and Maricourt to the Somme; but the fighting, especially in the north, was far from over on the Somme. Nor was the front line of 1 July 1916, which has become so familiar to students of the war, yet established in the northern sector of the battlefield.

Tour 1

A Car Tour of the Northern Somme Actions of August and September 1914

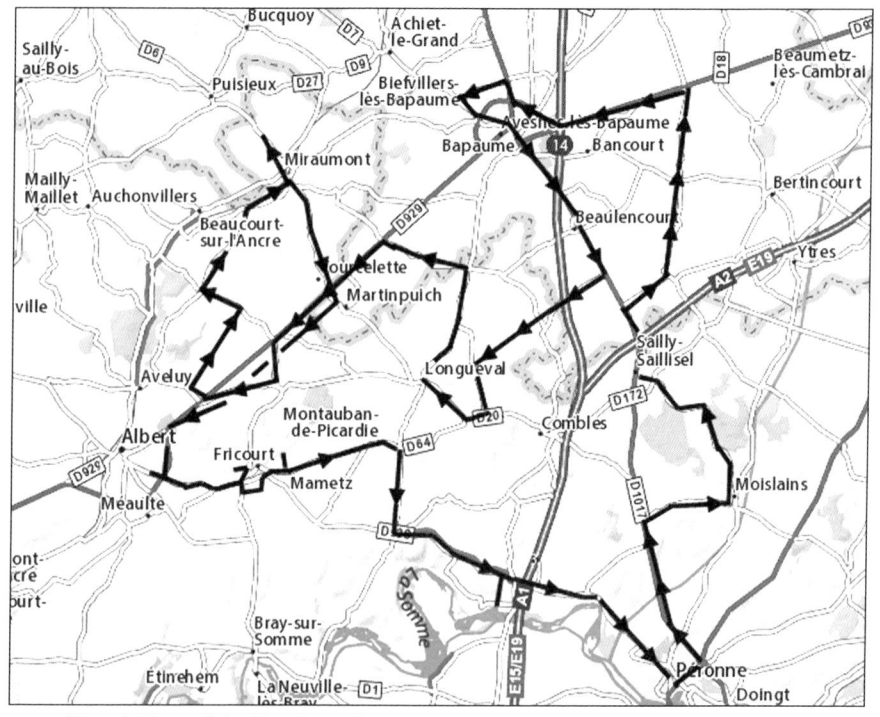

Tour 1. Tour of the Northern Somme Actions of August and September 1914: Route Overview.

Start the tour in the Grande Place (the *Place du Cmdt.Louis Daudre*) *at* **Péronne (1)**.

This is the area in which the entire *120e régiment d'infanterie* (including the reservists) publicly assembled on an annual basis prior to manoeuvres and where, amongst great festivities and ceremony on 12 July 1914, the town was awarded the *Légion d'honneur* for its role during the Franco-German War of 1870-71.

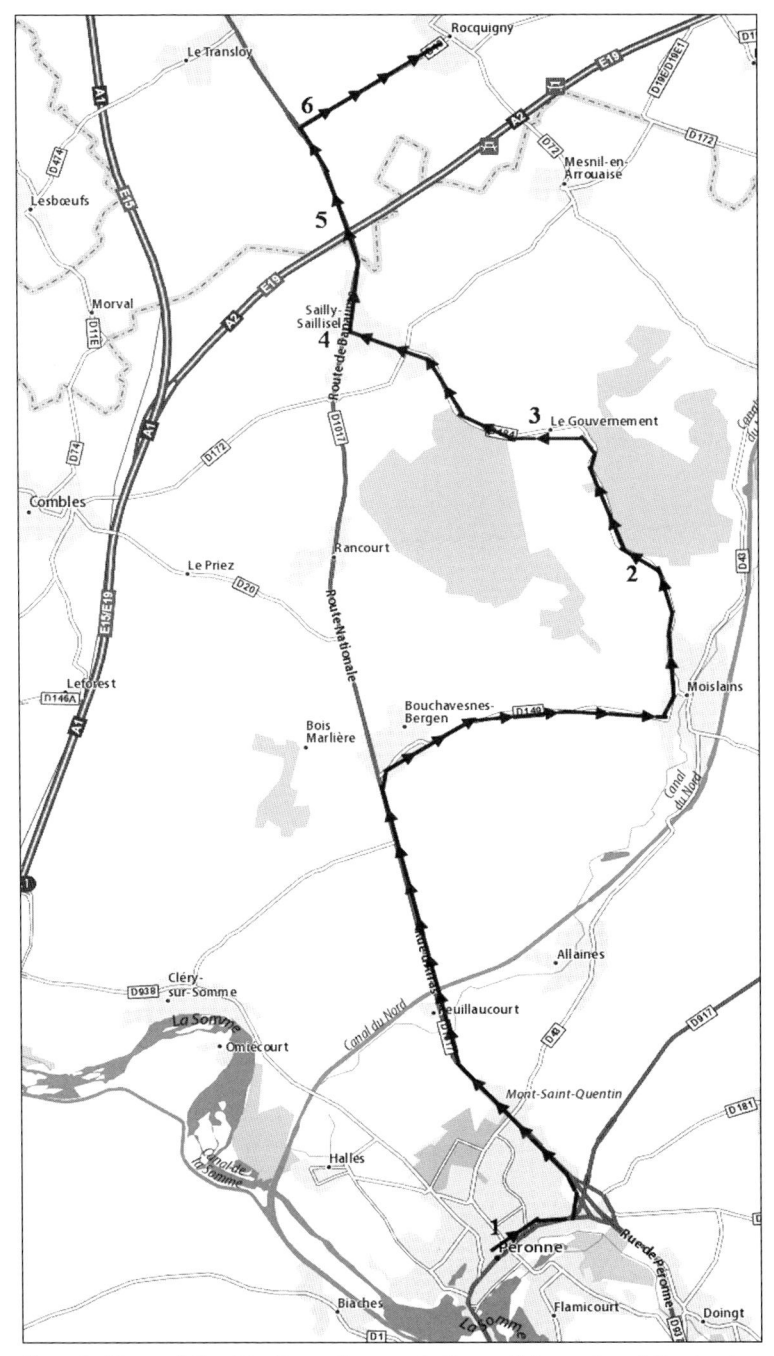

Tour 1: Tour of the Northern Somme Actions of August and September 1914 – Points 1 to 6.

49

Leave Péronne via the D1017 (signposted Arras and Cambrai) and continue along this road for 1,400 metres before turning left at the crossroads (yet remaining on the D1017) and following the signs leading to Arras, Bouchavesnes and Moislains.

Pass a large supermarket on the right and then crossing over a roundabout before actually leaving Péronne, the important vantage point of **Mont St Quentin,** *with its* **memorial to the 2ⁿᵈ Australian Division** *on the left, is traversed after 1.75 kilometres. Continue in the direction of Arras for a further four kilometres.*

As **Bouchavesnes-Bergen** *is reached, take the first right onto the D149 (the 'rue du 67RI') into the village and continue through it and on towards* **Moislains,** *which is reached after 3.4 kilometres. At the first junction in Moislains, turn left onto the D184 towards the town centre and go straight ahead at the first cross roads after 350 metres. After a further 100 metres, take the left fork at the Y junction and then the central road (of three) at the next (remaining on the D184 – direction Sailly-Saillisel). In one kilometre, you will arrive at* the **Cimetière militaire de Moislains**, which is better known as the **'Cimetière de la Charente' (2)**. **NB! Beware:** it is quite easy to drive straight past this cemetery, as it is set back a little distance from the road and there are hedges and trees that obscure the view.

The entrance to the *cimetière des Charentais* today.

The entrance to the *cimetière des Charentais* in 1915 during landscaping by the occupying German Armies.

This small cemetery was begun by the Germans in August 1914 following the '*Combat de Moislains*'and is located in the area in which the survivors from the *307e* and *308e régiments d'infanterie* were forced to take shelter from the devastating German cross-fire coming from the direction of Moislains and across the fields east and south west of the location of this cemetery. It contains the remains of 465 soldiers (mainly from the *307e* and *308e Régiments d'infanterie* of 28 August 1914), including numerous battalion and company commanders; 366 of the fallen, are buried in an ossuary at the rear, marked by a monument to these regiments. Unusually for a French military cemetery, there are a number of original headstones still to be seen.

From here, continue on the road to Sailly-Saillisel, skirting Bois des Vaux on the right. Over the fields to the left may be seen the eastern end of Bois Saint Pierre Vaast.

As you proceed, look into the fields to the left before the road bends to the right and imagine the massed ranks of the *307e* and *308e régiments d'infanterie* advancing through them and down the road towards

Moislains. Littered with French dead and dying, interspersed with the many field grey clad corpses of Germans who had attempted to follow up the French withdrawal only to be caught in these same open fields by the defensive artillery fire, by the conclusion of the action of 28 August this single field must have been a scène of utter misery and desolation.

Following the D184 as it curves to the left at a small crossroads. **Le Gouvernement Ferme** (3) *can be seen on the right some 300 metres beyond the crossroads.*

Le Gouvernement Ferme as it appeared in 1914, immediately following the August 1914 actions.

In the fields, some 300 metres to the south of the entrance to the farm and to the left of the road, was the location of the guns of the *34e régiment d'artillerie de campagne* that were attacked by a large patrol of Uhlans, thus removing their threat to the Germans just as the battle began further south and, out of direct sight, over the slight rise of the land that can be seen from this location.

Continue along the D184 through Sailly-Saillisel until the main Péronne-Bapaume road (D1017) is reached. Turn left and then, after seventy-five metres, take the first right onto the rue du Château. On the left, in the area of the industrial units and football fields, is the **site of the Château de Sailly-Saillisel** **(4).**

The scene of a desperate action in August 1914 - the Château de Sailly-Saillisel as it appeared in happier times.

Infamous for some of the most vicious close combat fighting of the entire war during October and November 1916, a taster of what was to come was experienced on 27 August 1914 when *122e brigade d'infanterie* were practically ambushed within the village, forcing a desperate house to house combat. The chateau and grounds were the scene of the 'last stand' of the *5e bataillon, 262e régiment d'infanterie* as, assisted by elements of the *219e* and *318e régiment d'infanterie* but still outnumbered at a ratio of six to one, they resisted German attacks and held this position for several hours before the survivors managed to disengage and withdraw.

Return to the D1017 and turn left. In 1.3 kilometres, after passing underneath the A2 motorway, find a safe place to stop. This location affords an excellent **battlefield view (5)** *of the August 1914 action before Sailly-Saillisel.*

Although, unfortunately, the A2 motorway bridge dissects the battlefield before Sailly-Saillisel and obscures the view somewhat in that direction, it actually does mark the limit of the advance of *17e compagnie (5e bataillon), 338e régiment d'infanterie* towards the village on 28 August 1914 – the point at which they, and the *20e compagnie*, were effectively destroyed by German defensive fire from Sailly-Saillisel prior to a German counter-attack. It is the location of the graphic description of the battlefield given by an eyewitness on pages 22–23 of this book. The fields either side of the road were littered with French corpses with clusters of bodies behind hay bales and in the ditches near the road where they had attempted to seek cover.

Continue in the direction of Bapaume for another 1,200 metres then turn right onto the D19 towards Rocquigny, where it is possible to safely stop on the right just after making this turn. *At this junction, another* **battlefield view (6)** *is afforded.*

At this position – **Cote 123** – it is possible to appreciate quite a wide expanse of the August 1914 battlefield in this area. As you face Rocquigny, the *338e régiment d'infanterie* advanced towards your position to the right of the road before turning towards Sailly-Saillisel and their fate ; while the *5ᵉ bataillon* of the *278ᵉ régiment d'infanterie*, with the *6ᵉ bataillon* advancing directly across the fields to their north, advanced to the left, sweeping towards Le Transloy at the main road. The *263ᵉ régiment d'infanterie* advanced directly towards Saillisel across the skyline, some 1,200 metres to your front right.

Turning to look across the main road, parts of Le Transloy can be made out just beyond the crest of the slope to the right, whilst the spire of Lesboeufs church can be seen on the horizon directly in front. To the left of Lesboeufs, also on the horizon, parts of Morval can be made out and, roughly equidistant between the trees of the two villages but slightly forward of the horizon, is the site of the Moulin de Morval, where carefully positioned German machine guns caused so much devastation amongst the *278ᵉ régiment d'infanterie* troops on 28 August in the fields to your front right. These same fields were the scene of devastating artillery and rifle fire on the *262ᵉ régiment d'infanterie* during their advance on Morval the previous day, 27 August, and on the *26ᵉ régiment d'infanterie territoriale* a month later, on 26 September.

Continue for two kilometres into the centre of **Rocquigny** *then turn left, through the route of advance of the 62e division d'infanterie of August 1914, onto the D20, following this road as it curves to the right at the extremity of the village towards* **Barastre**, *which is reached after another two kilometres, followed by* **Haplincourt** *– specifically targeted by the German 28. Reserve-Division on 26 September 1914 – 1,200 metres further on. Remain on the D20 as it skirts the eastern edge of the centre of Haplincourt for another 3.3 kilometres (passing Delsaux Farm [British] Cemetery) en-route after two kilometres until the main D930 (Bapaume-Cambrai) road is reached in* **Beugny (7)**.

A key location on the Bapaume-Cambrai road and, therefore, an important defensive point on the eastern approaches to Bapaume, the village of Beugny was defended by the *28ᵉ régiment d'infanterie territoriale* during their retreat from the vicinity of Cambrai, holding open

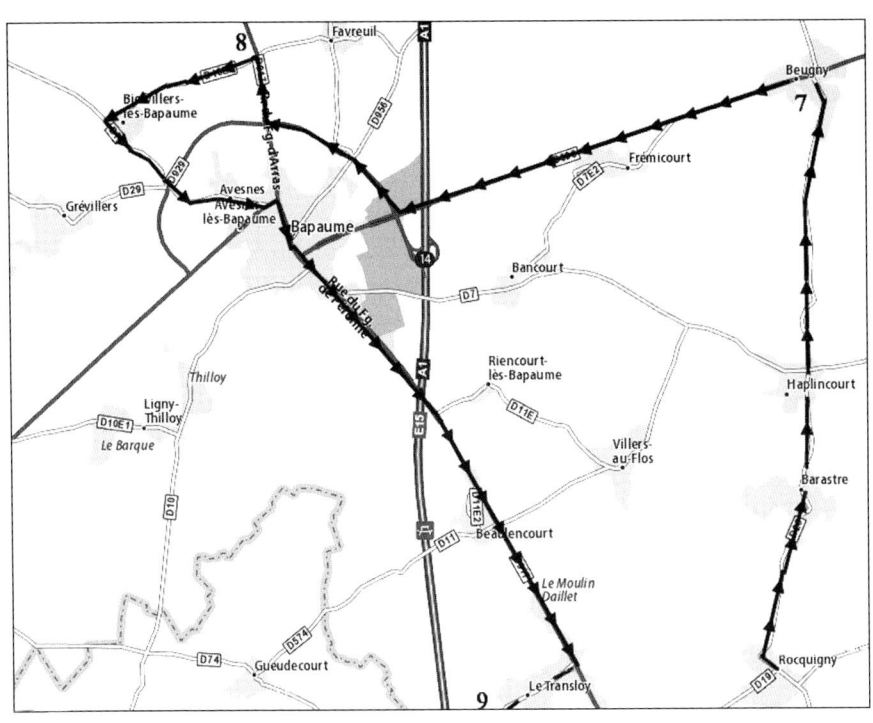

Tour 1: Tour of the Northern Somme Actions of August and September 1914 – Points 7 to 9.

A heavily disputed village during the first days of war on the Somme, and again in September – the main street of Beugny before the war.

the path for the *62ᵉ division d'infanterie* in their southerly advance on Péronne during the August battle. Abandoned by the territorials as their comrades approached, the village was harrassed by German cavalry patrols throughout the battle and, even though the focus of the action was further south, fell under German infantry occupation for several hours during the height of the battle. The village was thrust back into the front line a month later when it became the focus of several short but bloody encounters between the 26. Reserve-Division and the *84ᵉ régiment d'infanterie territoriale* as the Württembergers attempted to advance down the Bapaume-Cambrai road into Bapaume itself, whilst the French attempted to cover the retreat of their comrades. The village changed hands several times through 26/27 September but eventually had to be abandoned to the Germans after they began to break through to the south of this position.

Turn left onto the D930 towards **Bapaume** *and travel this route for five kilometres until the large roundabout east of Bapaume is reached. Turn right on this roundabout onto the D917, signposted Arras. At the next roundabout, after 700 metres, continue straight on (third exit), remaining on the D917 towards Arras. Yet another roundabout is encountered after a further 900 metres. Turn right here (first exit), remaining on the D917 to Arras. In one kilometre, at the first cross roads encountered, the* **1870-71 War Monument (8)** *to the 1871 Battle of Bapaume can be seen on the left.*

Located in the heart of the January 1871 battlefield, this monument is covered in the earlier tour in this book. However, it also marks the location in which major parts of the 26. Reserve-Division were congregated on 27 September 1914 following the entry into Bapaume and immediately prior to their push on Albert. From the mound of this monument the commander of the 26. Reserve-Division, General der Infanterie Franz Ludwig Freiherr von Soden, delivered orders to his subordinate commanders.

Turn left at this crossroads, onto the D10E3, towards Biefvillers – a significant village in the 1871 battle and part of the area vacated by the 88e division d'infanterie territoriale and I corps de cavalerie following the fall of Bapaume in September 1914 – which is reached after 1,500 metres. After skirting the northern edge of Biefvillers (and passing the 1871 memorial/mass grave) turn left onto the D7 towards **Bapaume**. *Travel straight on (third exit) at the new roundabout, and continue for 2.35 kilometres to a road junction in the suburbs of Bapaume. Here, turn*

Over 800 French soldiers who died in the August and September 1914 battles lie buried in this tiny plot of land: the mass grave, individual graves and memorial to the 'Combats of Le Transloy' located in the communal cemetery of that village.

left onto the D929 (rue d'Albert), then, after 130 metres, right onto the D917 towards the centre of Bapaume. Remain on this road (rue de Péronne) through the centre of Bapaume and continue for a further 5.5 kilometres until the village of **Le Transloy** *is reached.*

In Le Transloy, turn right onto the D19 (signposted Lesboeufs and Morval) and continue along this road for 1,100 metres until **Le Transloy communal cemetery (9)** *is seen over on the left.*

A monument, several individual graves and an ossuary (containing the remains of 792 soldiers) commemorate the '700 Braves' of the 'Combats de Le Transloy' of 28 August and 26-28 September 1914 that were fought near here. Although also commemorating the September action, the vast majority of burials date from August, when the *263e* and *338e régiments d'infanterie* of *123e brigade, 62e division d'infanterie* suffered 1,299 and 1,139 casualties respectively in the action of 28 August – fighting that lasted less than two hours. Out of the nearly 800 soldiers buried in the mass grave at Le Transloy, almost 700 are from the *338e régiment d'infanterie*.

Continue along the D19 towards Lesboeufs (noting that the road changes designation to the D74 soon after crossing the A1 motorway). In Lesboeufs, leave the D74 as it veers to the left and follow the C5 towards

The mass grave at Le Transloy as it appeared during the war.

… and in the 1920s.

Ginchy (also marked with a green CWGC sign, directing the traveller to Guards Cemetery). After 800 metres, **Guards Cemetery** *is passed on the right and, after a further 400 metres, the* **memorial obelisk to Captain Herbert Percy Meakin, 3rd Battalion, Coldstream Guards***, who was killed in action here on 25 September 1916, can be seen in the field to the right. Another British memorial, the* **Guards Memorial***, is passed after another 600 metres before the road turns to the right after 1,200 metres and into* **Ginchy***.*

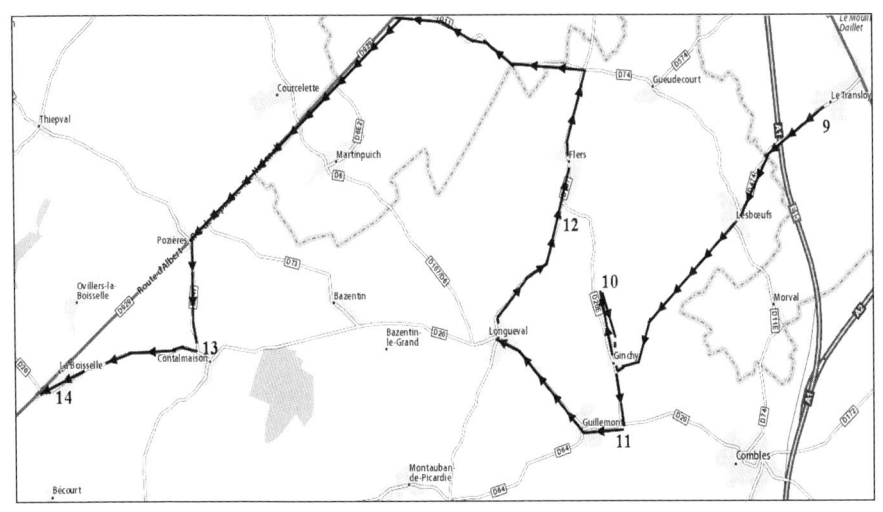

Tour 1: Tour of the Northern Somme Actions of August and September 1914 – Points 9 to 14.

At the first junction in Ginchy, turn right onto the Grande Rue. Passing the village war memorial and church, continue through Ginchy for 730 metres. Soon after passing the village cemetery, note the small copse and manicured lawn on the right. This marks the position of a **memorial to the *18e régiment d'infanterie territoriale*** (10).

Commemorating the actions of the *18e régiment d'infanterie territoriale* and their struggles with the Badisches Reserve-Infanterie-Regiment Nr. 109 for the possession of Flers and Ginchy on 26 September, this memorial specifically commemorates two soldiers from this regiment – 38 and 36 year old Parisians *sergent* Georges Pfister and *soldat 2.cl.* Pierre Georges Lejoindre (the widow of whom funded this memorial) of *11e compagnie (3e bataillon)*, who were both killed in action on this date. Neither man has a recorded grave location, but Georges Lejoindre is commemorated on his family grave in Père Lachaise Cemetery, Paris.

Return back down the same road to Ginchy and, at the crossroads, continue straight on onto the D20E. Some 900 metres along this road, there is another road junction upon which sits the truncated **memorial to the 20th**

Memorial to Sgt. Georges Pfister, Sdt. Pierre Georges Lejoindre, the *18e régiment d'infanterie territoriale* and their actions of 26 September 1914 near Ginchy.

59

(Light) Division (the cenotaph type structure on which it was originally fixed was taken down some twenty-five or more years ago, as it was unsafe). *Turn right at this junction and, after 150 metres, a* **memorial to the *265e régiment d'infanterie* (11)** *can be seen next to Guillemont's communal cemetery on the left.*

The *265e régiment d'infanterie* – known as *'le régiment Rose'* – came from the area of Nantes. Formed as the reserve regiment of the *65e régiment d'infanterie* in late July 1914, it consisted of reservists aged between 24 and 34 years of age (quite far removed from the 'elderly reservists' myth perpetuated in many texts), reinforced by a backbone of experienced regular soldiers who had been transferred to it upon its formation. As part of *121e brigade d'infanterie, 61e division d'infanterie* in August 1914, the regiment formed part of the Paris garrison intended to defend the capital and free the first line units from this duty. By 25 August, however, following the dramatic and unexpected turn of events during the German invasion of France, the regiment was ordered forward and arrived north of Arras the following day.

Memorial to the *265e régiment d'infanterie* and their actions of 28 August 1914 near Guillemont.

Part of the reserve element of *groupe d'Amade* (but soon to form part of the *6e groupe de divisions de reserve* (*groupe d'Ebener*) on 28 August), the regiment moved from Gavrelle, via Arras, to Bapaume to take part in the *bataille de Péronne*. After skirmishing with a patrol of Uhlans near Ginchy, they were part of the attack on Combles on 27 August, before moving back towards Waterlot Farm and holding the line between Ginchy and Guillemont on 28 August. Pushed back after five hours of tenaciously holding the line against overwhelming odds to Bois des Trônes before regrouping and withdrawing, the regiment suffered terrible losses during the day but also inflicted heavy casualties amongst the Germans, according to *médecin-major* Blondeau, who spent three days after his capture giving medical assistance to the German wounded of this battle; they thought that they had come up against an entire French corps rather than a brigade.

119 of the 28 August dead from *'le régiment Rose'* are commemorated by name on this memorial, including a separate plaque to *capitaine* **Maurice Hippolyte Marie Joseph Fockedey**, the commander of the 22*e compagnie* who was killed in action on the Ginchy plain that day. Maurice Fockedey was born in Lille on 3 October 1866 and was a graduate of the *École militaire d'infanterie Saint-Maixent-l'École* in 1891. Posthumously awarded the *Légion d'honneur* for his actions on 28 August, his citation reads:

Capitaine **Maurice Hippolyte Marie Joseph Fockedey, the commander of** *22e compagnie, 265e régiment d'infanterie.*

'A courageous captain with remarkable energy. On the morning of 28 August 1914, he gave his company an admirable example of coolness and bravery. He was killed at the head of his men during the day.'

His grave is unrecorded, but he is commemorated on several memorials in Lille and Nantes besides this plaque at Guillemont.

Note that, possibly rather confusingly to the modern eye, this memorial commemorates the men of the *265e régiment d'infanterie* of the *'XI Corps'*. This is not actually referring to their higher military formation, but rather to their military district of origin; in French military designations of the Great War period, unlike that of the British, Germans and Americans, etc., French military corps (*corps d'armées*) are given an Arabic numeral, eg. '6 *corps d'armée' – abbreviated as '6 C.A.'*, rather than the more commonly encountered Roman numeral identifier, XI Corps. For the French of this period, a Roman numeral refers to a military district or an army designation, eg *I Armée, II Armée*, etc.], not a 'corps' in modern understanding. In the case of this memorial, the reference is to the *XI Corps*' district (Nantes) rather than the military formation – *11e corps d'armée* – that was, at that time, fighting in the Meuse sector.

Continue into Guillemont and, remaining on the D20, turn right, towards Longueval, at the first major junction. After a kilometre, the site of what became known as **Waterlot Farm** *– a defensive point in both of the 1914 battles – is passed on the left before* **Longueval** *is reached.*

Turn right in the centre of Longueval onto the D197 (signposted Bapaume and Flers) and follow this road to the right as it leaves the village and skirts the north western section of Delville Wood. Just over two kilometres after leaving Longueval, and just as the village boundary of **Flers** *is reached, a memorial can be seen on the right. This is the* **memorial to the *17e* and *18e* régiments d'infanterie territoriale (12)** *and their actions at Flers, Ginchy and Lesboeufs on 26 September 1914.*

The memorial at Flers commemorating the 26 September actions of the *17e* and *18e* régiments d'infanterie territoriale.

These two regiments from Normandy (from Bernay and Évreux respectively; but containing a large number of men from the vicinity of Paris due to historical garrisons) made up *163e brigade d'infanterie* of the *82e division d'infanterie territoriale*. Consisting, mainly, of 35 to 41 year old men – most of whom had completed their compulsory, full time, military service by the turn of the century – the brigade spent the first month of the war guarding the river and canal crossings west of Lille. It began to move to the area of Amiens in the final days of August 1914 and then towards Courcelette and, east, to Lesboefs, Ginchy and Flers on 25 September. The battle of 26 September was the brigade's first action of the war and cost them dearly. Although the exact casualty figures for the *18e régiment d'infanterie territoriale* appear to be unavailable, the *17e régiment d'infanterie territoriale* sustained 290 casualties on this day, of which ninety-nine were missing or confirmed killed.

Travel through Flers and continue on the D197 for 2.1 kilometres to the crossroads with the D74. Turn left at this crossroads towards **Le Sars,** *which is reached after 3.5 kilometres. In the centre of Le Sars, turn left onto the D929 (the Albert-Bapaume road) and travel the 5.3 kilometres to* **Pozières***, where a left turn onto the D14, followed by another left onto the D20 after 1.75 kilometres, leads to* **Contalmaison (13)***.*

Damaged buildings in Contalmaison following the September 1914 fighting.

Strongly held by the *65e régiment d'infanterie*, supported by the *137e régiment d'infanterie,* Contalmaison was a key location that had to be captured if the German advance toward Albert was to have any chance of success. The village was attacked in force during the morning of 28 September 1914 by the Badisches Reserve-Infanterie-Regiment Nr. 109 and Württembergisches Reserve-Infanterie-Regiment Nr. 120 and finally fell at midday, forcing the French defenders back towards La Boisselle and Bécourt.

Continue along the D20 towards **La Boisselle (14)***, which is reached after 2.5 kilometres.*

Following the exact route taken by the Württembergisches Reserve-Infanterie-Regiment Nr. 120 after the fall of Contalmaison, La Boisselle was also strongly defended. Held by the *2e bataillon* of the *93ᵉ régiment d'infanterie*, supported by elements of the *64ᵉ* and *137ᵉ régiments d'infanterie* and the *82e régiment d'infanterie territoriale*, Reserve-Infanterie-Regiment Nr. 120 came under heavy fire about a hundred metres outside the village but, though enduring heavy casualties, eventually managed to force its way in. Fighting from house to house, the village was finally cleared by 5pm and the defenders pulled back to their previously prepared defences beyond the village cemetery (then located on what is now a small triangle of land between the D20 and D929 at the south western exit from the village and now the location of the Tyneside Memorial Seat) and the ground beyond an isolated farmhouse, soon to be infamous, located in the area known to the French as *l'Îlot de la Boisselle*. In 1914 this farmhouse was a relatively newly built building as the original was demolished in 1883 following the extensive damage it received in the skirmishes during the *affaire de Pozières* on 15 January 1871. Supported by devastating artillery fire on the village by the *51e régiment d'artillerie de campagne* the French held firm, despite vicious hand to hand fighting in and around the cemetery until nightfall. The German advance in this area was stopped.

Leave La Boisselle via the D20 and, remaining on this road, carefully cross the D929 in the direction of Aveluy and Authuille. At the road junction, reached 770 metres after crossing the main road, turn right onto the C8 towards **Ovillers (15)**.

The farmhouse at the *Îlot de La Boisselle* ('Granatenhof') following the intense fighting of September and October 1914, but prior to the onset of mine warfare.

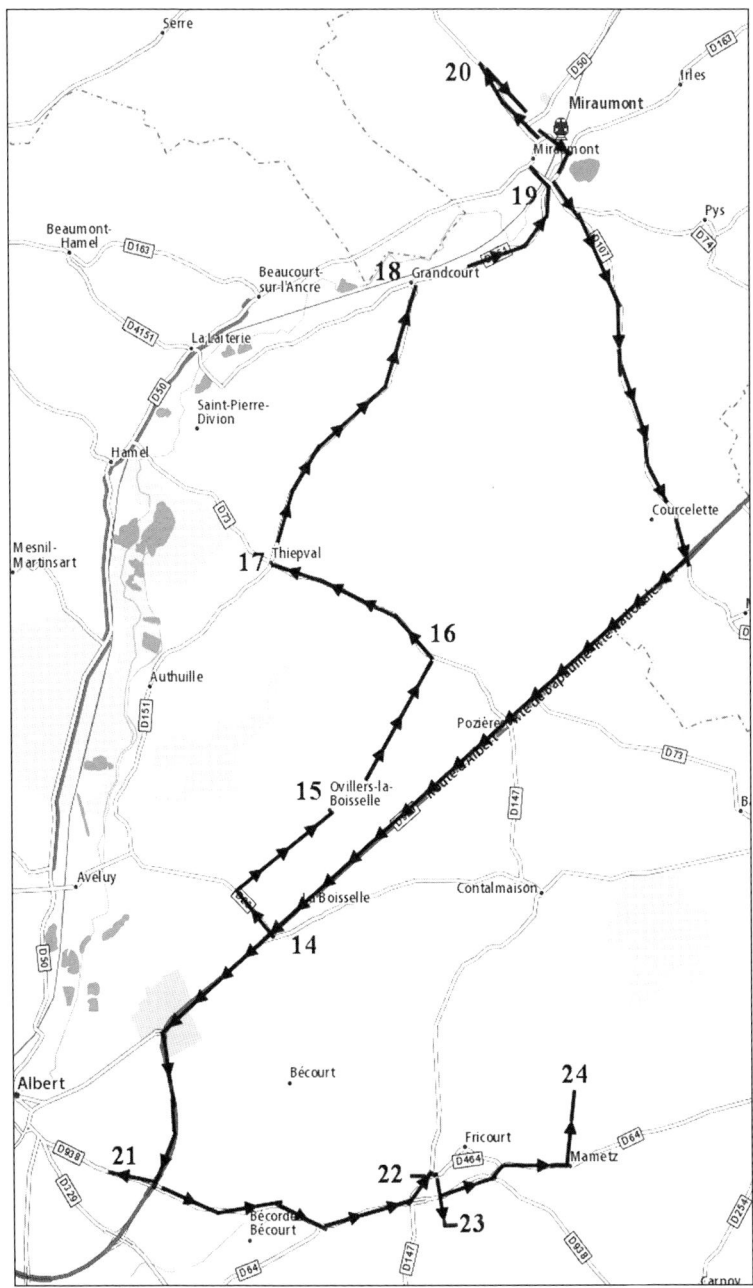

Tour 1: Tour of the Northern Somme Actions of August and September 1914 – Points 14 to 24.

Ovillers as viewed from the French front lines of September/October 1914, illustrating the expanse of exposed and open ground that separated the opposing forces.

Held by the *3e bataillon* of the *93ᵉ régiment d'infanterie* on the morning of 28 September and, like their *2e bataillon*, supported by elements of the *64ᵉ* and *137ᵉ régiments d'infanterie*, Ovillers was attacked from the east by the Württembergisches Reserve-Infanterie-Regiment Nr. 119. Holding the village until the late afternoon, the French were only forced to withdraw and abandon their positions after coming under increasingly heavy artillery fire, pulling back to pre-prepared positions on the slightly higher ground some 1,200 metres to the south/south west (approximately following the route of the D20 until the Ovillers turn off) and 500 metres to the west. French retaliatory artillery fire on the village, combined with their new positions forcing any further German attacks to have to cross a 'bowl' of extremely open territory also caused the Germans to dig in and here, again, the advance was completely halted by the evening.

At the fork at the eastern end of the village, follow the road to the right, back round to the D929 and then turn left towards Pozières. In Pozières, turn left onto the D73, signposted Thiepval. After 1.85 kilometres a small wooded parking area with a bas relief plaque will be encountered on the right. Though the plaque commemorates the 1916 actions, this refers to **Ferme du Mouquet (16)**, *which can be seen across the shallow valley behind it.*

More famous for the events of 1916, Ferme du Mouquet was the location of the headquarters of 51. Reserve-Infanterie-Brigade as from 29 September 1914 after French artillery forced it to vacate its original

Mouquet Farm, photographed later in the war but prior to the total destruction of 1916.

location in the château at Thiepval. The modern farm is slightly south of the original farm, which was located on the other side of the track leading to it.

Continue along this road for a further 1.5 kilometres to the crossroads at Thiepval. Turn left here onto the D151 and, after 300 metres, the (British) 18th Division memorial is reached on your right. This gives another opportunity for a **battlefield view (17)** *of some of the September 1914 fighting.*

View across the battlefield north of Thiepval showing the area fought over by the 10. Württembergische Infanterie-Regiment Nr. 180 and the *82e régiment d'infanterie territoriale* on 29 September 1914.

Looking towards the church and village of Thiepval, in 1914 your view here would have been obstructed by the buildings of Thiepval Château that would have straddled the road some 100 metres to your front and encompassed parts of the farm building you can also see. This, until the afternoon of 29 September 1914, was the brigade headquarters for 51. Reserve-Infanterie-Brigade. Left of here, the open ground upon which you can see Mill Road Cemetery and the Ulster Tower marks the area upon which the soldiers from 10. Württembergische Infanterie-Regiment Nr. 180 were forced to stop and dig in after it became apparent that Thiepval Wood was impenetrable due to wire defences and because it was under heavy fire from French troops and artillery massing across the Ancre valley to the north east on 29 September. These two features also mark the area in which the *82e régiment d'infanterie territoriale* was stopped by 3. Bataillon of Infanterie-Regiment Nr. 180 as they attacked up the slope from Hamel as part of *176e brigade d'infanterie*'s attempt to outflank Thiepval to the north on that same date. Across the field to your front, and directly behind the memorial, is Thiepval Wood, as it was known to the British; and as Thiepval Wald to the Germans. Slightly confusingly, on some French maps and records, it is sometimes referred to as Bois d'Authuille.

Return to the crossroads and, passing the eastern fringe of Thiepval, continue for another 3.5 kilometres along the D151 to Grandcourt and the site of the important **Grandcourt river crossing (18)**. *(Note that the present crossing may not be used by the public.)*

This is the scene where, covered by elements of 2. Kavallerie-Division, the 2. Bataillon of Reserve-Infanterie-Regiment Nr. 99 and two companies from the 3. Bataillon of Württembergische Infanterie-Regiment Nr. 180 fought with he *82e* and *83e régiments d'infanterie territoriale* for control of the crossing point on 28 September 1914, eventually taking complete control; however, other than for one short term breakthrough, they were unable to develop the gain due to the presence of French artillery and repeated French counter-attacks that continued into the following day. The Germans were forced to strengthen the area as a defensive position rather than press on with the attack.

The river crossing at Miraumont easily fell to the 2. Bataillon of Reserve-Infanterie-Regiment Nr. 99 who, with their third battalion moving to the right of the village, then proceeded towards the fortified farmhouse of Beauregard, north west of the village, to relieve the company of Jäger cyclists who were, at that time, in occupation. Soon after the relief was completed, French artillery made the position untenable and it was abandoned for relatively safer location of a nearby sunken road and entrenchments at the edge of Miraumont.

After a further two kilometres on the same road, Petit Miraumont is reached. At the crossroads here, turn left onto the D107 towards Miraumont. Immediately after passing underneath the (height and width restricted) railway bridge the site of the **Miraumont river crossings (19)** *are reached.*

One of the tactically crucial river crossings at Miraumont as it appeared in 1915.

With a similar story to the crossing at Grandcourt, the present rather insignificant looking Miraumont crossing was captured by the 2. Bataillon of Reserve-Infanterie-Regiment Nr. 99 on 28 September. They crossed the river but were forced into a defensive role soon afterwards by repeated counter-attacks conducted by the *82e division d'infanterie territoriale*.

200 metres beyond the river crossing site, turn right at the major junction onto the D50 (direction Puisieux and Achiet le Petit) and follow this road in this direction through Miraumont for 500 metres until it takes a ninety degree turn to the right. At this point, turn left off the road (by travelling

Beauregard Farm and dovecote in September 1914.

straight on!) onto the D107 (direction Puisieux) and continue for 800 metres until a small, but complex, junction of farm tracks meets the road on the right and a small area of scrub and woodland can be seen bordering the road on the left. This woodland is the site of the **Ferme de Beauregard (20)**

A heavily disputed position, Beauregard Farm was a substantial set of buildings – including a tall dovecote offering commanding views over the Ancre valley – protected by a thick wall. Practically undefended at the time of the German attacks of 28 September, it was occupied and held by a cyclist company from a Jäger Bataillon until they were reinforced by the 2. Bataillon of Reserve-Infanterie-Regiment Nr. 99. Shelled out of the position during the evening (in the same bombardment that forced the abandonment of the Miraumont river crossing), the farm then became a focus of attention for the *21e régiment d'infanterie territoriale*, who managed to briefly occupy the buildings before being pushed out themselves. The following morning, as the *82e division d'infanterie territoriale* launched successive, though ultimately unsuccessful, attacks throughout the day, the casualties mounted in this area but the line remained static. For the next five days, numerous costly attacks on the farm by the *18e, 21e* and *22e régiments d'infanterie territoriale* were conducted; but they all failed to dislodge the German defenders.

A particularly interesting casualty in these actions was *Soldat* Pascal François Félix ; a caster/moulder who was resident at Louviers, Normandy at the time that war was declared. Unremarkable in most aspects – he saw his compulsory service through with the *28e régiment d'infanterie* from 1896 to 1898 before passing to the *armée territoriale* in 1908 and moved to Louviers in 1912 before being mobilised into on 1 August 1914 – what makes him stand out is that he was born, on 27 November 1874, in New Jersey, USA and held dual US/French nationality. He was killed in action during one of the attacks at Ferme de Beauregard whilst serving with the *21e régiment d'infanterie territoriale* on 1 October 1914 and so it is possible that Pascal could be amongst the first combat deaths of a United States' citizen of the Great War.

After turning around, return through Miraumont the same way that has just been travelled but continue on the D107 through Petit Miraumont. After skirting Courcelette, the junction with the D929 is reached after 4.4 kilometres. Turn right – now following the route taken by the 26. Reserve-Division on 27-28 September towards the primary target of the September 1914 attacks – **Albert**.

In 7.7 kilometres turn slightly left at the roundabout (third exit), continuing on the D929 signposted 'A1 (Paris)'. At the next roundabout, after 1.75 kilometres, turn right (first exit) onto the D938 in the direction of Albert. 400 metres along this road, the **Nécropole Nationale d'Albert (21)** *will be seen on the right.*

The *Nécropole Nationale d'Albert.*

Created in 1923 and containing the remains of 6,293 French soldiers, this cemetery is a concentration of smaller cemeteries from across the entire Somme *département*. 2,879 of the dead are interred within four ossuaries which also house two burials of the British Empire. Another, separate, grave within the cemetery contains the remains of Labourer Wing Yu Shan of the Chinese Labour Corps, who died on 5 December 1918. Though the French graves range in date from 1914 right through to 1918, as might be expected the majority date from the 1914 – 1916 period, with a large percentage of these being from the October 1914 to August 1915, the latter date coinciding with the British Army taking over most of the Somme front north of the river.

After a further 650 metres towards Albert, the town's **Communal Cemetery** *is reached on the left of the road and the CWGC* **Albert Communal Cemetery and extension** *can be seen.*

The CWGC plot contains 862 British, Canadian, Australian and Indian First World War graves and twenty-five from 1940 and 1944. If the path to the right of the extension is followed through the cemetery, a *carré militaire* of French graves can be found. Signposted as the ***carré Breton***, this small cemetery is hidden behind a hedge and contains the remains of 115 soldiers, many from the *19e* and *118e régiments d'infanterie* but nearly exclusively hailing from Brittany and Normandy, who were killed in the vicinity of Ovillers-la Boisselle or died of wounds in Albert in 1914-15. A small monument at the entrance to the *carré* carries the simple inscription: '*A nos soldats bretons 1914 1918'*.

The *carré Breton*, tucked away in the communal cemetery of Albert.

Turn around and travel back along the D938 away from Albert, travelling straight on (second exit) at the roundabout. At the hamlet of St Quentin (Fricourt) – entered after three kilometres – turn left onto the D147 towards **Fricourt** *centre. After passing* **Fricourt British Cemetery** *on the left, take the next left turn onto the 'rue du 8 Mai 1945' and follow the road to the left where it forks. As the recycling yard is entered at the end of this road (where it is possible to turn around), note that the final building on the left before entering the yard is built on the* **site of Fricourt Station (22).** *The post-war station, which is visible to your front as you descend into the yard, was built in a similar design to the original, but some seventy metres further west.*

Fricourt railway station as it appeared pre-war. The scene of a desperate stand in September 1914 and a front line location into 1916, this spot soon became a constant source of harassment to the Germans holding Fricourt and was a hub of aggressive activity throughout 1914 and into 1915.

Stubbornly held by less than a *section* made up from stragglers and displaced men from the *65ᵉ régiment d'infanterie* on 28/29 September 1914, Fricourt Station became the scene of a last-ditch defence of the final substantially defensible building before Bécordel, on the south eastern approach to Albert. Giving the impression of being far stronger in size than they were, this section stopped the German attacks by much greater forces and forced them to dig in along the western and southern edges of the village of Fricourt. The station, though far from undisputed throughout, would remain in the French, then British, front line until the Somme battle of 1916.

Return along the rue du 8 Mai 1945 and go straight across the junction taking the lower (and smaller) of the two roads (the 'rue d'en Bas') to your front. Follow this road for 300 metres to the junction with the D938 and cross this main road, following the exact route of the Reserve-Infanterie-Regiment Nr. 40 attacks on 29 September and continuing up the small road opposite (which has, for many years, been marked with 'Ball Trap' [clay-pigeon shooting] advertisement boards) for another 600 metres through Bois d'Engremont (Bois Francais on the right of the road and Bois Allemand on the left). At the crossroads (where it is possible to park a car if needed) take the left-hand track, noticing the remains of the World War Two anti-aircraft positions (built by the French in 1939, but used and extended by the Wehrmacht between 1940 and 1944, forming part of the aerial defences of the French Armée de l'Air, then Luftwaffe, airfield at Méaulte) and bordered to the rear by slight depressions marking the remains of mine craters of 1915 vintage on the left, for approximately 400 metres. This height is **Cote 110 (23).**

Cote 110, with the trees of Bois Allemand and Bois Français clearly visible on its summit, as viewed from the Fricourt to Mametz road.

With the lower slopes partially occupied during the night of 28/29 September 1914 by Badisches Reserve-Infanterie-Regiment Nr. 111 and Reserve-Infanterie-Regiment Nr. 40 in an unplanned advance over the Albert – Péronne road under the cover of darkness, the main assault om this dominant position was launched on 29 September after news was received that Fricourt had been captured. Tenaciously defended by the *37e régiment d'infanterie* and the *2e bataillon de chasseurs à pied*, the advance up the slope under heavy rifle and artillery fire was laborious and costly, forcing an entrenchment of the positions once the peak was reached. Several counter-attacks continued throughout the day until the French themselves began to dig in opposite the newly dug German positions. Cote 110 would remain a heavily disputed position for the next nine months as is indicated by the remains of the mine craters that can still be seen within the trees of Bois d'Egremont.

Return to the crossroads of tracks at Bois d'Egremont, continuing westwards for 100 metres, with Bois Francais to your right. Here is located an entrance to the wood. Take this entrance and follow the path to the **Private Memorial to H. Thomassin** (49°59'23.1"N, 2°43'02.0"E).

Located in the French front line area of late 1914 to 1916 (with evidence of trenches and craters in the (private property) wood around the memorial), this is the tomb of *soldat* **François Henri Thomassin of the 26e *régiment d'infanterie*,** who was killed in action here, possibly whilst relaying a message to the officers in the front line at Bois Français on 30 September 1914. Born at St Nicolas, Meurthe et Moselle on 19 January 1880, he enlisted for his compulsory military service at Nancy on 4 November 1901, and was promoted to *soldat 1er Classe* in September 1902. He was discharged to the reserve in November 1904. A notary clerk

The tomb of *Sdt* François Henri Thomassin of the *26*e *régiment d'infanterie* in Bois Français.

in civilian life, he was mobilised for war service as a reservist on 2 August 1914 and, after service in Lorraine, saw action south of the River Somme at Dompierre before crossing to the north bank and Cote 110, where he would be killed in action within thirty-six hours of arrival in this sector. His remains were not identified after the war.

Return to the crossroads with the main road and turn right onto the D938 for 600 metres. Turn left onto the D64 towards **Mametz**, *following this road as it curves to the right into Mametz village.*

At this curve, the field to your front is the scene of where Reserve-Infanterie-Regiment Nr. 40, accompanied by Reserve-Jäger-Bataillon Nr. 14, moving slightly left to right across your field of view, accidentally attacked German held Mametz instead of Fricourt (obscured during their advance by the trees of Bois de Fricourt) in the darkness of the night of 28 September and sustained numerous casualties as the 'defenders' returned fire.

Upon arrival in Mametz, turn left onto the C4 at the village war memorial, signposted to Contalmaison and (by a green CWGC sign) the 38th (Welsh) Division Memorial. In 720 metres, the road forks (with the right-hand road leading to the Welsh memorial). Stop here (carefully!) and look back towards Mametz and across the fields for a **Battlefield view (24)** *of the 1914 actions here.*

With your back to the 38th (Welsh) Division Memorial road junction, look back up the road you have just travelled. The field to your right is the location of the advance of Reserve-Infanterie-Regiment Nr. 40 of 28 September. On that night this field was lit by burning hay bales, with the houses of Fricourt (in the distance to your right) and Mametz (over the crest of the slope to your front) providing similar illumination. With the dark expanse of Bois de Fricourt obscuring the light coming from Fricourt, the glow of Mametz became stronger as the advance continued; thus, from here, it becomes clear as to why the erroneous attack on Mametz occurred.

Go back to Mametz centre and turn left onto the D64, heading towards Montauban. After passing **Dantzig Alley British Cemetery** *on the left after 500 metres, a further two kilometres takes us to the* **Memorial to capitaine** **Henri Thiéron de Monclin**, *69e régiment d'infanterie* **(25)** *on the left, shortly before entering Montauban.*

Henri Louis Jules Antoine Thiéron de Monclin was born in the fashionable *7e arrondissement* of Paris on 13 June 1883. Educated at St

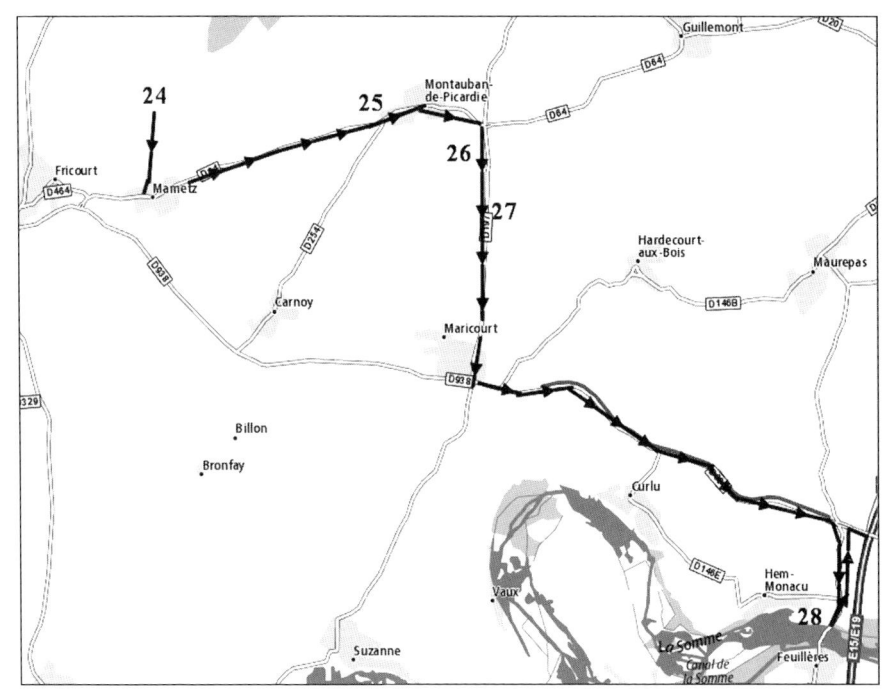

Tour 1: Tour of the Northern Somme Actions of August and September 1914 – Points 24 to 28.

Joseph de Reims school between 1895 and 1900, he entered St Cyr as an *élève officier* after voluntarily enlisting at Mézières in 1902. Following graduation, he was commissioned as a *sous-lieutenant* in the *2e régiment de Zouaves* in 1904 and served in Morocco, where he was promoted to *lieutenant* in 1906. In 1907 he gained combat experience during the occupation of Oudjda and against the Beni Snassen before the suppression of the revolt in Casablanca; and he took part in many smaller actions of the *Algero-Marocain* campaign over the next few years. On 24 November 1911 he was transferred to the *69e régiment d'infanterie* in Tunisia and served with them in Algeria until December 1913, when they returned to France. Soon after

Le capitaine **Henri Thiéron de Monclin,** *69e régiment d'infanterie.*

the declaration of war, he was in action during the Battles of the Frontiers and was wounded in the arm during fighting at Haut de Koeking, near Morhange, on 20 August 1914 and was then medically evacuated to

Bordeaux. Not content to remain in the rear, however, he discharged himself from hospital before his wound had healed and made his own way back to the front. Promoted to *capitaine* on 2 September, he had returned to his regiment within a couple of weeks of his wounding. He was soon back in the fray, commanding the *5e compagnie*; he was killed in action near the position of this memorial whilst covering the retreat of his regiment following their expulsion from Montauban on 28 September 1914. The regimental history of the *69e régiment d'infanterie* notes:

Memorial near Montauban to *Capt* Henri Thiéron de Monclin of the *69e régiment d'infanterie*. This was erected near to the spot where he fell on 28 September 1914.

'He was a fine soldier, that Monclin, one of the purest souls of our regiment. Having already been wounded once with a bullet in the arm during the fighting of August 1914 and evacuated to Bordeaux, he hurried his return to combat. The city where he was being treated presented too cruel a contrast – having seen suffering, he did not want the 'obnoxious' fun [of a city away from the fighting]. Fleeing the rear without being fully healed, he wanted to take up his place again in combat. Every day he would go down the lines as far as the aid post to have his wound re-dressed.

In Montauban, the company he commanded was up in the front line. The enemy attacked with fury. On the left and right [the French] were withdrawing, but no orders had been received by his company. He would die at this post.

Showing familiarity with his men, he shared a few chocolate bars and stated, 'It's over – we won't need any provisions'. *Capitaine* Monclin then made a large sign of the cross and stated 'My children. Our mission is to hold on here and we will stay until death. Let those who believe in God, pray.'

He then seized the rifle of a dead man and fired it like a soldier. A bullet hit him in the shoulder and, as his wound was dressed, he still tried to take aim – he did not even think!'

The enemy was gaining ground and a *sous-officier* talked of retreat, but the irrepressible captain silenced him. He still had enough strength to take his binoculars to observe [the situation]. A second bullet laid him dead!'

He was awarded a posthumous *Légion d'honneur*:

'Although already wounded, he showed heroic courage by refusing to have his wounds dressed and was killed with half of his company to protect the retreat of a battalion.'

An older brother, Léon, was killed in action before the war whilst serving with the *141e régiment d'infanterie* at El Feda, Morocco in September 1912; and a younger brother, André, was killed in action with the *147e régiment d'infanterie* at Bois Trapèze on the Champagne front in February 1915. Henri is buried in the communal cemetery at Beaucourt-sur-l'Hallue.

Continue through Montauban to the crossroads with the D197 leading to Maricourt. Turn right onto the D197 and look across the fields to the left and right for another **battlefield view (26)**

An appreciation of the position of **Montauban** on its low ridge may be had here from the remains of the old Montauban brick works (the scrubland to the right of the road). Attacked and captured by the *3e bataillon* of the *69e régiment d'infanterie* on 27 September 1914, the French held the village under repeated German counter-attacks into 28 September when, under the cover of fog and with their flanks dangerously exposed due to the loss of ground either side of the village, they were forced out. Several counter attacks were made in an attempt to recapture this prime location throughout the day; but they all failed, and the village remained in German hands until July 1916.

Exactly 1,620 metres from the crossroads, the German army dug in across this road. A **battlefield view (27)** *of this sector at the end of September 1914 can be afforded from this point on the road.*

This is the location of the German front line as it would remain until July 1916. The flag poles of the Franco-British (1916) memorial can be seen to the front. This marks the French front line position at the end of the 1914 actions. At this point, as you face the memorial, the German front line spread across the field to your right to about half way between your location and the elongated wooded area on the horizon (Talus Boisé). It then moved northwards to skirt this woodland and out of view, proceeding in a westwards direction as far as Mametz and Fricourt. To your left, it crossed the field eastwards before sweeping south parallel with, but about 150 metres from, Bois de Maricourt, which is the nearest woodland to your front left.

Continue along the eastern edge of **Maricourt** *– held by the 69e and, then, the 45e régiments d'infanterie under sustained German attacks throughout 27 and 28 September – to the junction with the D938 and turn left towards Péronne, following this route for exactly five kilometres until you come to a major crossroads at Bois de Hem. Turn right here towards Hem-Monacu on the D146. After 1,000 metres, the* **Monacu and Feuilléres river crossings (28)** *are reached.*

Maricourt as it appeared in December 1914.

An important river crossing that separated the northern and southern battle areas, the *11e division d'infanterie* attempted to capture and hold this location to facilitate the movement of troops – especially cavalry – between the two zones in an attempt to relieve Péronne on 25 September. However, with the I. Königlich Bayerisches Armee-Korps having made the first moves, the bridges were already in German hands and, other than forcing the Bavarians to evacuate for a short while, all attempts by the

Monacu Farm. An infamous location during the 1916 battle, but an underused strongpoint covering the Somme crossing between Hem and Feuilléres in August 1914. Whoever held this farm could dominate this major, important crossing; the French abandoned it.

A view from the Somme canal bridge at Feuilléres. From this point, other bridges traversed another 300 metres of slow flowing river and impenetrable marshland and was the most important Somme crossing between Péronne and Cappy.

11e division and elements of the *10e division de cavalerie* to wrest this position from their hands were to prove futile.

Return to the D938 crossroads and turn right towards Péronne which, after passing through Cléry-sur-Somme, is reached in another seven kilometres.

End of Tour

GPS Waypoints, August and September 1914 Tour

1 – 49°55'46.23"N, 2°56'4.93"E
2 – 50° 0'3.86"N, 2°57'40.37"E
3 – 50° 1'3.52"N, 2°56'36.51"E
4 – 50° 1'44.73"N, 2°54'35.20"E
5 – 50° 2'23.46"N, 2°54'44.73"E
6 – 50° 3'0.53"N, 2°54'18.24"E
7 – 50° 7'11.17"N, 2°56'4.69"E
8 – 50° 7'18.37"N, 2°50'39.44"E
9 – 50° 3'17.12"N, 2°52'55.28"E
10 – 50° 1'44.50"N, 2°49'44.84"E
11 – 50° 0'50.58"N, 2°49'55.09"E
12 – 50° 2'38.15"N, 2°49'11.09"E
13 – 50° 1'25.49"N, 2°43'45.38"E
14 – 50° 1'12.89"N, 2°41'38.90"E
15 – 50° 1'51.33"N, 2°41'51.59"E
16 – 50° 3'2.99"N, 2°42'45.52"E
17 – 50° 3'9.26"N, 2°41'7.85"E
18 – 50° 4'58.30"N, 2°42'34.61"E
19 – 50° 5'29.03"N, 2°43'51.19"E
20 – 50° 6'6.49"N, 2°43'18.05"E
21 – 49°59'46.53"N, 2°39'46.17"E
22 – 49°59'45.37"N, 2°42'25.65"E
23 – 49°59'14.85"N, 2°43'24.32"E
24 – 50° 0'12.71"N, 2°44'20.94"E
25 – 50° 0'16.03"N, 2°46'17.53"E
26 – 50° 0'6.85"N, 2°47'29.77"E
27 – 49°59'20.01"N, 2°47'27.63"E
28 – 49°57'5.16"N, 2°50'54.85"E

Chapter Three

Final Adjustments and the Stabilisation of the Line, September-October 1914

Alhough attention had begun to focus to the north by 30 September, with titanic struggles taking place around Arras, the Artois, Ypres and the Yser over the coming weeks, the situation as far as both the French and German armies were concerned was far from ideal in the sectors on the Somme and southern Pas-de-Calais fronts. Realising that, as had happened further south, a prolonged, positional campaign was becoming likely, a struggle for the most favourable and advantageous ground upon which to conduct such a campaign began to ensue. Small scale, local, offensives would continue throughout the Somme sector, but it would be in the north of this sector where the most dramatic alterations to the line took place. As far as the troops located on the whole of the Somme front north of the river were concerned, the fact that they were no longer engaged in a defined 'battle' as such was nothing more than a case of semantics. In this sector, and especially so in the northern parts along the Ancre valley, 30 September would simply be a continuation of the events of the previous few days.

In the south, below Fricourt and Mametz, the front line held by Reserve-Infanterie-Regiment Nr. 40 was lit up by French searchlights prior to first light in an attempt to illuminate the German positions and dazzle the defenders. Followed by an infantry assault, the lights, unfortunately for the attackers, also illuminated their own positions and, though the *26e régiment d'infanterie* managed to break through into Fricourt and engage in close combat amongst the buildings of the village, over 160 casualties were incurred, and the ground could not be held. At Cote 110 another *11e division d'infanterie* attack was stopped by the machine guns of the Königlich Bayr. 5. Infanterie-Regiment 'Großherzog Ernst Ludwig von Hessen' and Reserve-Jäger-Bataillon Nr. 8 before it could even really begin, resulting in the capture of forty prisoners who had taken cover behind a low embankment and were unable to retreat. At Fricourt Station, the (now reinforced) defenders from the *65ᵉ régiment d'infanterie* made several attacks against the south east corner of Fricourt, each of which was preceded by an artillery bombardment. All along the line between the Somme and the Ancre and along the Ancre valley north

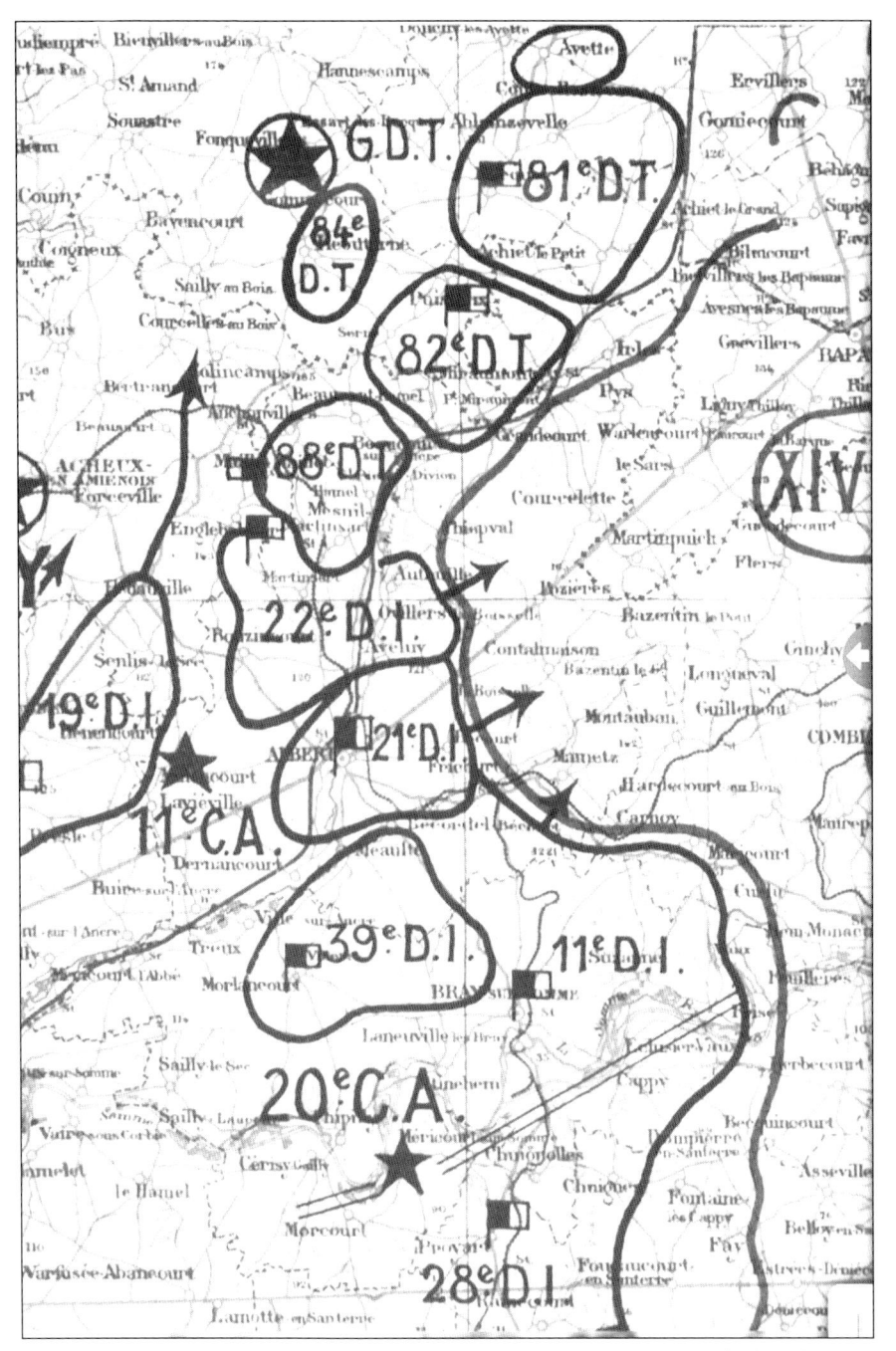

French situation, 30 September 1914. (*Les Armées Françaises dans la Grande Guerre*)

Rudimentary French fire trenches circa September/October 1914. Whilst the front line infantryman initially fought out of ditches, scrapes and shallow slit trenches, to their rear the *génie* were busy constructing more substantial systems in more advantageously defensive locations. Many of these systems would become the front lines by the end of September and early October.

east of Thiepval between Grandcourt and Miraumont, numerous positional attacks, reconnaisance patrols, fire fights and probing assaults were conducted by the French, all of which were, eventually, repulsed.

With no headway being made by the French infantry, artillery, which had been heavily reinforced by fresh batteries arriving in the sector over the previous couple of days, became the dominant factor in this sector and the shelling intensified throughout the day. Mametz, Fricourt, La Boisselle, Ovillers, Pozières and Thiepval were all targeted and, with varying intensity of fire, all suffered severe damage throughout the day. Fricourt Château was all but destroyed, as was the château of Thiepval ; and Mouquet Farm, the regimental headquarters of Infanterie-Regiment Nr. 180 and the brigade headquarters of 51. Reserve-Infanterie-Brigade after they had been shelled out of Thiepval Château the previous day, was set alight. In the skies, French aircraft appeared to have a free reign on the 30th, flying low over German positions and dropping steel flechettes and bombs on the men and targets below. They even managed to destroy part of General Franz von Soden's – the commander of the 26. (Württembergische) Reserve-Division – billet in Martinpuich, causing him the loss of several personal items, along with his pride. Throughout the day, however, German artillery attempted to counter their French counterparts. Initially unsuccessful, several reinforcement batteries arrived in the sector during the afternoon and began a bombardment of the French rear areas as far as Albert, where several buildings were set alight. German infantry reinforcements also began to arrive, with the 7. Division of IV. Armeekorps arriving on the northern flank of XIV. Reserve-Korps and the 1. Garde-Infanterie-Division disembarking at St Quentin en route for the Somme. By evening an artillery and infantry stalemate had developed along all the line south of Thiepval to the River Somme and entrenchments on both sides were improved, strengthened and deepened. This situation would continue, relatively unchanged, into the next day.

The ruins of Thiepval Château following the bombardments.

Around mid-day on 2 October, and much to the relief of the XIV. Reserve-Korps, who were beginning to feel threatened by French pressure on their northern flank near Miraumont (especially in the vicinity of Beauregard Farm, which had been attacked, yet again, by the *18ᵉ régiment d'infanterie territoriale* with great losses due to German artillery fire the day before), the Gardekorps began to arrive near Bapaume. The following day, 1. Garde-Infanterie-Division progressed from between Noreuil and Vaulx-Vraucourt to the line north of Miraumont opposite the *81e* and *82e divisions d'infanterie territoriale* and the flank was secured to the extent that it was felt that a further push could be made in this sector. Almost immediately upon arrival, they began to make a move on Puiseux and Serre, north of Beauregard Farm via Achiet le Petit, pushing the *81e division d'infanterie territoriale* out of Achiet during the first few hours after arrival. After encroaching on the northern flank of the *82e division d'infanterie territoriale*, the *21e régiment d'infanterie territoriale* moved forward into positions south and east of Puiseux, with the *2e bataillon* in the line, the *3e bataillon* holding the area between Toutvent Farm and Serre and the *1er bataillon* en route from Corbie.

A relatively peaceful night was spent in these positions before, at around midday on 3 October, a violent bombardment on Puiseux began, heralding a German attack at 5pm. Though the attack was held up by French artillery around the area of the Puiseux-Achiet road, Bucquoy, to the north, was lost by the neighbouring *88e division d'infanterie territoriale* and the attack progressed on to the village of Gommecourt, leaving the positions at Puiseux dangerously exposed. After coming under heavy fire from the area of Beaucourt in the south, Achiet to the east and Bucquoy to the north during the morning of 4 October, the north east corner of Puiseux fell after the defenders began to run low of ammunition. An assault directed from the area of Beauregard Farm finally forced the *21e régiment d'infanterie territoriale*, covered by two companies from the *1e bataillon,* out of Puiseux around 1pm and they fell back towards Hébuterne beyond a protective line established by the *22e régiment d'infanterie territoriale* to the east of Serre. Fighting in Puiseux would, however, continue into the evening as the final remnants of *12e compagnie, 21e régiment d'infanterie territoriale*, who had been holding the buildings and grounds of the château, finally and gradually withdrew via La Louvière Farm and made their way towards French lines through enemy occupied territory. By 3pm, the main thrust had reached the eastern approach of Serre and the *22e régiment d'infanterie territoriale* was driven out of the trenches defending this village, forcing a general retreat towards Hébuterne and Sailly-au-Bois. There the shattered regiments managed to reform and, after collecting stragglers and isolated groups, moved forward again to a defensive line on the low slopes before Hébuterne. A counter-attack on Serre during the afternoon met with abject failure, but confirmed that the Germans were digging in on the slopes opposite; these positions remained practically immovable for the next eight months. The operations of 4 October beween Puiseux and Hébuterne cost the *21e régiment d'infanterie territoriale* 478 officers and men killed and missing, yet the blood letting in this area during the first year of the war was far from over.

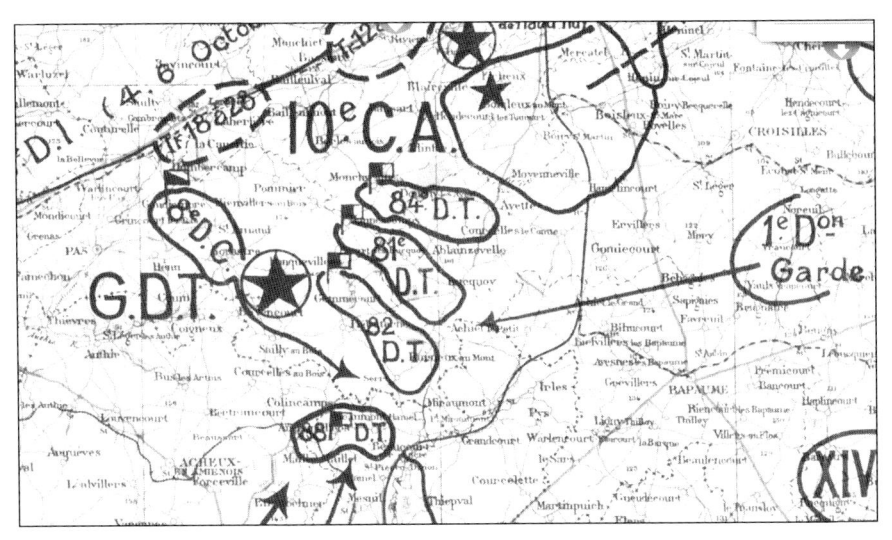

Attack of the 1. Garde-Infanterie-Division, 3 October 1914. (*Les Armées Françaises dans la Grande Guerre*)

Whilst this *1er bataille d'Hébuterne* was in progress, the battalions of Reserve-Infanterie-Regiment Nr. 99 took up positions, under heavy artillery fire, near Beauregard Farm and before Beaucourt in anticipation of joining the assault and gaining a line between the heights east of Beaumont to the Ancre river crossing southwest of Beaucourt. In the very early hours of 5 October, reinforced by elements of Reserve-Infanterie-Regiment Nr. 110, a night assault was conducted aginst the *88e division d'infanterie territoriale* (and *8e division de cavalarie*, who had been rushed forward from Gaudiempré in order to plug the gap south of the *82e division d'infanterie territoriale* caused by the fighting around Puisieux) that demanded an advance of some 3,000 metres. Before Beaumont-Hamel, good progress was made under the cover of artillery fire and, with the French defenders here only putting up a token resistance, the advance progressed rapidly on to Cote 143 (later known as the Redan Ridge) and the decision was made to make a move directly on Beaumont-Hamel.

The village was entered at 5:30am, to the near total surprise of the French defenders, who had not realised that the Germans had got so close. Consequently, around a hundred French prisoners were taken and, after forcing some entrenched defenders out of the southern part of the village, the advance was continued in the direction of Auchonvillers, where a battalion of the *84e régiment d'infanterie territoriale* was assembling for a counter attack. This concentration was observed from the heights of Hawthorn Ridge and fire was laid down on the village, forcing the French to seek shelter in the buildings. A French attack was made, however, but it was weak and ineffective and was beaten back by rifle fire from Cote 143.

Throughout the morning the French artillery shelled the Germans near Beaumont-Hamel. This was combined with a German bombardment of the village ; because of the rapid advance of the previous day, the gunners were not notified of its capture. The effect was to force the German infantry to seek shelter and dig in. Despite mounting casualties, Reserve-Infanterie-Regiment Nr. 99 was reinforced during the evening by troops from Reserve-Infanterie-Regiment Nr. 110 and two Bavarian regiments; Kgl. Bayr. 5. Infanterie-Regiment and Kgl. Bayr. 17. Infanterie-Regiment (respectively of the 4 and 3 Königlich Bayerische Divisions). By this time, Beaumont-Hamel and the surrounding heights were firmly in German hands.

German memorial to the 1914 fallen from Reserve-Infanterie-Regiment Nr. 99. Erected by their comrades in Beaumont-Hamel.

At Beaucourt, however, the story was different as, though progress was made to the north of the village, the village itself was strongly barricaded and defended. Under a hail of fire, much of which was emitting from a *section de mitrailleuses* from the *116ᵉ régiment d'infanterie* firmly established in Beaucourt Château, the second

The ruins of Beaucourt after the passing of the 1914 actions.

Battalion of Reserve-Infanterie-Regiment Nr. 99 managed to break into the village and engage in a desperate house to house battle before finally managing to advance to the western edge. One company was engaged in a frenetic battle on the railway embankment at the southern edge of the village, constantly harassed by and unable to progress due to the machine guns at the château. At around 6:30am the château and grounds were finally cleared and an advance became possible. By the end of the day, Beaucourt Station and the Ancre valley were secured and the newly captured ground began to be consolidated.

Slightly further south, the *21e* and *22e divisions d'infanterie,* who had managed to push the French front line slightly forwards to the north and south of Ovillers and La Boisselle by occupying unoccupied land between the lines, had entrenched on Cote 141 (west of Authuille, south of Thiepval) and the heights above Ovillers. This, combined with the strong French outpost position on the south bank of the Ancre at St Pierre Divion, posed a significant threat to Thiepval – which was at the head of a small salient at that time – and the communications northwards towards the Beaumont Hamel area. Consequently, orders were issued to the Germans for the capture of the area between St Pierre Divion and Hill 141 to straighten the line and assist in making the Thiepval position more secure.

Launched by 51 Reserve Brigade (and Reserve-Infanterie-Regiment Nr. 119) against *44e brigade d'infanterie* during the evening of 5 October, this attack initially resulted in a total success as, completely surprised, the French were driven from St Pierre Divion and, through Thiepval and Authuille Woods, to the river. Only the village of Authuille remained in French hands in this sector (even Hamel, north of the river, was evacuated). French artillery was still hitting pre-selected targets from before the assault, ranged on Thiepval but not the forward line, proving them for once to be ineffective. The German attack, however, could not be pressed due to events taking place far to the north. Thiepval Wood, considered too swampy to be defensible, was later abandoned, as was Authuille Wood, which was too exposed to French gunners (as had been painfully experienced in the not too distant past). Just before 11pm, parts of the *19e* and *118ᵉ régiments d'infanterie* launched a vigorous attack on Cote 141 from Authuille but this was easily beaten back by Reserve-Infanterie-Regiment Nr. 121, holding the crest. A similar event occured the following morning that left hundreds of corpses strewn across the slopes as the French dug in opposite.

On 6 October, artillery ruled the day, preventing any major advance, as consolidation continued. Trench digging took place along Redan and Hawthorn ridges and the captured villages were prepared for defence. Along the Ancre a slight advance on the village of Hamel was made by the second battalion of Reserve-Infanterie-Regiment Nr. 99; however, the artillery preparation was cancelled when it was noticed that there were French children – though no French soldiers – still in the village. The advance, without artillery, went on nonetheless and Hamel, confirmed as unoccupied by French troops, was temporarily occupied. However, all impetus for the attack had now disappeared and the village was soon abandoned, the German line moving back to the higher ground on the river bank north east of Hamel. The French, at that time holding a line established between Auchonvillers and Mesnil, moved the *116ᵉ régiment d'infanterie* in to reoccupy Hamel the following day. Neither side had the strength any longer to continue the attacks, though the French developed a tactic of feigning an assault by shelling lengths of front line with high intensity for fifteen or twenty minutes and targeting specific areas to the rear giving the impression of a forthcoming attack. The Germans were reasonably content, the French rather less so, with the positions held and the line now stabilised both north and south of the Ancre.

In the southern section of the front, the line from the River Somme to Mametz was more settled, with only slight adjustments as both sides either dug forwards or pulled back slightly, usually without much exchange of fire, to gain the best possible topographical advantage. Slightly to the north west of this sector, Fricourt Station was a scene of constant patrol activity. The *6e compagnie* of the *160e régiment d'infanterie* launched a rather ambitious, but doomed, surprise assault on

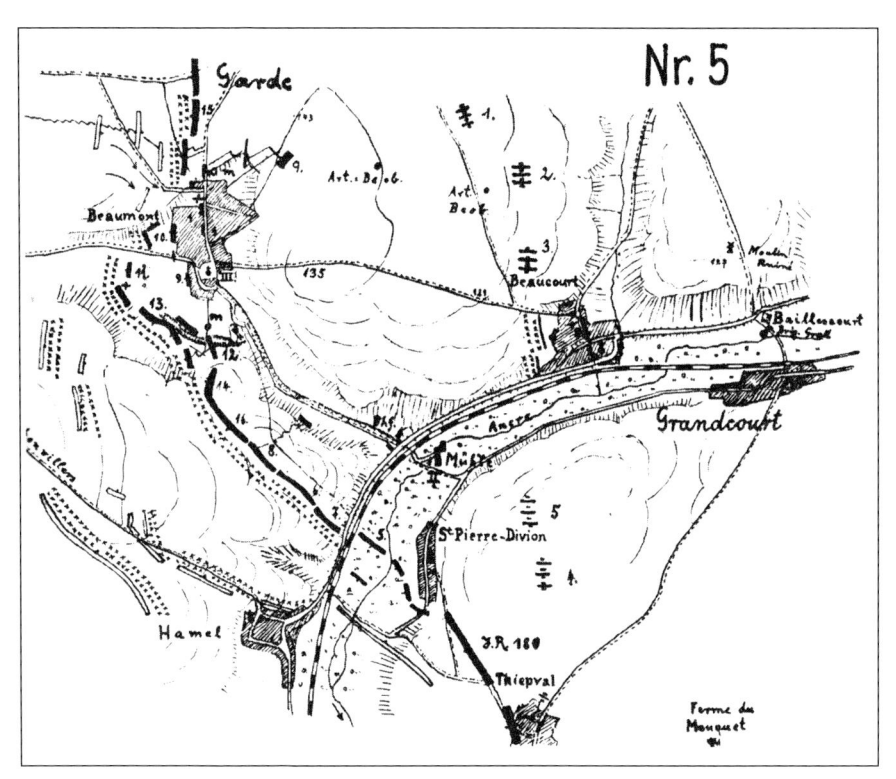

Situation between Beaumont Hamel and Thiepval, 6 October 1914.

Fricourt from hère on 4 October. The positions on Cote 110 were also still heavily disputed for several days as the French held the crest of this advantageous position; the Germans pushed slightly forwards in an attempt to gain at least a foothold on the hill. This jostling for position culminated on 12 October with an attack by *2 bataillon, 156e régiment d'infanterie* that resulted in the final establishment of the French line on the crest and the occupation of the woodland that became known as Bois Français on the western slope. Another small wood, slightly north of Bois Français, remained in German hands until July 1916 and, almost inevitably, became known as Bois Allemand. So tenaciously were these woods held over the coming months that the No Man's Land separating the two lines in this sector was only twenty-five yards wide.

To the north, orders were issued on 7 October to the 28. Reserve-Division to attempt an assault on the French positions in the village of Bécourt and on neighbouring Cote 106 which, apart from being an ideal general observation position, was serving as the 'eyes' of a particularly troublesome French battery of the *39e régiment d'artillerie de campagne* that was located on the La Boisselle to Bécourt road.

The rallying point of Reserve-Infanterie-Regiment Nr. 111 during the early hours of 8 October: Bécourt Château before the war.

The attack was launched from positions to the north of Fricourt at 11.30pm on 7 October against the *160e régiment d'infanterie* by Reserve-Infanterie-Regiment Nr. 40 and Reserve-Jäger-Bataillon 14, with Reserve-Infanterie-Regiment Nr. 111 as the main support close behind. The attackers steadily advanced in the moonlight but realised that they were heading in the wrong direction when they came across a patrol from Reserve-Infanterie-Regiment Nr. 120 just below La Boisselle. After adjusting direction, they then moved towards Bécourt, coming under heavy fire on their left flank as they approached to within 500 metres of the woodland surrounding the village. A company of Reserve-Infanterie-Regiment Nr. 40 was ordered to engage on this flank as the remainder of the attackers continued to proceed towards Bécourt. However, this company was soon pinned down and isolated from the main assault body as the fighting on the flank increased in intensity. The main body themselves came under fire 200 metres from the woodland, but they managed to struggle through it towards the open ground near Bécourt Château from where, after a quick reorganisation, an attack on Cote 106 was launched.

As the attackers approached Cote 106 they were hit by intense rifle fire from the flanks and from a network of trenches to their front as the *160e régiment d'infanterie* received rapid reinforcement from the *26e régiment d'infanterie*. An attempt to storm the hill was made, but this met with abject failure and the French managed to reoccupy some of the trenches lost during the advance, effectively cutting off and surrounding the attacking detachment on Cote 106. With messages unable to get through to the German lines, support was unavailable even though a battalion from Reserve-Infanterie-Regiment Nr. 120 at La Boisselle attempted to give assistance several times but was unable to break through the French positions. It was decided at this point to call off the attack and attempt to get back to the German lines but, after five attempts – each of which resulted in the Germans being forced back into the wood (which also happened to be under German artillery fire in a misguided attempt at assistance) – it became apparent that only small groups of men and individuals had any real chance of getting through. By 8am on 8 October, the bulk of the isolated unit had been forced to surrender. Soon afterwards, the company that had been isolated and pinned down on the flank during the first few hours of the attack managed to reach the wood, where they realised that the battle was lost and began to make their own way back to the German lines. Though individual stragglers and groups of men from this action would gradually return to the lines throughout the day, the cost had been high. The Second Battalion of Reserve-Infanterie-Regiment Nr. 111 suffering the most; at the end of the day, they could only muster 150 men fit for duty. The regimental history of the *160e régiment d'infanterie* does not give precise casualty figures, but states that, between themselves and the *26e régiment d'infanterie*, they took ten officers and 400 men prisoner during the night of 7/8 October 1914. It is quite probably an exaggeration, but it gives an indication of how cataclysmic the events of that night were for the attackers. This failed attack would be the last major operation (on the surface anyway!) conducted by the Germans for some time to come in this sector and they now began to deepen, strengthen and fortify their positions all along this part of the line. However, though the era of mobile warfare had now ended, along with any foreseeable chance of its return, all along the Somme front, the French were not quite as content as the Germans to just simply sit back, fortify and wait.

 A network of trenches developed, becoming more intricate and complex as the weeks went by; deep dugouts were constructed, some using natural chalk cave/quarry systems underneath the area, particularly in the area of Beaumont-Hamel and Cote 143, many others using deep cellars of the buildings in the front line villages and farms. Reinforcements were gratefully received and battalions that in some cases had been in almost constant combat since the end of September were rotated out of the line for a much needed rest and resupply. On the French side, entire divisions were replaced, moved or reshuffled. Some, in as much need of rest and replenishment as any other, were simply moved from one area of intensive combat to another, taking part in further battles to the north as the 'race to the sea' continued. This was a clear indicator of the desperate nature of military events further north at the time. As the situation became more controlled into November, however, and more fresh troops direct from training depots became available, the rear areas of the Somme front became heavily reinforced.

Barricades and trenches set up within the streets and ruins of Somme villages, October/November 1914. Scenes such as these were typical on both sides of No Man's Land in many of the front line villages of this sector as buildings and other features were adapted as fortifications.

Chapter Four

Hébuterne to the River Ancre: late October 1914 – July 1915

There was a slight flurry of activity to the north of this sector on 8 October 1914, when the 1. Garde-Infanterie-Division failed to dislodge the *81e division d'infanterie territoriale* from Foncquevillers and Hannescamps and thereby settled the northern flank of this sector, the remainder of the month and into November mainly passed relatively quietly. There was sporadic (but, occasionally, heavy) artillery fire and increasingly aggressive patrol activity as positions were consolidated and, especially in the German held villages of Serre, Puisieux and Beaumont-Hamel, fortified.

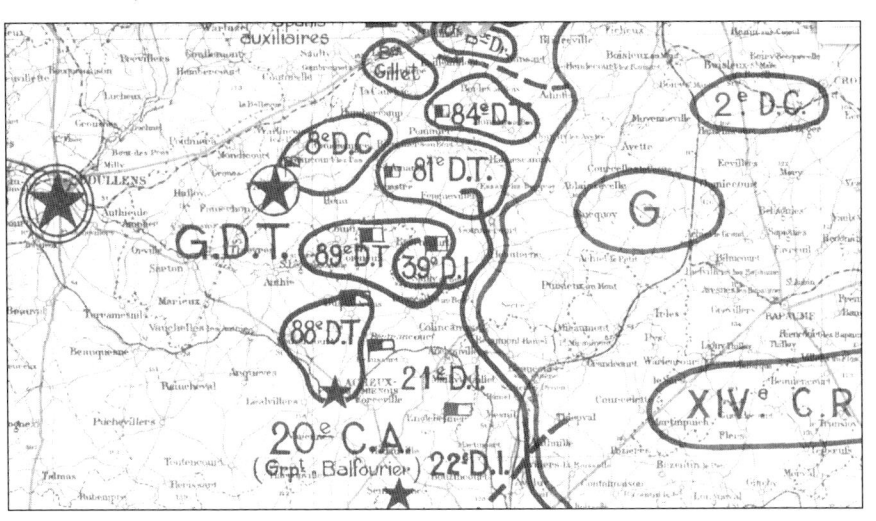

French situation, 8 October 1914. (*Les Armées Françaises dans la Grande Guerre*)

From the north to the south (Hébuterne to the Ancre), the *39e, 21e* and (parts of the) *22e division d'infanterie* held the line by the last week of October. The loss of Serre and much of Cote 143 earlier in the month and the commanding dominance these positions enjoyed of the whole front down to the Ancre was a constant aggravation to the French. An

A trench haircut near Hébuterne, 26 October 1914.

attack by the *65e régiment d'infanterie* on the Reserve-Infanterie-Regiment Nr. 110 at Beaumont Hamel on 25 October was repulsed by German defensive artillery fire before the German front line was even reached.

Another attack on 29 October, launched by the same régiment, on Cote 143 met with a similar fate when it came under fire from artillery located near Serre. The situation was not helped by the French infantry becoming entangled in three rows of barbed wire. This second attack was notable for the fact that (according to the regimental history) the attackers were all equipped with body armour. A third attack was conducted by the *21e division d'infanterie* (with elements of the *56^e division d'infanterie* in support) along their entire front from La Signy Farm to Hamel on 19 November ; but it was again repulsed. It was rapidly becoming clear that, even after increasingly heavy shelling, using coventional methods of warfare in this sector were ineffective. With the resources available and with the tactics that had been employed, it seemed that the fortified ridges and villages in this sector were impregnable. Other methods would be required.

In mid October, soon after the lines in the area became semi-static, the *sapeurs et mineurs* of the *11/1 compagnie du 6e régiment du génie* (first company of the eleventh battalion, sixth Engineer Regiment) and, temporarily, the *11/3 compagnie* of the same regiment, arrived at billets in Mailly-Maillet and Hébuterne. Here, and along the line to the south of Beaumont-Hamel, they began constructing saps and galleries towards and under the German lines – particularly close to the French on Cote 143 – initially to act as listening posts and possible jump off points for infantry assaults. However, the failures of recent surface attacks led to a change in approach. Already in the Argonne and, more recently, by four mining companies (*14/1, 14/2, 14/3* and *14/6*) of the *4e régiment du genie* south of the River Somme between Frise and Lihons, the heads of the galleries, once under German lines, were packed with explosives and detonated, destroying German trenches and defences, demoralising the defenders and leaving gaps in the defences open to surface assault. The Germans had the same idea and also began to tunnel towards and under the French trenches. Indeed, it was the Germans who instigated one of the first attacks preceded by the detonation of a mine during the war – in the Argonne on 13 November 1914; on the Somme, it was the French who struck first.

Tunnellers in training. The *4e régiment du genie*, immediately pre-war, practicing the skills to which they would become so adept from late 1914. The *4e régiment* served south of the Somme river during 1914-1915.

Immediately preceding a general attack along the line to the south of the Ancre on 17 December 1914, and to act as a diversion for this assault, two mines dug by the *11/1 and 11/3 compagnies du genie* were detonated just in front of the German front line and barbed wire on Cote 143, approximately 500 metres south of the Serre road, destroying a German listening gallery. However, it also detonated a German mine and thus destroyed part of the French front line in the process! It was followed by a badly timed small scale diversionary assault launched by the *7e* and *8e compagnies* of the *137e régiment d'infanterie*, some of whom were in the open at the time of the mine detonation on Infanterie-Regiment Nr. 99 and the area held by Reserve-Infanterie-Regiment Nr. 119. The attack was easily fended off by the use of trench mortars and rifle fire at the cost of seventy-one French casualties from the ranks of the attackers, including thirty-four that were taken prisoner during the German counter attack that followed. Though the numbers do not seem high, this single day resulted in just over a third of the entire casualty numbers sustained by the *137e régiment d'infanterie* in this sector since mid October: approximately one man in every four of the attackers was a casualty.

Following this first firing of mines, a systematic pattern of static warfare progressed into 1915. Artillery was now the dominant weapon of the battlefield all along the line from Hébuterne to the Ancre, interspersed with sporadic aggressive raids, patrols and frequent use of trench artillery and snipers. An example of the nature of the warfare was a several company sized assault on the night of Christmas Eve 1914. Beaumont-Hamel came under heavy French shelling that preceded an infantry attack, easily beaten back. On Cote 143/Redan Ridge, underground warfare continued, the French detonating a further mine on New Year's Eve and the Germans responding by detonating their first mine there on 3 January 1915. Blow and counter blow continued unabated up to and beyond the arrival of the British in the sector. The ridge became a moonscape of craters, resulting in only marginal changes to the lines but with a greater impact on the topography. Approximately forty mines, counter-mines and camouflets were dug and detonated during the course of the next six months of French occupation in the sector; such blasts were often followed by short, sharp, small scale actions to capture the lips of the resultant craters.

Between Hébuterne and the shattered ground of Cote 143 the daily routine of trench holding continued into the spring of 1915, albeit with the French high command still enviously coveting the dominating position afforded to the village of Serre, lost the previous October. Preparations were begun by *XI corps d'armée* to make a large scale assault in this area in April 1915 in order to eradicate the Toutvent Salient and, perhaps, even push on to take Serre and the high ground upon which the village sat. However, much to the disappointment of the corps commander at that time, *général de division* Maurice Baumgarten, these were cancelled at the last minute – partially as a result of increased German aggression in the area and partially because of a failed attack in the vicinity of Beaumont-Hamel on 11 April.

However, on 9 May 1915 the *2e bataille de l'Artois* opened to the north of Arras which, after some intial successes, rapidly began to bog down into what was becoming a typical attritional battle on the Western Front and a focal point for German reinforcements. With that sector being reinforced so heavily, the French offensive was jeopardised and required a quick and effective solution. For this reason, the Somme battlefield was brought back to centre stage in French thinking.

The *bataille de Toutvent* (*2e bataille d'Hébuterne*): 7 to 13 June 1915
Généralissime Joffre was informed by his intelligence staff in mid May 1915 that the quantity of German reserves that were being sent to the Artois sector, where the *bataille d'Artois* was in full swing, roughly equated to those being sent to the whole of the Eastern Front. With progress in this major French offensive at risk, he decided that diversionary action needed to be taken quickly and ordered a local offensive in the Somme area.

On 17 May, he sent a telegram to the *Second Army* (*général* Noël Édouard Marie Joseph de Curières de Castelnau) in which he suggested the types of operations that could take place:

> 1. The execution of several localised 'body blows' and multiple, small scale, surprise actions in various sectors both to unsettle the enemy and to enable the identification of any changes in his order of battle.
> 2. A more significant, more concentrated, operation that would have to be executed at very short notice, using only the resources (troops, guns and munitions) that were available in that location at that present time.

Général de Castelnau wrote to Joffre on 18 May suggesting that the second option, if it was to take place around the area of Toutvent Farm, would benefit from the preparations made in this area for the proposed, but cancelled, *XI corps d'armée* attack of April in support of actions in the Chaulnes sector, south of the Somme. With the forming up trenches already dug and associated weaponry already in situ, de Castelnau decided upon this option and at this location. He stated, however, that he

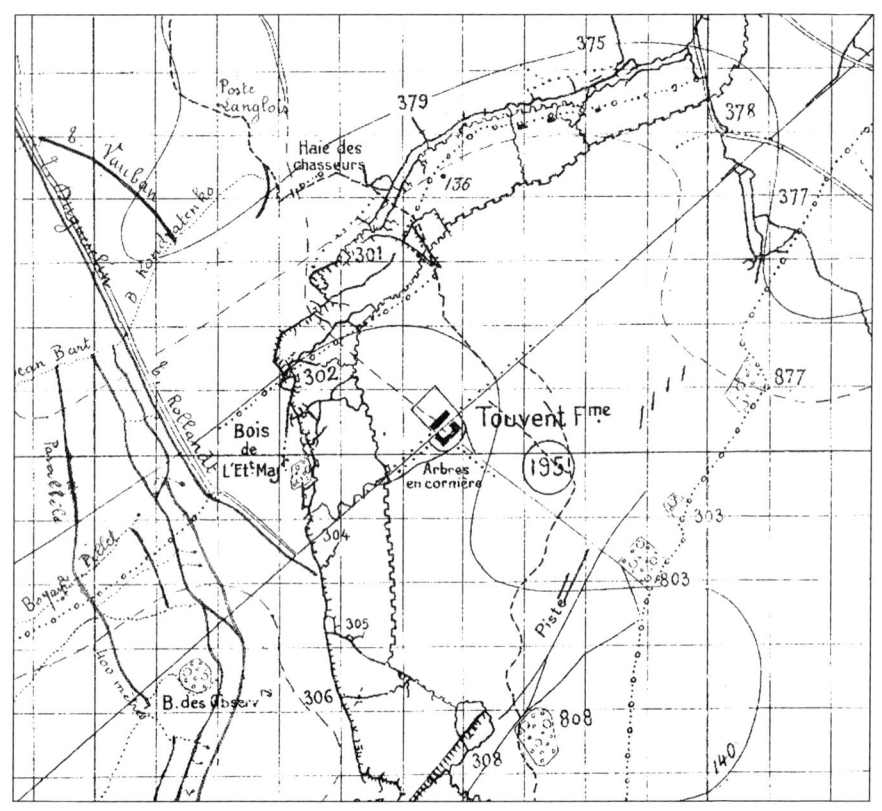

Touvent (Toutvent) Farm trench map extract, 7 June 1915.

could only make one division (the *21e division d'infanterie*) available for the operation and that, with his limited resources in heavy artillery, the attack could only hope, at best, to capture the German first lines and their associated defences and then settle in and consolidate the captured ground.

Approved by Joffre on 24 May, the attack at Toutvent Farm would become another example of the much criticised 'attritional' or 'nibbling' (*'grignotage'*) type of operation that appeared to be a typical tactic at this stage of the war. The nature of these attacks was to a large extent dictated by the French Army's severe shortage of heavy artillery, a situation unchanged from when the war broke out.

As time went on after his initial suggestion, however, de Castelnau became increasingly optimistic; far more optimistic than Joffre, it must be said! He began planning for an extension and widening of the offensive should the German line be broken. He put the *21e division d'infanterie*, the *53e brigade d'infanterie* (from the *27e division d'infanterie*) and one battalion from the *56e division d'infanterie* in the line in preparation for the opening day. In anticipation of a breakthrough, he also ordered the *1er corps de cavalerie* to move closer to the front line and, on 28 May, the *51e division d'infanterie* was moved from its encampment in the area of Doullens and placed into second line positions ready to assist the cavalry in their exploitation of any breakthrough. This divison comprised reserve regiments recruited from areas relatively local to the forthcoming operation: the *243e regiment d'infanterie* from Lille, the *233e regiment d'infanterie* from Arras and the *327e regiment d'infanterie* from Valenciennes. For artillery support, de Castelnau managed to accumulate twenty-two batteries of 75s and eight heavy batteries, supplemented by six further batteries of 75s and six heavy batteries from the *56e division d'infanterie* area to the north. Available trench artillery consisted of fourteen heavy and sixteen light *canons de 58*. With a total of just fourteen heavy batteries, along with a pitifully small amount of trench artillery, the *bataille d'Hébuterne* would be, in terms of guns, amongst the most lightly supported of the larger French operations on the Western Front of the whole war. The prospective battlefield was described in the *XI corps d'armée* diary as:

> '...a salient of German trenches formed between the Serre-Hebuterne and the Serre-Mailly Maillet roads, with the first line covered by a network of wires and fougasses. The second line, about a hundred metres behind the first, is complete and seems very strong. The centre of the battlefield is marked by the fortified farm house of Toutvent. The village of Serre is positioned at the top of a long glacis, about 1,500 metres behind the German forward trenches...'

The artillery preparation plan provided for a bombardment of two days. Due to the likelihood of the loss of the element of any surprise, the artillery of the neighbouring *corps d'armées* was to be equally active. This aimed to muddy the waters as to where exactly the infantry blow would fall. It was considered that this two day bombardment would be sufficient to allow for accurate ranging and targeting of specific targets and would destroy all of the enemy's main points of resistance. On the day of the attack the whole front was to be shelled immediately prior to the assault, was to be followed by a systematic move of the barrage forward as the infantry advanced. The flanks of the attack were to be constantly shelled in order to prevent German reinforcement of the area; several batteries were reserved for specific location targeting as and when called upon by the advancing infantry. It was a relatively sophisticated artillery plan.

The attack was initially planned for 2 June; but on 31 May it was postponed until 5 June. On 3 June the artillery preparation began but, following a further postponement of the attack on the 4th, this was halted. The attack date was finally set for 7 June and the artillery barrage began again on the 5th. However, due to the lack of heavy ammunition, it was realised that it would not be as effective as desired and an extra 1,000 rounds of 155mm ammunition was rushed forwards to the two *155 C* batteries, increasing their effective fire rate. On this first day a squadron of Morane-Saulnier fighters was also placed at the disposal of *XI corps d'armée* to assist in the protection of its artillery spotting and reconnaissance aircraft.

The effectiveness of the artillery now that more heavy ammunition was available increased significantly. The *journal des marches et operations* (war diary) of *Second Army* noted during the evening of 5 June its particular effectiveness in practically neutralising the strongpoints at Points 302 (east of Toutvent Farm), 305 (south south east of Toutvent Farm), 307 (south of Toutvent Farm and slightly east of, as it would later become known to the British, Matthew Copse), and 311 (due south of the eastern section of Matthew Copse). It also noted that works in the area along the length of the *Haie des Chasseurs* and the whole area to the north of Bois de l'Etat-Major had been severely disrupted. On 6 June the bombardment was switched to concentrate on ancilliary defences and barbed wire entanglements. However, plans were disrupted slightly by violent German counter-battery fire and a retaliatory bombardment of the French front line in front of Hébuterne.

Prior to the infantry assault on 7 June, *Second Army* issued strict orders (possibly with de Castelnau in mind!) to emphasise to the attacking formations and units that this was not to be a large scale offensive and that the attack on the Toutvent Salient was one with limited objectives and in support of the major offensive north of Arras. They were reminded that, with very little in terms of support, especially in the availablity of heavy artillery, it would be unthinkable, even in the case of total demoralisation of the enemy or decisive successes elsewhere, to continue the action beyond the planned assault. It was with this injunction in mind that during the afternoon and night of 6 June the infantry formed up in their jump off trenches for an attack to be launched in the early hours of the morning of 7 June 1915. They had been issued with steel skull caps to be worn under the *képi* (the *cervelière* – commonly referred to by the average French soldier as the '*bol de soupe*').

The initial assault was to be carried out by three regiments of the *21e division d'infanterie* in what would be the centre sector of the battlefield. These regiments (listed from north to south) had the following objectives;

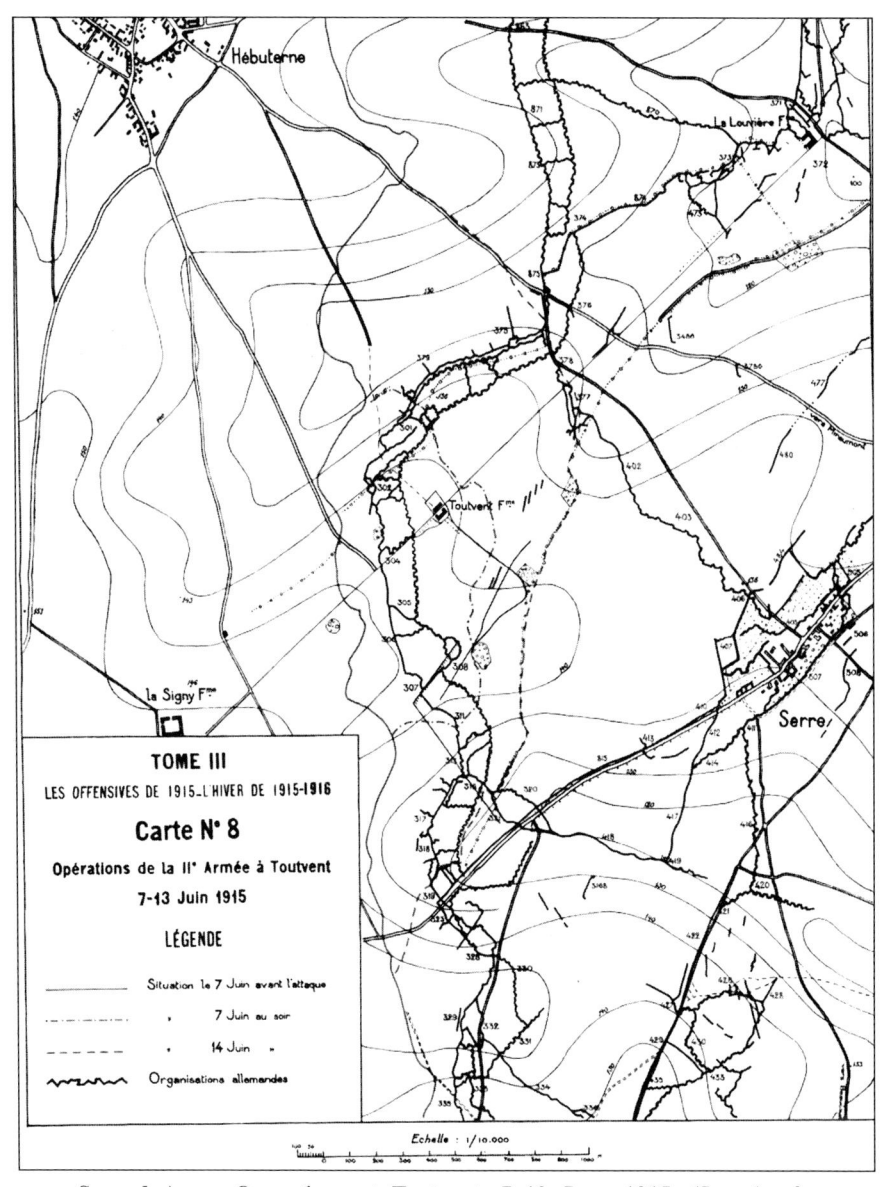

Second Army Operations at Toutvent, 7–13 June 1915. (*Les Armées Françaises dans la Grande Guerre*)

other than those for the *93e régiment d'infanterie,* all were German front line positions:

137e régiment d'infanterie (from Fontenay-le-Comte): The line from Point 301 to Bois de l'Etat-Major.

93e régiment d'infanterie (from Bar-le-Duc): Toutvent Farm and the line down to Point 306.

64e régiment d'infanterie (from Acenis and St Nazaire): The line from Point 306 to Point 311.

Each regiment deployed two battalions for the attack and were arranged so as to form four waves:

1. The first wave formed up in wide, but shallow, recently dug trenches located in No Man's Land just in front of the French front line (referred to as *parallèles de départ* – parallels of departure) and barbed wire. These trenches were furnished at the front with short ladders and had a shallow slope to the rear to ease access for following waves.
2. The second wave was located in the French front line trench. This had ladders arranged every ten metres along its length and, to its immediate front, gaps cut every ten to fifteen metres through the barbed wire to allow easy access to the forward parallel of departure. Ten, metre wide, bridges (one per section) were placed over the trench to allow succeeding waves to cross.
3. The third wave was some forty metres behind the French front line in another recently dug parallel of departure trench of similar design to that of the first wave. This wave would advance across the open ground to the French front line and also make use of the communication trenches leading to it. Those advancing in the open would cross the line using the bridges, those in the trenches would use the ladders.
4. Sixty metres to the rear of the third wave a third parallel of departure trench had been dug that accommodated the fourth wave. These were to follow the third wave in a similar manner.

In the sector of the *137e régiment d'infanterie* the first and second waves were made up from the *1er bataillon*. Ordered to cross the first two lines of German trenches without stopping, they were then to consolidate their positions between Toutvent Farm and Point 379. The role of the *3e bataillon*, making up the third and fourth waves, was to sweep up behind the first two waves, eliminating any pockets of resistance left behind by the swift advance and then assist the *1er bataillon* in the consolidation of the newly won territory and defend against any German counter attacks.

With everyone in position by 2am, the attack was launched at 5am but German artillery (evidently not taken completely by surprise)

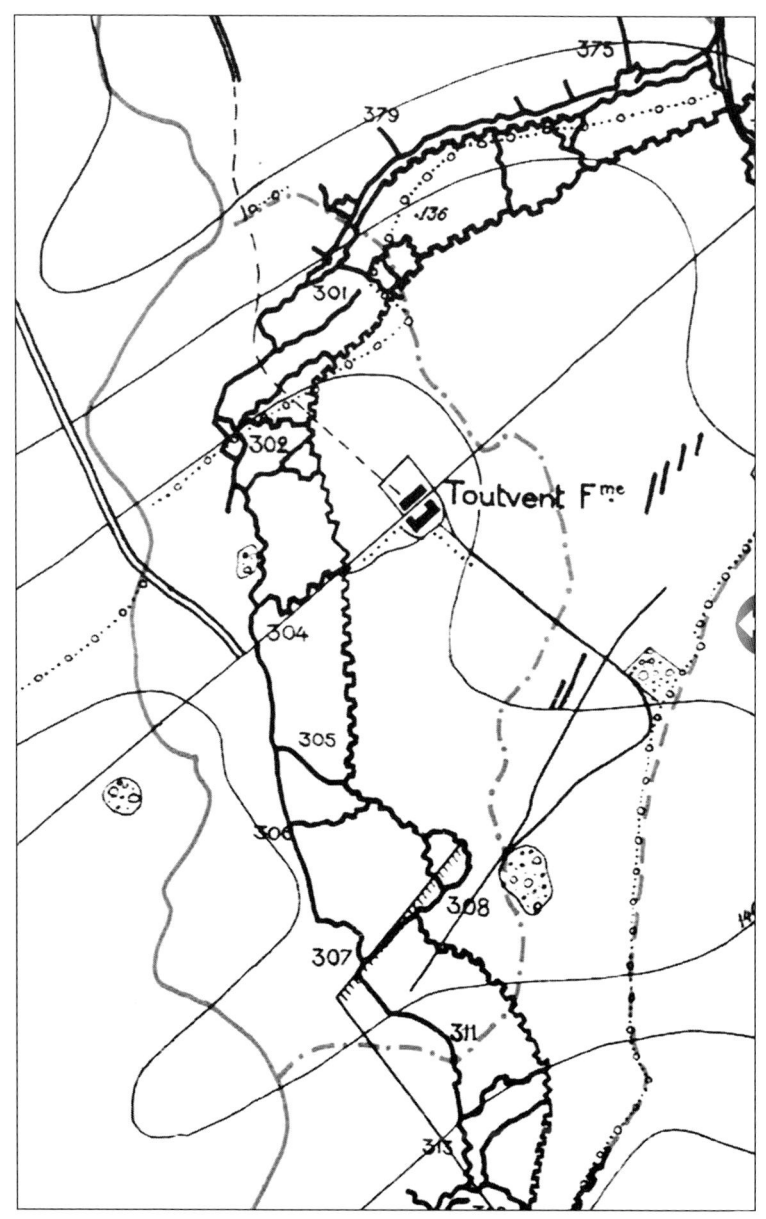

Toutvent detail, illustrating first day gains near the farm. (*Les Armées Françaises dans la Grande Guerre*)

violently bombarded the French front just as the *clairons* sounded the attack. On the left flank, the *2e compagnie* managed to advance before the shells hit their positions; but in the centre and on the right an advance was only possible in fractions. To their rear, the barrage damaged the communication trenches leading to the front line, with the dead and wounded only adding to the congestion and chaos.

Despite this, the *137e* still managed to break through the barrage and advance as planned. Within five minutes of the launch of the attack, the German lines had been breached and the third and fourth waves followed the first and second waves into the second line of German trenches and began to consolidate. In some areas officers had difficulty in restraing their men from continuing the assault, intent as they were on pursuing the fleeing Germans and to get to grips with the German batteries that had caused so much destruction minutes earlier.

Losses, however, were heavy. Although the *1er* and *3e compagnies* managed to get established in the positions between Toutvent and the *Haie des chasseurs*, within the *2e compagnie* all the officers had been killed and the *4e compagnie*, in confusion, found itself located in the same position as the *3e*. The left flank, left open and exposed due to the mix up of units, was reinforced by two companies of the *2e bataillon* (the reserve battalion in this initial assault) and then by another two companies from the *3e bataillon* once its commanding officer had been assured that the German trenches to the rear had all been completely cleared.

These four companies on the left flank pushed up the German trenches and managed to advance to Point 379 before then erecting trench blocks and setting up defensive positions within a German communication trench in case of counter attack. The expected German counter attack materialised at about 11am; however, it was launched through the trench network and not across open country in a frontal attack as had been expected. Focussing on Points 375 and 379, the defenders of the barricades were overwhelmed by a shower of hand grenades and began to fall back. However, *12e compagnie* arrived and reinforced the pressed defenders and then attacked themselves, managing to push the Germans back once again after a vigorous grenade battle at the barricades. During the evening, despite several other smaller scale German counter attacks, the *137e régiment d'infanterie* was firmly established in the old German trenches.

To the immediate south of the *137e régiment d'infanterie*, the *93e régiment d'infanterie* had been given, potentially, the most difficult task of the three attacking regiments. The mission of the first two waves (*2e bataillon*) was the capture of the fortified Toutvent Farm and the trenches to its immediate east.

Despite also being hit by the disruptive German barrage, the *93e* still managed to start according to the schedule and advanced in double columns across No Man's Land at 5am, holding the German second

German communication trench south west of Toutvent Farm, captured by the French on 7 June 1915.

trench by 5.21am. By 5.30am telephone communications from the old German front line were established and the first call was made to the French command by *Capitaine* Poitou-Duplessy, a reassuring message that simply stated, 'All is well'. After a further ten minutes the second German trench was consolidated and numerous prisoners sent rearwards. By this point the reserve companies had also begun to arrive to reinforce those in the new front line and at 7am a connection was established with the *137e régiment d'infanterie* on the left. It would take a further hour to achieve the same with the *64e régiment d'infanterie*, on the right.

According to a further communication from *capitaine* Poitou-Duplessy timed at 08.45, the situation of the *1er bataillon* (third and fourth waves of the initial assault) was that they were in occupation of the German front, rear and communication trenches to a point eighty metres east of Toutvent Farm, with the *1er* and *4e compagnies* holding the German firing trenches and the *2e* and *10e compagnies* (the *10e compagnie* being from the *3e bataillon*) located in the German communication trenches. The trenches had been consolidated and the digging of communication trenches back towards the old French front line had started. However, German shelling disrupted this work severely and destroyed the parapet in some places; but several trenches were eventually completed and links established not only between the original

A strongpoint that quickly fell on the first day of battle; the ruins of Toutvent Farm, June 1915.

front lines but also with the *137e* and *64e régiments d'infanterie* to the left and right.

More success was to be found south of the *93e*, in the sector of the *64e régiment d'infanterie*, where it was reported that all the German wire had been cut by the French preliminary bombardment. Here, despite heavy German fire during the opening minutes, by 5.15am Points 306 and 307 had been captured by the first two waves and progress on Point 311 made. By 6.30am the first two lines of German trenches, Points 306, 307, 308 and 311 were all solidly occupied and held by the French.

According to the original planning for this battle (and in line with Joffre's recommendations), the battle should now have ended following this first day's successes. By its end the French held about 1200 metres of captured trenches, ranging from Points 379 to 311, with the troops organized along a new front line from Point 379, through the hill crest approximately 300 metres east of Toutvent Farm, down to the western edge of the small wood in front of Point 308 and on to Point 311.

Two major German counter attacks at 4.30pm and 11.30pm were relatively easily repulsed with the aid of artillery; but the situation was still precarious. The French suffered many casualties from German artillery fire at this point and were, seemingly, highly dependant upon their own artillery for protection from the German guns. Hauptmann Leuchtenberger, the commanding officer of 1. Komp of Infanterie - Regiment Nr. 170, noted:

'… the enemy has penetrated eastwards beyond Toutvent. A violent artillery bombardment has forced him to retreat back to the farm, but he still held the conquered ground at 9.30. Heavy artillery will force him to evacuate [it].'

It would certainly appear that effective counter-battery fire of the French guns was the one thing that countered Leuchtenberger's prediction, allowing French infantry to remain in the newly conquered positions.

In the light of initial success, orders were issued by *XI corps d'armée* around midday on 7 June for the regiments in the area to reorganise in the newly captured territory and prepare for a further attack on 8 June on the trenches in the area of Points 375 to 377 and on Points 313 and 316 (immediately to the north and to the south of the actions of 7 June). The *53e brigade d'infanterie*, who had played no role in the first day's events, was to be used. The order stated, however, that the ridge to the east of Toutvent Farm should first be defensively organised in order to provide a good, solid base from which to launch an assault directly on the village of Serre in order to present the French Army with an advantageous position for any future operation in the area. On the other hand, it was acknowledged that it would be unlikely that such a scenario, in which German positions to the south of Serre would be placed at a major disadvantage, would be readily accepted by them and it was expected that the possession of the village and the western slopes would be hotly contested. However, whatever might happen in the near future, it was apparent that as the French defence of the new line was so reliant upon artillery protection in the current situation, further advances were

Shallow trench within the 'Apostles Copses' before Serre after the battle of Toutvent. Compare this image with the modern image in the tour section.

necessary. General Order No.471 was issued by GQG (ie the French Supreme Headquarters), stating that the offensive should be resumed on 8 June with the objective of capturing Serre from the north.

Général de Castenau was concerned both about introducing *53e brigade d'infanterie* into the offensive and for an attack in the general direction of La Louvière Farm. Without adequate artillery preparation, he considered that the attack had a very slim chance of success and therefore instructed *XI corps d'armée* to take adequate time to prepare. He stated that the attack on Points 375-377 was subordinate to the preparatory work that it would necessarily entail; he was prepared to delay matters, if necessary, in order to assure success in his goal of capturing the small area of land bordered by Points 379, 375 and 377 and parts of the communication trench connecting Point 377 with Serre. He ordered that the commanders should study all the arrangements for this attack and, though it should be carried out as soon as possible, it should only happen when they were certain of success and after the ground already captured was completely secure.

However, it would appear that de Castenau's concerns were mistakenly overlooked by *général* Maurice Baumgarten, the commander of *XI corps d'Armée*, following a telephone conversation between himself and *lieutenant-colonel* Joseph Écochard of the *75e régiment d'infanterie* at 9pm on 7 June, in which Baumgarten was trying to obtain information regarding the chances of success and the possibility of a delay. Écochard told him that a detailed reconnaissance of the area had proven impossible and that he could not accurately account for any obstacles that the attackers might encounter; but he also said that he did not think that a delay of a few hours would improve the situation. On the contrary, he suggested, it might actually be advantageous to attack as soon as possible, allowing the use of the maximum amount of daylight. Upon receiving this reply, Baumgarten ordered the attack to proceed in the early hours (3.30am) of 8 June but gave Écochard the freedom to modify any arrangements at the last minute if necessary.

Écochard left his PC (*poste de command* – command post), located in the quarries to the south of Hébuterne, at 11.30pm to reach his regimental start point in the new front line held by the *137e régiment d'infanterie*. The communication trenches were blocked by the troop build up, wounded being transported back to the rear and by many corpses, which prevented quick progress and he only completed his journey – of less than a mile – at 1.45am. The *1er bataillon, 75e régiment d'infanterie* moved forwards about the same time and were, likewise, obstructed; it rapidly became obvious that not all of the attacking troops would be in place by the scheduled start time. At 2.45am, therefore,

Écochard decided to delay the attack and contacted the artillery to postpone their prepararatory bombardment. The halting of the barrage, however, alerted the Germans. Suspecting an impending attack, they responded by heavily shelling the French front lines which, in turn, ended all thought of delaying the attack as it would probably be less costly to attack than to stay in tightly packed trenches under a German barrage.

At 3:30am precisely on 8 June, following a short resurgence of the French artillery bombardment, the *75e régiment d'infanterie* – supported by two battalions of the *140e régiment d'infanterie* – were launched into battle. The four leading companies (*1e, 3e, 8e* and *6e compagnies*) reached the German lines and managed to drive back the enemy, quickly reaching and even, unwittingly, advancing beyond their goal – Point 377. They only realised that they had gone too far when they came under fire from all sides, including French shells that was hitting captured targets behind them. They then retreated some 150 to 200 metres, bringing them back to their objective.

Although the leading four companies had progressed well so far, they were soon cut off from the rest of the regiment due to the following waves becoming caught up in a bitter hand to hand battle within the German positions; the advance faltering. On the left flank, one company began to crumble but its commander, *capitaine* Raoul Guérin, led a furious fight back after shouting: 'We are the left support point. If necessary, we will be killed to the last.' During the stand, *capitaine* Guérin and two other officers were killed, amongst others from the company, and the offensive spirit was broken.

All along the line the battle began to favour the German defenders and it seemed that the four advance companies surrounded at Point 377 would become permanently isolated and either killed or captured, so *lieutenant-colonel* Écochard called for two reserve companies from the *3e bataillon* (the *10e* and *12e compagnies*) to move forward to assist in the fighting and to attempt to break through to the isolated companies. By this point, however, *10e compagnie* had become almost ineffective because of the casualties suffered during the German shelling and reaching the front line appeared to be an impossibility. To add to the problems, parts of the *137e régiment d'infanterie*, upon seeing the approaching companies, believed that they were being relieved and began moving away from the front line, further blocking the communication trench in the process and adding to the utter confusion of the situation.

It soon became impossible to establish a link with the isolated companies and fighting died down both to the front and on the right, so that it appeared that they had been captured. At 1pm an officer managed to creep through German held territory to these companies. He returned safely and now that it was established that the companies were still in action, a larger scale breakthrough was attempted at 2pm. Once again, this attempt – carried out during a heavy thunderstorm – ended in failure and German pressure appeared relentless. French commanders, despite units being mixed up and short of grenades and ammunition, planned a new attempt to reach the beleaguered men on the night of 8/9 June, this time led by the *140e régiment d'infanterie*; again, it failed. Fighting continued throughout 9 June with no better results before the assault was resumed in full on the night of 9/10 June. The trench junction at Point 377 finally fell to the French – who managed to retain a precarious hold on to it – on 11 June. By then, though, it was too late for the isolated companies, who had managed to hold on against overwhelming odds for the best part of two days.

At the southern end of the battlefield, while the *75e* and *140e régiments d'infanterie* were fighting their fruitless yet costly battle in the north, the offensive was widened. In order to enlarge the breach made in the enemy positions and push closer to Serre, fresh units were called forward to pursue the attack. *101e brigade d'infanterie* of the *51e division d'infanterie* (*233e*, *243e* and *327e régiments d'infanterie*) was tasked with pushing forward to a line between the Sucrerie-Serre road to the south and the Hébuterne-Puisieux road to the north.

With the *243e* and *327e régiments d'infanterie* in the front line and the *233e* in reserve, extra artillery was brought up for the preliminary bombardment. It began at 4.30am on 10 June, with the assault scheduled for 7am; but this was postponed until 1pm due to thick fog that hindered the artillery obervers. At 5pm on 10 June the two regiments advanced but, after being caught up in unbroken German barbed wire, lost momentum and failed to gain a foothold in the German second line trench. A confused and intense close quarter grenade battle took place in the German lines overnight and fighting continued, under an intensive bombardment, throughout the next day but with practically no forward movement towards the objectives or Serre. A large German counter attack in the sector held by *6e bataillon* of the *243e régiment d'infanterie* was successfully repulsed during the afternoon of 11 June, but this was followed by three more attacks over night and into the morning of 12 June, during which the Germans, at heavy cost, managed to regain a tiny portion of ground.

Joffre realised by the evening of 12 June that an attack on Serre was very unlikely to succeed and decided that the planned attack on the village would no longer take place. Operations in the Toutvent area would, from then on, be limited to actions that were strictly necessary for the French to establish themselves in an indisputable way on the captured positions.

These 'necessary actions' would mean that smaller scale, yet no less violent, actions would take place for a short while longer at the most vulnerable points – that is in the northern and southern limits of the fighting area.

On 13 June, the *101e brigade d'infanterie* attacked yet again. Launched at 2.15am by the *233e* and *327e régiments d'infanterie*, with the *6e bataillon* of the *243e régiment d'infanterie* in support, they attacked with such venom that the Germans were caught unprepared and gave up considerable ground. Capturing the second line of German defences by 9.15am, it appeared that the route to Serre might now be open. However, having suffered such heavy losses over the previous few days – both in men and *materiél* – it would probably have been suicidal to press the advantage. During the afternoon, after taking 1,669 casualties within the three regiments of the brigade, the attack lost momentum and the men of *101e brigade* began to consolidate their new positions, which now passed through Points 875, 378 and 377, down the hedgerow and creek that ran in front of the (later named) Apostles Copses, past the 'Deux Arbres abbatus', through Points 316, 321, 319 to a point just below the Serre road, where it met the pre 7 June front line. Advanced posts were also held at Points 320 and 322. With most of the engaged units relieved by 15 June, the battle ended with the French holding a line that, when inherited by the British at the end of July, would be the start point for the sufferings of the Pals battalions of the 31st Division a year later.

German prisoners from Toutvent being marched into captivity through Amiens, June 1915.

The battle did at least partially achieve one of its original aims, as some German reserves actually were diverted from the fighting in the Artois. According to the French Official History – *Les Armées Françaises dans la Grande Guerre* – ten German officers and 621 soldiers were taken prisoner, though the actual figure, if the total amounts claimed in the various unit *journaux des marches et operations* are to be believed, could have been as high as 1,016. A significant number of the enemy were killed; one French batallion alone claims to have buried over 1,200 German corpses from a 400 metre stretch of battlefield. However, though the French had eliminated a potentially difficult salient in the line and had placed themselves in a more advantageous position, Serre (the secondary – and later – aim) and its high ground had not fallen. The battle had been costly, too, for the French.

Though it started off with great promise – a well organised limited attack, with effective use of the very limited means available – it soon turned into an horrific attritional battle as a result of the change in focus and intent. Take, as an example, just one regiment, the *137e régiment d'infanterie*. It was one of the main players involved on the first day, took part in the consolidation on the second, was only peripherally involved in action on the third, was relieved for a day and was then back in the line between 11 and 15 June in a purely defensive role, holding captured positions. Its losses amounted to eight officers killed and twelve wounded, sixteen NCOs killed with forty three wounded and one missing, thirteen corporals killed, fifty eight wounded, one missing, and 131 soldiers killed, 750 injured and twenty three missing: a total of 1,047 men *hors de combat* for a single regiment. The total French casualties from all units for the battle, according to the official history, amounted to fifty nine officers and 1,701 men killed or missing and 115 officers and 8,475 men wounded – 10,350 casualties for a battlefield less than two miles in length and a thousand yards in depth – and this may be a conservative figure. Twenty-five 75s and five heavies were knocked out by German counter-battery fire.

Throughout the battle and all the suffering, the stoic bravery and tenacity of the French soldier shone through. The final words should be left to one of their opponents – the commander of 1. Bataillon, 9. Badisches Infanterie-Regiment Nr. 170, Hauptmann Güßmann, who, according to the *journal des marches et operations* of the *21 division d'infanterie*, spontaneously declared to a French officer;

'Sir, you have undoubtedly sent elite troops against us. I was up in my battalion's front line trench at the moment of the attack, and I have never seen troops who launched themselves into an assault with more courage and drive.'

This statement can be found (in French) cast in bronze on the memorial located in the *Nécropole Nationale de Serre-Hébuterne*. Although the area over which the battle was fought would be under almost constant bombardment for the remainder of June, during July it became, almost unnaturally, a quiet back-water sector where a 'live and let live' attitude became routine. It was into this situation that the British Third Army began to arrive at the end of the month, relieving the battle weary *21e* and *22e divisons d'infanterie*, who had both been in almost constant action of varying degrees of intensity on the Somme since September 1914. They had fought between Hébuterne and Fargny on the north bank of the River Somme; and, within a few weeks, occupied a section of line to the south of the river, between Frise and Foucaucourt, for a couple of months after the arrival of the British XII Corps in September 1915. (This was not the first British occupation south of the River Somme, however, as 14 Brigade, 5th Division, were located at Frise for a short while during August 1915.)

The arrival of Third Army was intended primarily to relieve some of the pressure on the over-stretched French Army, freeing up divisions for rest or relocation to more critical locations along the Western Front. The Somme, now regarded as a rather placid sector, was regarded as an ideal nursery location for new formations in which to gain trench experience and training. To the average French *Pitou*, however, the reasoning was, perhaps, less complex and more functional; the Somme was a sector that was in need of defending and as, in his opinion, the British were far more adept at sitting back and defending rather than attacking, they were the ideal army to hold this sector! This was an attitude that would remain unchanged amongst the rank and file of the French Army until the Battle of the Somme was fought nearly a year later.

Flanked by the veteran *56e division d'infanterie* to the north and the untried *154e division d'infanterie* to the south, the British 4th and 48th (South Midland) divisions, of Third Army's VII Corps, began to relieve the *21e division d'infanterie* in the Hébuterne to the Ancre sector from 20 July. One of the first British battalions to move into the Somme front line were the territorials of the 1/6 Royal Warwickshire Regiment, who partially relieved the *92e régiment d'infanterie* in front of Hébuterne on 21 July. A few days later, via Albert, the 51st (Highland), the 18th (Eastern) and the 5th divisions of X Corps began to move into the area of the *22e division d'infanterie, 151e division d'infanterie* and (part of) the *28e division d'infanterie,* between the Ancre and the Somme, on the night of 30/31 July. Much of the French divisional artillery and engineers remained behind for a few more weeks to support the British as they acclimatised to their new area.

Tour 2

Hébuterne to the Ancre 1914-15 Walking and Driving Tours

Split into two sections, **the first part** *of this tour comprises a* **walking/bicycle tour of 9.2 kilometres**. *For the less enthusiastic walker, about half of it can be accessed by car, with the remainder of the stands located within 500 metres of a vehicle parking point. This part of the tour is a circuit – beginning and ending at the same location – and can be completed as a separate, stand alone, tour if required.* **The second part,** **16.1 kilometres in length,** *should be completed using some mode of motorised transport as, apart from the actual distance covered, it ends at a point some significant distance from where it starts. However, the end is within easy striking distance of a couple of decent refreshment stops!*

During the first part of the tour, sites concerned with some of the more significant events of the French occupation of this sector – namely the 2e bataille d'Hébuterne and the mine warfare on Cote 143 – will be visited or viewed. The second part is more concerned with the period of static trench holding but will also, hopefully, enable the visitor to look at one site, particularly well known and frequently visited by the British, with a fresh set of eyes.

Part 1
Begin the tour at **Serre Road Cemetery No. 2 (1)** *to the south west of the village of Serre on the D919 Mailly-Maillet to Serre road, where there is usually ample space in front of the cemetery to leave your vehicle.*

Serre Road Cemetery No. 2, along with Nos. 1 and 3 and several other CWGC cemeteries in the area, was begun in May 1917 after the battlefields of the Somme and Ancre were cleared by V Corps. The wartime burals are in Plot I, Rows A to G. After the war this became a concentration cemetery and the bulk of the graves were added after the Armistice, brought in from (usually, but not always) nearby battlefields and from six smaller cemeteries from the area. Presently, there are 2,426 casualties of the Great War, mostly dating from 1916, buried or commemorated in this cemetery, 1,728 of which are unidentified.

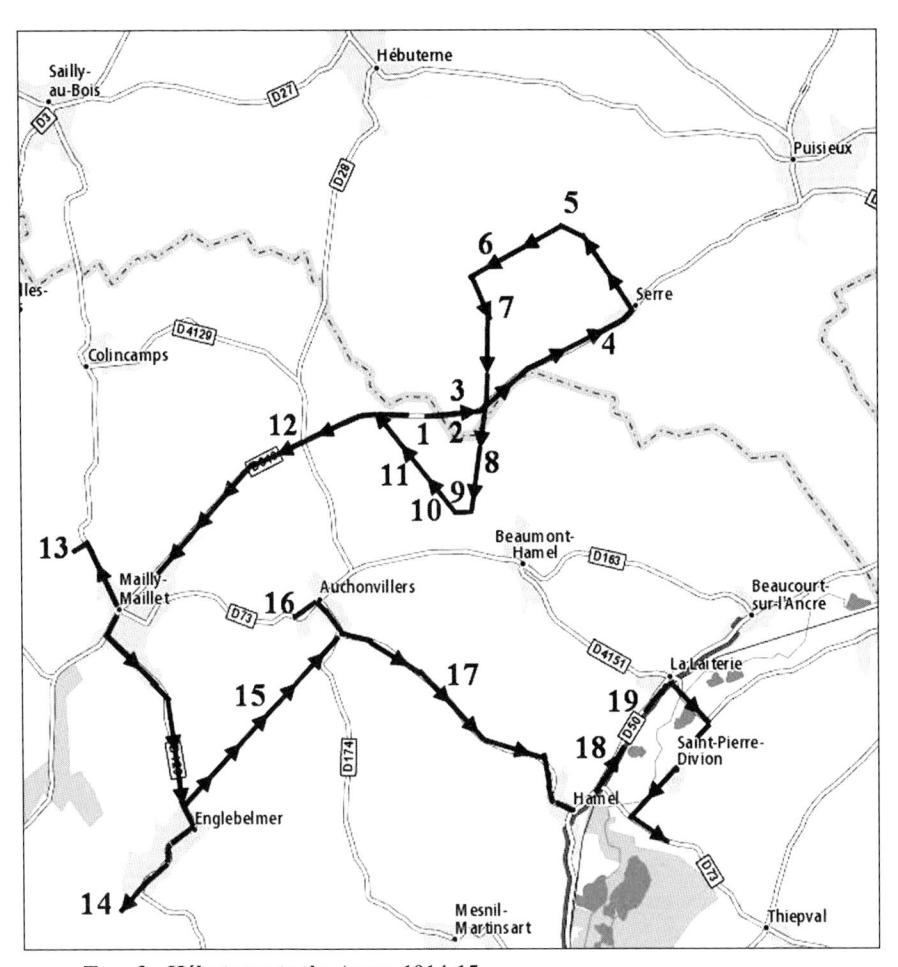

Tour 2: Hébuterne to the Ancre 1914-15.

It is located in the No Man's Land of mid 1915 to early 1917; the right hand corner of the cemetery as you face it marked the French/British front line and the rear, left corner marked the German. The cemetery also marks the southern extremity of the *bataille de Toutvent* of June 1915, with the pre-battle French front line located at a point where a track reaches the main road about 150 metres away, in the direction of Mailly-Maillet and ran due north (and south) from that point. Note that here, the German line was not pushed back during the battle. The French simply advanced their front line trench, narrowing No Man's Land, to connect with the new, mid-June 1915, line that ran parallel with the northern edge of the road towards Serre to a point about half way between here and the nearby French cemetery before switching slightly northwards, skirting the back walls of the French and British cemeteries and turning north again towards the 'Apostles Copses' that are just visible on the horizon.

Walk along the D919 towards Serre, through the centre of No Man's Land of 1915-17, passing the **private memorial to Lieutenant Valentine Braithwaite of the 1ˢᵗ Battalion, Somerset Light Infantry** *on the right, just outside the eastern boundary wall of the cemetery, and just south of the head of the infamous* **Heidenkopf Redoubt.** This was formed after *101 brigade d'infanterie* captured Point 319 on the other side of the road, directly behind the French cemetery (but failed to capture Point 323 at this approximate location) on 13 June 1915, causing the Germans to abandon a short section of trenches to the north and turning what was once merely a communication trench and short stretch of front line into the northern defence of what would, by July 1916, become a fortified mini salient and a formidable obstacle.

After 230 metres a **small memorial plinth** *can be seen on the right.* This is dedicated to three soldiers whose remains were found here in October 2003. Two were German soldiers from Reserve- Infanterie-Regiment 121, Vizefeldwebel Albert Thielicke and Landwehrmann Jakob Hönes, who were killed nearby on 11 and 13 June 1915 respectively; and one was an unknown British soldier of the King's Own (Royal Lancaster) Regiment, believed to have died on 1 July 1916. Unveiled in June 2006, the memorial has impressions of the regimental insignia of both units on its sides.

Landwehrmann Jakob Hönes.

The plinth commemorating Albert Thielicke, Jakob Hönes and the unknown British soldier.

A further 200 metres brings you to the French **Chapelle de souvenir Serre-Hébuterne (2)***.* Built in 1936, this chapel perpetuates the memory not just of the French soldiers who fell in the *bataille de Toutvent*, but also the Germans. A plaque on the steps approaching the chapel commemorates the soldiers from the *21e, 27e, 51e* and *56e divisions d'infanterie* who fought and died here in June 1915 and commends the dead of both sides to rest in peace. Other memorials at the chapel include one to *Aumônier militaire* Joseph de la Rue, who served as a chaplain to both the *233e* and *243e regiments d'infanterie*; and one to Kgl.

The memorial on the wall of the *Chapelle de souvenir* that commemorates the regiments who took part in the June 1915 battle.

French *Chapelle de souvenir*, Serre.

Bayerisches Reserve-Infanterie-Regiment Nr. 1, who garrisoned this sector during the winter of 1916/17. A commemorative service takes place at this chapel every year on 7 June.

Cross the road to visit the **Nécropole Nationale de Serre-Hébuterne (3)** *and, if desired,* **Serre Road Cemetery No. 1***, 100 metres to the north east (where there is space for parking should it have proven impossible to park at Serre Road Cemetery No.2).*

The rear wall of both of these cemeteries mark the location of the French front line of 13 June 1915 and the location of Point 319.

The *cimetiére nationale de Serre-Hébuterne* (now officially the *Nécropole Nationale de Serre-Hébuterne*) was, in common with the British Serre Road cemeteries, begun during the V Corps clearances of the battlefield in 1917. The remains of about 150 French soldiers from June 1915 were discovered and buried towards the rear of the present cemetery near to where, also in 1917, a small memorial (still present) was erected in memory of the fallen from the *243e regiment d'infanterie*. In 1919 the

Containing many of the dead from the June 1915 battle, the *Nécropole Nationale de Serre-Hébuterne*.

Imperial War Graves Commission took over the care and maintainance of the cemetery and a *Comité du Souvenir* was formed by ex-servicemen from the *243e*, who returned to the battlefield annually in a search for the remains of their fallen. By 1922 the cemetery contained more than 500 burials and by 1925 had become an officially recognised cemetery on land now owned by the *Comité du Souvenir du 243ᵉ regiment d'infanterie*, although (unusually) it was still maintained by the IWGC. After the discovery of more isolated graves from other regiments, a large monument to the dead was erected in 1925, followed, in 1933, by the cemetery being granted national status and handed over to the state in a solemn ceremony on 11 June 1933. The cemetery now contains 834 French burials from the 1915 battle, mainly from the *243e* and *327e Régiments d'infanterie,* including 240 in the ossuary.

Continue towards Serre for one kilometre, passing the approach track to the Sheffield Memorial Park and its associated cemeteries and noting the **expansive views across the October 1914 battlefield** *to your right as you proceed. In June 1915, a long communication trench that led to the front line from the village ran along the northern edge of this road. Soon* *after entering the Serre village boundary, turn right at the calvary and follow the road for 100 metres until the first bend is reached and the trees on the left are passed.*

From this **viewing point (4)**, an appreciation of Serre's dominance over the battlefields to the south west can be made whilst looking to the east and along the road to your front gives a panoramic view of the battlefield of the *21ᵉ* (and *22ᵉ*) *régiments d'infanterie territoriale* of 4 October 1914.

Return to the D919 and turn right, continuing your journey into Serre for another 275 metres, passing the **memorial to the Pals of the Sheffield City Battalion** *(12th (Service) Battalion, York and Lancaster Regiment) who died before Serre in 1916, until the first side road is reached.*

Turn left onto this side road (rue du Château d'Eau – or Serhab Road as it was named on British trench maps) and continue for 1,300 metres, noting, as a farm is approached on the left, the long expanse of woodland to your front left.

This woodland, once the site of the 'Apostles Copses', marks the **French front line at the end of the *bataille de Toutvent*** and the British launch point for the 1916 Battle of the Somme in this vicinity. *When the farm on the left (Fme Pierrard) has been reached,* you are in the vicinity of the main German first line defences of June 1915 to February 1917 that ran due north (your front right) and to the south west from here. Up until June 1915, the German second line trench – which also served as a communication trench for the front line to the north – ran parallel with the road upon which you are walking. Located fifty to sixty metres into the fields on your left, only open fields, the copses and a natural ditch separated this area from the front line at Toutvent.

Beyond the farm, continue along the road, noting that the fields to your front right, ie to the right of, and beyond the next farm that you are approaching, mark the area of the northern limit of the battle of June 1915. Having just walked from its southern limit, this illustrates the compact size of this battlefield. This farm is the post war **new Toutvent Farm (5)** *which, located near Point 875 (captured by 10e brigade d'infanterie in June 1915), sits in the No Man's Land of June 1915 to February 1917. The French/British front line was to your left or, more precisely, on the road as it passes the present farm, the German front line about 150 metres to the right.*

In June 1915 the second row of German front line trenches crossed the present location of the farm, which is located exactly on a trench intersection, Point 378, attacked and captured by the *137e régiment d'infanterie* on 7 June, who then fought off desperate counter attacks throughout the remainder of the day

Just before the farm is reached, the road bends to your left before sweeping to the right. At this point, which marks the French front line in this vicinity at the end of the first day of the attack, take the track to the left. This is marked by the twin telegraph poles on the occasions that the track cannot be made out! Follow this track, passing through Point 377 (also captured and defended by the 137e régiment d'infa*nterie on 7 June) after fifty metres, for 670 metres until an overgrown area of rough ground and rubble, conveniently marked by a small clump of trees, is reached on the right. This is what remains of the original* **Toutvent Farm (6)**.

Toutvent Farm as it appears today.

Held by elements of the *3e bataillon* of the *21ᵉ régiment d'infanterie territoriale* during the *1ᵉʳ bataille d'Hébuterne* in October 1914, the farm was evacuated after a small exchange of fire following the fall of Serre on 4 October and occupied by the Germans who dug in between the farm and the nearby copse (bois d'État-Major). After the position was strengthened over the next eight months, it was defended by two rows of trenches to its east and by three to the north and by heavy wire entanglements. Captured by the *2e bataillon, 93e régiment d'infanterie* as part of the first wave assault on 7 June 1915 and heavily bombarded prior to German attacks attempting to recapture the position, the French, though forced back slightly, managed to hold on to the ruins of the farm for the remainder of the day and the remainder of the battle. An excellent view of much of the 1915 battlefield, from north to south, may be had from here.

Continue along the track for a further 140 metres before taking the track to your left. Before making the turn, however, note that in the field 100 metres to your front right once stood **Bois d'État-Major** *(under British occupation it became Staff Wood), a German front line position from October 1914 to June 1915. The buildings, visible to your front at a distance of about 1,000 metres, form* **La Signy Farm***; rebuilt on its original location after the war, it served as a battalion headquarters during the Bataille de Toutvent.*

Take the track to your left and continue for 420 metres until the corner of the **Sheffield Memorial Park (7)** *is reached.*

As you descend this track, note that the two rows of German front line trenches here (encompassing Points 304, 305 and 306) were located 100 metres to your right and that, for the first 300 metres of this path, you are walking through the territory captured by the *93e régiment d'infanterie* on 7 June. Looking in a south westerly direction as you walk, you can also observe the site of the actions of the *64e régiment d'infanterie* on the same date and sites of Points 306, 307 and 311, some 400 metres to your right.

Once the corner of the memorial park is reached, look back up the hill towards the site of Toutvent Farm on the crest, marked by the clump of trees. The French front line by the end of 7 June was about half way down this slope, with the Germans still holding the copses and the slopes within the park. Until this date, other than for a few scrapes, there were

Toutvent Farm (on the horizon) as viewed from Railway Hollow CWGC Cemetery. The front line by the end of 7 June 1915 ran across the field (left to right as viewed) below this position at about the mid-way point.

Sheffield Memorial Park (compare this image with the contemporary image on p. 109).

no trenches in the area of the memorial park so, on 7 June, the German defenders began hurriedly to entrench the summit of the slope and made use of an ancient, tree lined ditch that ran across the crest and along the eastern edges of the copses for some distance.

Fighting on this slope and into the bottom of the valley continued between 7 and 11 June, with the Germans finally being forced off the crest on 13 June following the *101e brigade d'infanterie* advance to the south west. Positions were consolidated and a new front line trench dug slightly forward of and the within the copses.

Though the area is primarily concerned with the events and the Pals units of the British 31st Division here on 1 July 1916, the small **Railway Hollow Cemetery**, located in the valley behind the memorial park, significantly also has evidence of French actions in the sector during the *Bataille de Toutvent*. There are the graves of two Frenchmen – thirty-five and thirty-four year old *soldat*s Louis Lesourd and Georges Palvadeau of the *64e régiment d'infanterie*, who both died of wounds on 7 June 1915. Trenches that were originally dug by the French and Germans during the June 1915 battle before being improved and deepened by the British can also be seen within the woodland north of, but attached to, the memorial park. (There is also evidence of them within the memorial park, but time has been less kind to these to the point that they are almost indiscernable). Shallow remains of the ditch used as a defensive position by the Germans on 7 June can also be seen along the front of the copse.

Railway Hollow Cemetery: the two French graves from 7 June 1915.

Once the park and area have been explored, continue along the track for 620 metres until the main D919 road is reached and turn right. After 100 metres, opposite Serre Road Cemetery No.1, take the road to the left, following the CWGC signs to the Redan Ridge group of cemeteries. Follow this road for 1,000 metres until the track to Redan Ridge Cemeteries No. 3 and No. 1 is reached. Take this track, passing Redan Ridge Cemetery No. 3, *and continue to* **Redan Ridge Cemetery No. 1 (8).**

As you walk this track (not recommended for a car!), note that you are within the German front line of December 1914 that was held by Reserve-Infanterie-Regiment Nr. 119 – the French line being just 100 metres to your left – and you enter No Man's Land approximately half way between these two cemeteries. The two mine detonations of 17 December 1914

Undulations on Redan Ridge; located near Redan Ridge Cemetery No.1, these slight dips are all that remain of the Cote 143 mine craters of 1914 and 1915.

took place in this area, followed by the failed assault by the *7e* and *8e compagnies* of the *137e régiment d'infanterie*.

Redan Ridge Cemetery No. 1 sits in the middle of the No Man's Land of 1914-1916 and is the final resting place of 154 casualties of the Great War, of which eighty-one are identified, mainly from the 1-2 July 1916 and the November 1916 attacks in this area and is another cemetery that was constructed during the V Corps clearances of the battlefield during the spring of 1917. Situated on the crest of Cote 143, this was the scene of much of the mine warfare of 1914 and 1915, which continued beyond the British arrival in the sector and on into early 1916. Though the mine craters have all been back filled since the end of the war, evidence of some of the 1915 craters can still be seen on some of the undulating land around this cemetery, especially the scrub area to the immediate south, where the remains of March and April 1915 detonations can be found.

Return down the track and turn right on the metalled road towards Beaumont-Hamel. After 400 metres, take the track to the right, known to the British as Watling Street, towards **Redan Ridge Cemetery No. 2 (9)** *which is reached after 350 metres.*

Containing the remains of 279 Great War dead, 155 of these are identified British soldiers. The cemetery, again dating from the V Corps clearances

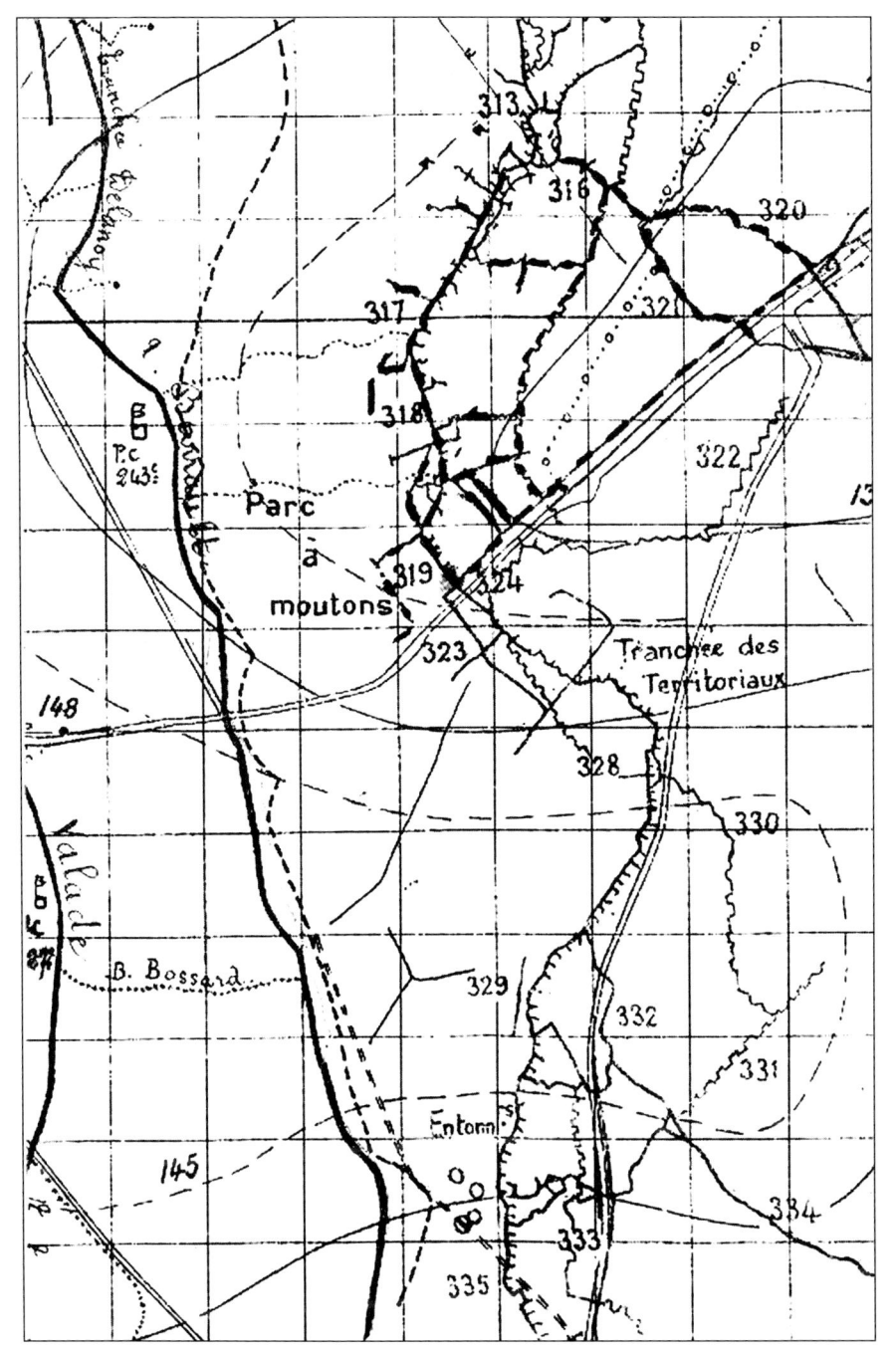

June 1915 trench map extract illustrating mine craters on Cote 143 and the area of the Serre road.

of 1917, lies in the centre of the 1914 – 1916 No Man's Land and lies on the southern slope of Redan Ridge/ Cote 143. Looking north from the back wall of this cemetery (towards Redan Ridge Cemetery No.1 on the crest). The German lines ran roughly following the road northwards 100 metres to your right and the French lines were parallel to them, about 200 metres to your left, with the gap between them narrowing as the crest of Cote 143 was approached. You are looking over the stretch of No Man's Land where the majority of the mine warfare of 1914 -1915 in this area took place and which was one of the more dangerous spots on the French Somme front during this period.

Continue along the track, noting after eighty metres that the track that you pass to your left is the northern extremity of the **Sunken Lane (10)** *made famous by the film of the 1st Battalion Lancashire Fusiliers taken on 1 July 1916. (The site of this footage can be visited, if desired, by following this side track for 380 metres.) As you continue along Watling Street, note the extensive battlefield views to your right, more especially so after 400 metres.*

This is the area, approximately 250 metres behind the French first line, from which the *11/1 génie* sank some of their **earliest mine shafts in November 1914 (11)**. From here, looking due east towards Redan Ridge Cemetery No. 1 and south east towards Redan Ridge Cemetery No. 2, an appreciation of the French battlefield around Cote 143 can be had.

Continue along Watling Street for another 580 metres to the junction with the D919. Turn right and, after another 640 metres, you will reach *Serre Road Cemetery No.2, and your vehicle.*

Part 2 (continuation)
From Serre Road Cemetery No.2, drive westwards along the D919 in the direction of Mailly-Maillet until a crossroads, once the site of a small hamlet but now dominated by large farm building, is reached after 1.7 kilometres. 180 metres beyond this crossroads a small track to the right leads to a British military cemetery that can be seen in the fields just beyond. The field to the right of this track is the site of the pre-war sugar factory that gave its name to the cemetery, **Sucrerie Military Cemetery (12).**

The sugar factory originally served as an aid post and brigade headquarters for the *21e division d'infanterie* from the winter of 1914/15;

The shell riddled Mailly-Maillet sugar factory as it appeared during the later war years.

a small cemetery was, therefore, established at the present location of Sucrerie Military Cemetery by the early spring of 1915. During the *Bataille de Toutvent* the cemetery was enlarged and, by July 1915, contained some 285 burials from both the *21e* and *51e divisions d'infanterie*. When the area was taken over by the British 4th Division at the end of July 1916 they continued to use this French cemetery for their own dead. The French graves were removed after the war and the cemetery now contains the remains of 1,103 British and Dominion soldiers.

Continue along the D919 to Mailly-Maillet for 2.3 kilometres and, at the first crossroads before the war memorial, turn right onto the D129, signposted with a green CWGC sign to Mailly-Maillet Communal Cemetery Extension. Follow this road for 900 metres until the communal cemetery (on the left) is reached.

Attached to the communal cemetery, **Mailly-Maillet Communal Cemetery Extension (13)**, which now contains the remains of 122 British soldiers, three New Zealanders and one Canadian, was started by the French Army in June 1915. Prior to the influx of burials during the *Bataille de Toutvent*, burials were conducted in the communal cemetery itself and mainly consisted of engineers, including the Redan Ridge Tunnellers of the *11/1 compagnie du 6e régiment du genie*, who were headquartered in Mailly-Maillet between 15 October 1914 and June 1915. By the time this sector was taken over by the British, there were fifty-one French graves in this cemetery. All of them were removed after the war.

Return to the crossroads and turn right onto the D919 through the centre of Mailly-Maillet. After 240 metres, turn left onto the D129 towards Englebelmer, On your way through Mailly, note the magnificently carved sixteenth century west façade of Mailly-Maillet's parish church, a quite extraordinary survival of the war. It was safeguarded by the erection of massive sand bag walls on both sides, interior and exterior, of its west end. Further down the road and off to the right is a recently restored mausoleum of the mid eighteenth century. After 1.8 kilometres a small crossroads, marked with small wayside chapel, is reached just after entering the northern boundary of Englebelmer.

[*Here, if desired, a detour can be made to another CWGC cemetery that was originally a French burial ground by continuing through this crossroads and following the D129 as it sweeps to the right through Englebelmer itself to* **Englebelmer Communal Cemetery (14)** *which is located on the right of the road, 1,200 metres after leaving the western boundary of the village.*

Containing fifty-two British and Dominion war graves (plus a further 150 in the attached Communal Cemetery Extension) of the 1916 to 1918 period, the French were the first to use this cemetery for their dead; there were eleven burials near the southern boundary of the cemetery in the first half of 1915. These graves were removed post-war.]

Turn left at the crossroads in the direction of Auchonvillers (or turn right if the extra visit was made).
   After 540 metres, at the end of the first row of trees on the left of the road, an iron crucifix can be seen on the left, next to which a recently erected headstone marks the **isolated joint grave (15)** *of colonel Paul Costebonel and capitaine Aimé de Fontenay, who were both killed near here in 1914.*

The son of a school teacher, **Paul Léon Costebonel** was born in Bioule (Tarn-et-Garonne), on 1 February 1855 and enlisted into the army at Montauban in 1875, immediately applying for officer training at St Cyr. After attendance at St Cyr between 1875 and 1877, he began his military career in Tunisia and Algeria and then joined the staff of *l'École supérieure de guerre* at St Cyr. Promoted to *chef de bataillon* in 1904, he became Professor of military topography at *l'École supérieure,* followed

The isolated grave of Paul Costebonel and Aimé de Fontenay on the road to Auchonvillers.

by various other assignments and promotions before being given the command of the 62e *régiment d'infanterie*. On 7 August 1914 he left Lorient with his regiment and took part in actions during the Battles of the Frontiers and the Marne before arriving on the Somme as the commanding officer of *43e brigade d'infanterie*. *Colonel* Costebonel was severely wounded by the detonation of a large calibre shell near his post, forward of Cote 151 and south east of Auchonvillers, during the fighting between Auchonvillers and Hamel on the night of 5 October 1914 and died of his injuries, aged 59, in a field ambulance west of Auchonvillers a few hours later, on 6 October. He was mentioned in *général* de Castenau's Army order of the day:

'…very seriously injured in combat on 5 October, he particularly distinguished himself in a critical moment by his bravery, energy, calmness and his observation. Due to his personal actions, his brigade held their ground under an intense cannonade. He was a fine example of the highest military virtues and died in the ambulance on October 6, 1914.'

Costebonel was made a *chevalier* in the *Légion d'honneur* in 1908.

Aimé Edouard Louis de Fontenay was born at St Rémy la Varenne, Maine-et-Loire, on 5 January 1876. A student at the time of his enlistment, his (deferred) compulsory military service began at le Cholet on 14 November 1899, where he was enlisted into the *77e régiment d'infanterie* as a *soldat 2e Classe*. Promoted to *caporal* in September 1900, he passed to the reserve in November of the same year. In November 1901 he was promoted to *sergent* in the reserve before being commissioned as a *sous-lieutenant de réserve* in October 1903 and then to *lieutenant de réserve* in February 1908. On 1 August 1914 he was mobilised back into full time service and, soon after arriving at his depot on 3 August, was promoted to (temporary) *capitaine* and transferred to the *62e régiment d'infanterie* and the staff of the brigade headquarters of the *43e brigade d'infanterie*. He was killed in action by the detonation of a shell on the brigade headquarters at the *moulin de Vitermont* (in the field opposite the location of this grave, approximately 170 metres to the south east) at 5am on 5 October 1914. He was awarded a posthumous *Légion d'honneur*. Note his incorrect date of death and regimental details on the headstone. These details were taken from his *mort pour la France fiche individuelle* (which quite often contain errors) and contradict both his service records and the brigade war diaries.

Continue along the road for 1.65 kilometres and turn left onto the D73 into Auchonvillers. Remaining on the D73, turn left in the centre of Auchonvillers after 340 metres, following the signs towards Mailly-Maillet and **Auchonvillers Military Cemetery (16)***, the approach path of which is reached on the right after another 330 metres.*

This is another CWGC cemetery that was started by the French Army in June 1915, there were twelve French burials (located against the back boundary of the current cemetery) here when the British began to use the cemetery in August 1915. The nearby farm was used as an aid post. The French graves were removed post-war and, out of a total of 528 burials, it now contains the remains of 487 identified British, New Zealand and Newfoundland war dead of 1915 to 1918.

Auchonvillers church as it appeared in 1915.

Return to the junction in the centre of Auchonvillers and turn right, in the direction of Hamel and Mesnil, but also signposted for the Newfoundland Memorial Park. At the Y-junction in 330 metres, remain on the D73 (left) in the direction of Hamel and continue on this road until the **Newfoundland Memorial Park (17)** *is reached in 1,300 metres.*

One of the more highly visited areas of the Somme battlefield, increased footfall from visitors over the past decades has led to measures restricting access to certain areas within the park. Luckily, however, one of the (reinforced and preserved) areas in which the vistor actually can walk is through a small section of the front line trench of 1916 that is located to the front of the Newfoundland Caribou Memorial and Memorial to the Missing. The site is understandably geared to the remembrance and commemoration of the tragic events here of 1 July 1916 (with lesser, but still obvious commemoration of the events of November 1916). It is very easy not to realise that, though there are various front line trenches (representing different dates) in this preserved section of the battlefield, with some parts labelled with sign posts, sections of the original front line trench that was constructed by the French Army in October 1914 and

Aerial view of the Newfoundland Memorial Park illustrating the location of the (originally) French dug front line trench. Initially a number of shorter, unconnected trenches, the trenches were joined and extended from mid October 1914 onwards.

held by them for a further eight and a half months, to the end of July 1915, have also been preserved, including a small section where the visitor is able to walk through.

Though the trenches within this park have been dug and re-dug several times throughout their history (including post-war), a section of the original French front line can be seen winding its way to the northern boundary of the park from in front of the Caribou monument. The front line was altered and straightened during the British occupation (both prior and post 1 July 1916); the small, signed, section of front line that has been

The French built front line trench.

'floored' and preserved for the visitor to walk through was originally dug as a system of short fire trenches and scrapes by the *piou-pious* of the *84e régiment d'infanterie territoriale* between 4 and 5 October 1914 and was deepened, connected, elongated and improved by the *116e régiment d'infanterie* and *65e régiment d'infanterie* from that date. Over the following months, units of the *21e division d'infanterie* rotated in and out of the trenches in this area as the network of trenches improved and were developed westwards towards the rear. Other than patrol activities, attacks here were infrequent into the summer of 1915 but, on the occasion when they did occur, they were all small scale harassing actions with no real hope (or desire) for any breakthrough from either side. Casualties were relatively light in this area over the period of French occupation after December 1914. They were, however, constant throughout that period and in no way could it be considered that this was a 'live and let live' sector.

Continue on the D73 towards, and through, the village of Hamel – occupied, abandoned and reoccupied by the 116e régiment d'infanterie on 6 and 7 October 1914 before becoming a French front line village up to the British occupatation of the sector. At the junction with the D50, reached after 1,600 metres, turn left (sign posted Beaucourt and Thiepval) for 550 metres until **Ancre British Cemetery (18)** *is reached, beyond the new road arrangement, on the left.*

Originally called 'Ancre River No.1 British Cemetery, V Corps Cemetery No. 26', this cemetery, as its original name suggests, was another of the V Corps battlefield clearance cemeteries of 1917. Containing 2,543 burials, 1,211 are of identified British army and naval, Newfoundland, Canadian and New Zealand casualties, along with one German. It is situated in the centre of a low valley that marked the No Man's Land of 1914-1916. Views can be had of the battlefield from the back wall: the French line up to July 1915 – originally dug by the *116e régiment d'infanterie* – was located approximately 200 metres to the left of your view and the German line – dug by the Reserve-Infanterie-Regiment Nr. 99 – the same distance to the right, the lines climbing the slope towards the Hawthorn Ridge.

Continue towards Beaucourt for another 930 metres and the entrance to **Beaucourt Station (19)**. *The battlefield of* Reserve-Infanterie-Regiment Nr. 99, the *116e régiment d'infanterie*, the *83e régiment d'infanterie territoriale* and the *84e régiment d'infanterie territoriale* in September and October 1914 *– can be seen on the right.*

Turn right at the crossroads, found after another 100 metres, onto the D4151 and from there to one of the all-important river crossings of 1914.

The scene of a vicious and prolonged action in October 1914; Beaucourt railway station as it appeared before the war.

A right turn at the T-junction after 560 metres will take you through to St Pierre Divion (with some evidence of German workings in the bank alongside the road) and another T-junction after 1,300 metres. Turning left at this junction takes you back onto the D73 and in the direction of quite likely some much needed refreshment at the **Ulster Tower** *or the* **Thiepval visitors centre***!*

End of Tour

GPS Waypoints, Hébuterne to the Ancre 1914-15 Tour

1 – 50° 5'47.25"N, 2°39'4.30"E   2 – 50° 5'56.84"N, 2°39'22.42"E
3 – 50° 5'57.60"N, 2°39'21.67"E 4 – 50° 6'9.49"N, 2°40'8.39"E
5 – 50° 6'48.87"N, 2°39'31.41"E 6 – 50° 6'32.46"N, 2°39'9.78"E
7 – 50° 6'21.13"N, 2°39'23.29"E 8 – 50° 5'33.83"N, 2°39'8.21"E
9 – 50° 5'19.40"N, 2°39'8.14"E   10 – 50° 5'20.04"N, 2°39'3.50"E
11 – 50° 5'30.67"N, 2°38'49.59" 12 – 50° 5'36.51"N, 2°37'35.47"E
13 – 50° 5'8.66"N, 2°35'47.18"E 14 – 50° 3'24.66"N, 2°36'15.74"E
15 – 50° 4'3.10"N, 2°37'4.06"E   16 – 50° 4'49.77"N, 2°37'36.95"E
17 – 50° 4'20.36"N, 2°38'51.64"E 18 – 50° 4'3.69"N, 2°40'4.51"E
19 – 50° 4'26.68"N, 2°40'31.90"E

Chapter Five

The Ancre to the Somme: mid October 1914 – June 1916

Like the events north of the Ancre, from the end of the first week in October 1914 a short period of comparative calm followed once the frenetic and desperate actions of the 'race to the sea' period had moved northwards towards Arras and then, eventually, into north western Belgium. Trench lines were dug, extended and reinforced as villages were fortified and defences deepened. Behind the lines roads were repaired and constructed and light railways built to keep what was rapidly becoming a static front well supplied. Fresh artillery batteries, especially behind the French lines, arrived almost daily, as did plentiful supplies of ammunition and, as the recalled reservists of August and September 1914 were gradually freed up from their interior and (re)training duties by the early mobilisation of the Class of 1914 on 1 September, 'human resupply', in the form of reinforcements and relief for the battle weary front line troops, became plentiful. This led to an increase in aggressive patrol activity between any set piece, pre-planned actions.

All was far from idyllic, however. The increase in artillery (and shells) led to heavier use of this arm in order to harass the enemy as much as possible and the actual location of the lines, especially the French front line, provided issues on both sides of No Man's Land. After the actions of 5 – 8 October, the French line was still, so far as the high command and the front line troops were concerned, far from ideally situated; it was still located on lower lying ground within the marshy soil of Bois d'Authuille and on the slopes too far from the rapidly strengthening fortifications of Ovillers. The Germans had their own concerns: the French encroachment into the south west edge of the village of Fricourt, where French outposts were invariably situated in buildings on the fringe of the village; the slightly disadvantageous position on Cote 110; exposure on the plains north of Maricourt and the ideal artillery ground beyond from which the French could harrass the German held Somme River crossings as far as Feuilléres and the northern section of German line south of the river; and the pressurised situation at La Boisselle were constant thorns in their side. Attempts to eradicate the issues at all of these places would follow in the coming months.

The village of Fricourt photographed from Cote 110 during the early summer of 1915.

The first of the major assaults intended to alter the situation took place at La Boisselle after a short, but intense, bombardment at 7:40am on the morning of 18 October. The *1e* and *2e bataillons* of the *160e régiment d'infanterie* (of the *78e brigade, 39e division d'infanterie*), under the command of *chefs de bataillon* Lebreton and Pesme, launched an attack directly upon the village almost immediately after arriving in the front line from Corbie, where they had been resting and refitting after seeing considerable action earlier on the month. Despite the ferocity of the preliminary bombardment, it proved insufficient to silence the German defenders and, assisted by artillery, German machine gunners halted the attack almost as soon as it had begun. Further attempts at 8.30am and at 2pm met with the same fate, costing the *160e régiment d'infanterie* 194 casualties; forty-three of these were killed outright, 145 wounded and six missing.

Exactly one week later, on 25 October, and following a week of sustained French artillery activity, another attempt was made. This time a joint *22e* and *53e division d'infanterie* attack was made at points along the whole line between Ovillers and Mametz. It was specifically targeted at the area between La Boisselle and Fricourt, held by the Reserve-Infanterie-Regiments Nrs 109 and 120. However, the results were the same. The French attackers hit a virtual, but no less impenetrable, wall of artillery and machine gun fire in No Man's Land and, after sustaining many casualties, were forced to return to their starting positions. It was now clear that in this sector, as had been discovered north of the Ancre, constant all-out attacks across the open would, most likely, end in nothing more than costly failure and other tactics would be needed. From this point into December, and as wet weather set in in early November, operations would become smaller, more local, affairs. For example, *329e régiment d'infanterie* managed to break through the German lines beyond the Moulin de Fargny on 30 October and advance onto the *Chapeau de Gendarme* before being shelled off this height; or, from the German viewpoint, at Fricourt on 4 November, when, with the use of heavy minenwerfer mortars and artillery, Reserve-Infanterie-Regiment Nr 110 finally managed to push the *205e régiment d'infanterie* out of the village entirely, even using the mortars to destroy the railway station from where many of the French aggressive actions originated – though the station remained in French hands.

The main activity began to be driven underground. Even on the surface, as trenches were pushed forwards (and rearwards, into more intricate spider-webs of trench systems), the spade and pick became the main weapons of choice. Covered by a diversionary infantry assault on 19 November (which was easily repulsed) conducted by the *22e division d'infanterie,* intended to keep the Germans occupied around Ovillers and La Boisselle, the French line was sapped forward a hundred metres or so on to slightly higher and more favourable ground above Ovillers. A similar event took place to the south of La Boisselle on 28 November, with a diversionary attack carried out by the *53e division d'infanterie* that enabled the French front line to be pushed forward another 300 metres away from Bécourt. At La Boisselle itself, advances were made without an actual attack; the French managed to sap to within three metres of the German lines at the *Îlot* during November and into early December. As was the case north of the Ancre, tunnellers from the *11ᵉ Bataillon de sapeurs-mineurs* (*6ᵉ régiment du génie*) switched from digging trenches, saps and dugouts and began constructing fighting tunnels and mine shafts near and east of Cote 110 (Carnoy to Bois Français, Fricourt). Here, the *mineurs* of *11ᵉ bataillon de sapeurs-mineurs* (initially from various companies until the sector was established and taken over by the *11/3 compagnie du genie* in its entirety) began to sink shafts at the end of November, compelling the German pioniere in the area to follow suit. *11/4 compagnie du génie,* after a period of undertaking counter-mine measures to control the German pioniere who had already been detected tunnelling under the French lines in the vicinity of the *Îlot*, found themselves similarly employed at La Boisselle within the next few weeks, finally relieving the part of the *11/3 compagnie du genie* that had started the workings in that sector.

The ending of large scale French attacks during November resulted in increased German patrol activity that extended into December, with the aim of obtaining information as to French intentions. Other than this, and an increase in French artillery activity, the front was, rather unnervingly for the Germans, quiet for the first couple of weeks of December. However, this all changed on 17 December. Heralded by the mine detonation and limited attack near Beaumont-Hamel, the French launched a general attack all along the line between the Ancre and the Somme rivers.

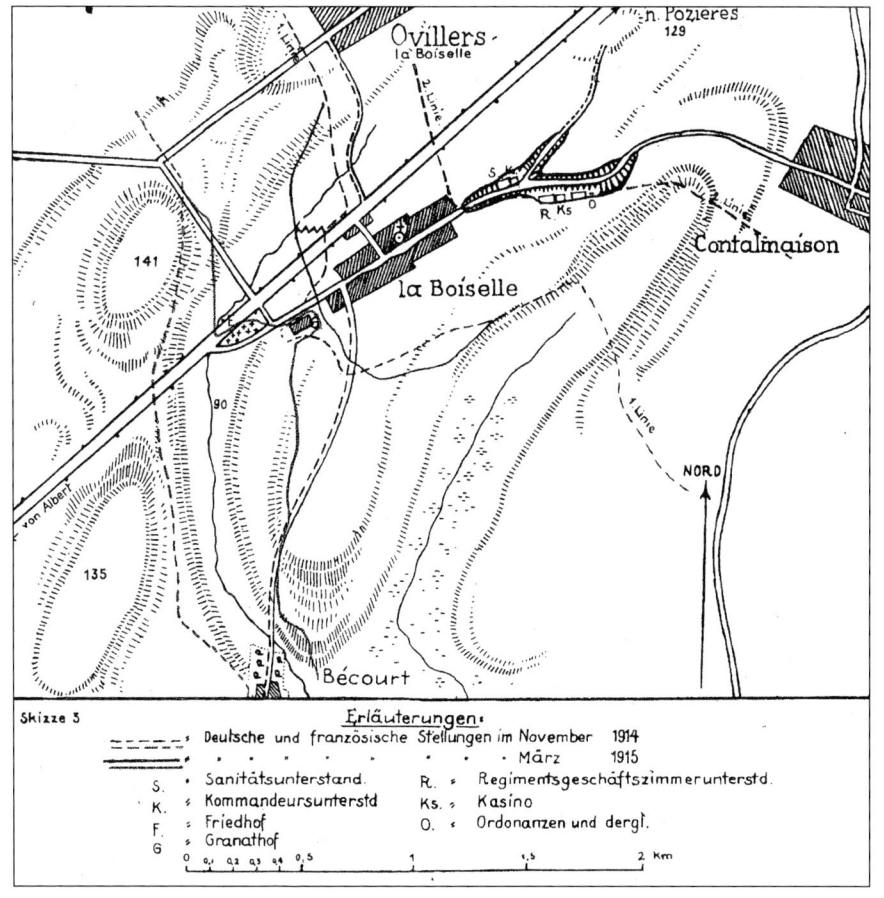

La Boisselle, November 1914 to March 1915.

From the Ancre to La Boisselle, the *22e division d'infanterie* was reinforced by *41e brigade* (*64e* and *65e régiment d'infanterie*) from the *21e division d'infanterie* and, from there to the Somme, *53e division d'infanterie* was reinforced by *16e brigade* (*115e* and *117e régiments d'infanterie*) from the *8e division d'infanterie*, who had been transferred to this sector from just north of Montdidier specifically for this attack. In reserve, in and just behind Albert and covering the whole of the southern sector, were the *82e division d'infanterie territoriale*.

French guns had been shelling heavily, but sporadically, all along the front and the immediate rear for some weeks now and there was no specific prior artillery bombardment of any note in an attempt to maintain an element of surprise. In addition, the nightly wire cutting patrols had been able to complete their tasks adequately. The *XI corps d'armée* (and

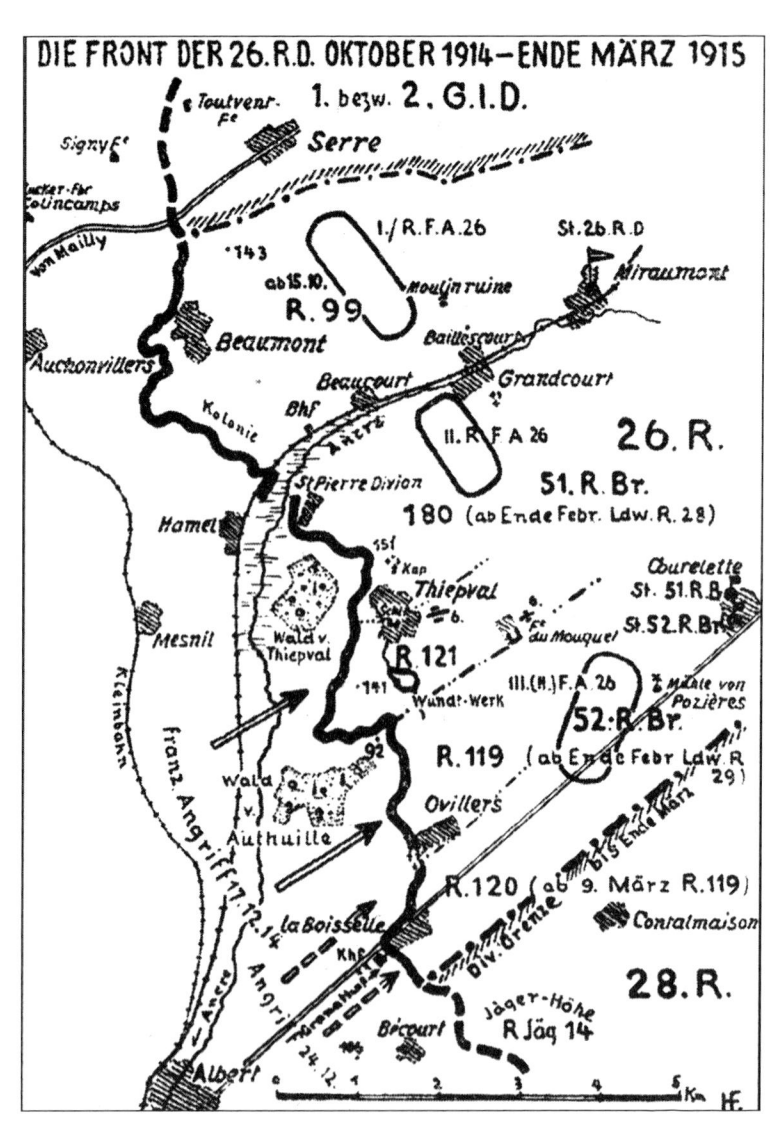

26. Reserve-Division front, October 1914-March 1915, illustrating the French attacks of 17 and 24 December 1914. (*Die 26. (Württembergische) Reserve-Division im Weltkrieg 1914–18*)

the unattached *53e division d'infanterie*) launched their attack at 6am. In the north, from Thiepval to Ovillers, supported by elements of the *64e régiment d'infanterie*, spread thinly along the whole line from Beaumont-Hamel down to La Boisselle and the *62e régiment d'infanterie,* located in reserve at Aveluy and Authuille, the *19e régiment d'infanterie* confidently advanced against the strongly held villages of Thiepval, Ovillers and La Boisselle.

On their left flank, before Thiepval, they immediately came under heavy fire from Infanterie-Regiment Nr. 180 and Reserve-Infanterie-Regiment Nr. 121 on the slopes below Thiepval Wood, stopping the attack there dead in its tracks before the German wire. Further south, some progress was made in front of Bois d'Authuille and on to the heights to the north of Ovillers. The infantry advanced up to and even in the German lines to the north west of Ovillers. However, the attackers here were then exposed to heavy fire from Reserve-Infanterie-Regiment Nr. 119 and Reserve-Infanterie-Regiment Nr. 120 and the advance faltered as German artillery fired a barrage on the French rear. This stopped reinforcements from getting forward and prevented any withdrawal by the soldiers in the fighting zone, who were also being shelled. West and south west of Ovillers a similar scenario unfolded as the attacking troops from the *19e, 118e, 64e* and (in support) the *65e régiments d'infanterie* were cut down in swathes by the cross-fire coming from Ovillers and La Boisselle to the south. The French managed to reach the western edge of Ovillers but were forced to stop there as the German guns swept the battlefield. Many survivors had to wait until the relative safety of the night before they could return to their own lines. A *section*, made up from a hundred volunteers from the uncommitted *116e régiment d'infanterie*, under the command of *sous-lieutenant* Pichon and placed under the orders of the *19e régiment d'infanterie*, was cut up before Ovillers. Just thirty-four men returned.

The ruins of Ovillers in early 1915.

French trenches in the ruins of La Boisselle cemetery, early 1915.

At La Boisselle, the *118e régiment d'infanterie* managed to rush the village cemetery but was prevented from advancing further by thick barbed wire defences and the weight of fire coming from the front and the north east. They managed to hold the position overnight; German defences were broken the following morning and the *118e* advanced a few more metres and dug in in at the eastern edge of the cemetery. Advances on the neighbouring *Îlot* during the day had proved impossible.

Further south, a smaller scale assault at Cote 110 by two *compagnies* of the *205e régiment d'infanterie* was made as a diversion to the main French attack at Mametz and Montauban. Mametz was to be directly assaulted by *105 brigade d'infanterie* (*205e, 236e* and *319e régiments d'infanterie*), with the *2e* and *3e bataillons* of the *45e régiment d'infanterie* to their east tasked with the capture of Cote 125, which lay between Mametz and Montauban. Montauban itself was the target of the *117e régiment d'infanterie*, attacking from the direction of Carnoy, and of the *228e régiment d'infanterie*, from the direction of Maricourt. In support, located between Maricourt and Carnoy, was the *5e bataillon* of the *329e régiment d'infanterie*. In the most southerly sector of the attack – Maricourt – the *115e* and *224e régiments d'infanterie* were to strike towards Hardecourt-aux-Bois.

Mametz, held by Reserve-Infanterie-Regiment Nr, 111 and Reserve-Jäger-Bataillon 14, was assaulted at 5am on 17 December. Under heavy fire and sustaining numerous casualties, *105 brigade d'infanterie* was held up in front of the German wire before the village but to their east their flank units and *45e régiment d'infanterie* managed to break through the German front line and advance on Mametz behind the positions held by Reserve-Jäger-Bataillon 14. This led to a vicious, traverse by traverse, fight in the trenches leading to the village. Mametz was entered by 7am but, after several counter attacks, during which the Germans managed to penetrate as far as the centre of the village, it was proving impossible to hold the gains without reinforcement. German artillery began to sweep the rear of the French positions and so reinforcements could not get through, which in turn prevented further attacks of any major scale during the afternoon. By evening, following heavy street fighting within Mametz, the French defenders, mainly from the *236e régiment d'infanterie,* were boxed in the buildings near the village church and forced to surrender. Several attempts to relieve the trapped defenders were made during the afternoon and further attacks to recapture Mametz were made into the early hours of 18 December. However, due to the effectiveness of the German guns and the reinforcement of the German line during the previous afternoon and night, all failed, leaving the corpses of hundreds of French soldiers strewn in No Man's Land south of the village.

Further east, Montauban and its defenders from Reserve-Infanterie-Regiment Nr. 40 came under heavy shell fire during the morning of 17 December, alerting them to the forthcoming operation. When the fighting began at neighbouring Mametz an hour before the attacks along the remainder of the line, they had time to prepare their defences hurriedly and were even able to give assistance to the critical situation a kilometre and a half to the west. Thus, when the *117e* and *228e régiments d'infanterie* launched their frontal assault on the German lines, other than on their right flank, they were cut down in No Man's Land almost as soon as they reached the German wire. Immediately north of Maricourt, however, the right flank of the *228e régiment d'infanterie* and the left flank of the *115e régiment d'infanterie* managed to break through the German front line and advance several hundred metres up the Maricourt to Montauban road before being forced to dig in because of suppressive fire from machine guns on their flanks and the presence of German reserves arriving at their front. During the afternoon a German counter-attack from the direction of Bernafay Wood was successfully repelled; but further advance proved impossible.

To the east of Maricourt, the right flank of the *115e régiment d'infanterie*, located in the Bois de Maricourt, and the *224e régiment d'infanterie* to their south, attacked towards Bois Favière and Hardecourt-aux-Bois respectively at 7:05am, supported by a smaller attack across the plain south of the road towards Curlu. Both of these regiments came under heavy fire from fully prepared Bavarian troops and their perfectly sited multiple machine gun positions to the north of Bois Y and west of Bois d'en Haut as soon as they left their trenches and, at very high cost (the *224e régiment d'infanterie* sustained 324 casualties within the first half hour of the attack), made no progress in the area.

By nightfall on 17 December, the disastrous attack had been temporarily called off all along the line and, apart from at La Boisselle and to the north of Maricourt, the surviving French troops were either back in their starting positions or were trying to get back to them. Casualties amongst the attackers had been huge and No Man's Land from the River Ancre all the way to the Somme was littered with the corpses of dead Frenchmen – some 500 or so lying before the German wire in front of Ovillers alone. The *19e régiment d'infanterie* was particularly badly hit, taking approximately 50% casualties in this day's action: 302 of its officers and soldiers were killed and over 800 missing or wounded.

The following day several German counter attacks were made along the line, most of which achieved nothing more than establishing more securely their own positions. One attack north of Maricourt, however, conducted with the use of incendiary grenades, pushed the French out of some of the positions that they had captured the previous day. These positions were, in turn, retaken during the morning by a French counter-attack from the west by the *45e régiment d'infanterie*. A final, easily repulsed, attack in this sector at Carnoy took place on 21 December, during which the French lost another 1,200 men, including prisoners. A truce was arranged here for both sides to recover their dead and wounded. French attacks also took place on Mametz and Fricourt on this same date, following which the line became static. Realising that further such attacks would, most likely, be just as costly, the commander of the French *Second Army*, *général* de Castelnau, called off the offensive on 24 December 1914. With its ending, both sides paused to consolidate their positions along much, but certainly not all, of the front in the sector. On Christmas Day 1914, in a very rare occurrence on the French front and in what seems to have been an isolated incident in this sector, some soldiers from the *205e régiment d'infanterie* even took part in a festive truce with their opposite numbers from the Badisches Reserve-Infanterie-Regiment Nr. 109 and their neighbouring Jäger-Bataillon near Cote 110, swapping cigarettes and chocolates in the spirit of the season. This incident was of very short term duration, however; by evening, the French artillery had begun to bombard violently the whole German line and the situation returned to its pre-Christmas state.

Though the general offensive had been halted, fighting continued at

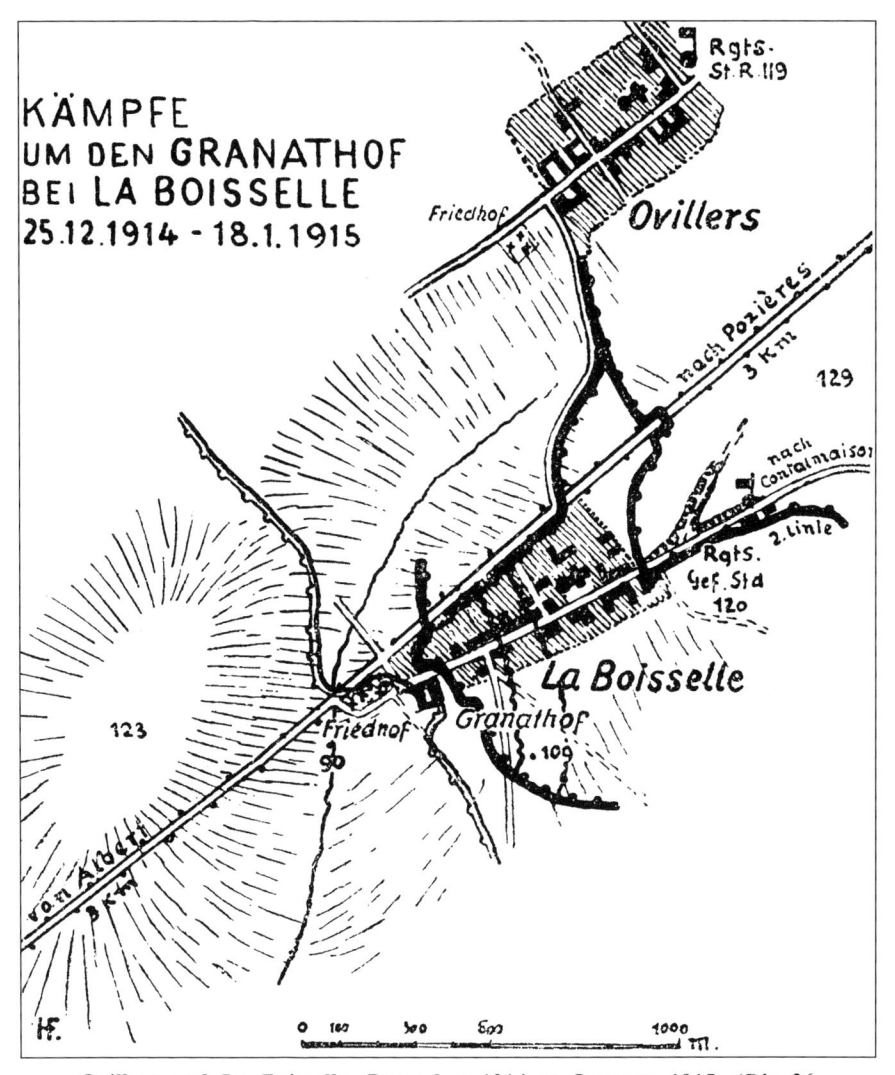

Ovillers and La Boisselle, December 1914 to January 1915. (*Die 26. (Württembergische) Reserve-Division im Weltkrieg 1914–18*)

La Boisselle. On 24 December, the village was heavily shelled, preceding a strong assault against Reserve-Infanterie-Regiment Nr. 120 by the *118e*, *62e* and *64e régiments d'infanterie* and during which the *Îlot* was finally captured. The *64e régiment d'infanterie* even managed to penetrate the German defences as far as the village church. A concealed gun halted them and, with the threat of being cut off during a counter attack, forced them to withdraw back to the eastern edge of the village cemetery. Heavy shelling of the village continued throughout Christmas Day 1914, whilst the *11/4 compagnie du génie* began to sink four mineshafts at the newly captured *Îlot*. On 26 December an attack was carried out on La Boisselle by *7e* and *8e compagnies* of the *65e régiment d'infanterie* prior to their relief that night from the area of the cemetery. Although fruitless, the attack was rare in that the French casualties were light, with just two dead and thirty-two wounded. The following day, suspecting that tunnelling work was under way, Reserve-Infanterie-Regiment Nr. 120 launched an attempt to retake the *Îlot* but were thwarted by effective frontal and flanking fire from the *64e* and *118e régiments d'infanterie*. The Germans gradually transformed La Boisselle into a fortress, but niggling actions continued into 1915 as several French attacks during January resulted in German local counter attacks and further (failed) attempts to recapture the *Îlot,* specifically on 8 and 14-15 January 1915.

The Granathof: the farmhouse at *l'Îlot de La Boisselle* in early 1915.

The first mines at La Boisselle were detonated by the Germans. On 2 January, their first mine on the Somme, intended to be blown under the *Îlot*, was laid too short and detonated under their own trenches, which they had evacuated prior to detonation. They were more successful with their second mine; but, though it was blown under the French lines this time, it was not powerful enough and caused very little damage. On 10 January at 2:50pm, the *11/4 compagnie du génie* blew their first mine of the war directly under the German defences on the road leading into the village. The blast was followed up by an infantry attack of three *compagnies* in size. However, as was becoming the normal situation in the area, it was eventually beaten back by artillery and overwhelming rifle and machine gun fire, ending in heavy fighting around the ruins of the *Îlot* farm buildings which, precariously, remained in French hands.

On 11 January the Germans blew a 600 kg charge under the *1er* and *9e bataillons* of the *118e régiment d'infanterie*, killing forty Frenchmen and provoking a short, sharp fight for the crater. This action was followed in the evening by a short truce in order that both sides could recover their dead and wounded from the events of the previous two days.

Just under a week later, just after midnight on the morning of 18 January, 'Bataillon Todtenberg' – a composite unit made of four companies from Reserve-Infanterie-Regiment Nr. 120, supported by Reserve-Infanterie-Regiment Nr. 119 giving flank protection and accompanied by groups of Pioniere skilled in the art of demolition – took part in a surprise attack on the *Îlot* and the area of the La Boisselle cemetery, which was held, once again, by the *7e* and *8e compagnies* of the *65e régiment d'infanterie*. After stealthily moving across the (very narrow) No Man's Land, the unaware French sentries were silenced and the raiders swarmed into the French trenches at the principal target of the *Îlot,* killing or capturing much of the defending garrison before it was even fully alert. The attackers were less successful at the cemetery, becoming caught up in the wire entanglements and coming under heavy small arms fire; however, supporting German artillery, which lay down a crescent shaped bombardment around the *Îlot* and cemetery, prevented French reinforcements getting forward and the positions eventually fell. The French artillery remained silent throughout the action due to uncertainty about where the front line was at that particular time. Alongside the infantry, who were slowly eliminating the few pockets of French resistance, German pioniere were able to proceed with their own mission, packing the deep cellars, dugouts and mine shafts with explosives, ready for demolition. Their work was completed within two hours and a single long whistle blast signalled a return to the German lines; within five minutes, the *Îlot* and cemetery were empty. Once all the German troops were either back in their own lines or, at the very least, clear of the *Îlot,* the charges were blown and, though not all of them detonated successfully, the French tunnel system and defences through the cellars and several mine shafts were destroyed. This forced the *génie* to dig new shafts into their systems further back and bought the Germans in the sector several weeks of relief from the threat of French mining activities. During the raid, the two companies of the *65e régiment*

The ruins of the village of La Boisselle.

d'infanterie sustained losses of fourteen dead, twenty-six wounded and 105 missing. Total German casualties amounted to thirty-four killed, wounded and missing.

Immediately after the 18 January action, French artillery laid an eight hour long bombardment of the German lines as the *65e régiment d'infanterie* reoccupied the shattered remnants of their defences, increasing their pre-attack strength by moving three companies from the *1er* and *3e bataillons* into the front line at the cemetery and the *Îlot*, with a further three companies from the same battalions immediately to their rear in support.

Underground fighting continued through February and March. A trio of German mines were blown on 7 February near the *Îlot*, held by companies from the *2e bataillon, 19e régiment d'infanterie*, that damaged, but failed to destroy, the French defences there. In an unwittingly unfavourable location, a detachment of troops from the Reserve-Infanterie-Regiment Nr. 120 advanced to occupy the craters and demolished houses but were stopped by French artillery and rifle fire before finally being driven back by a French counter attack during the afternoon. Probably much to the surprise of the German defenders, who had thought that French mining had been more severely damaged by the actions of 18 January, these blows soon brought a rapid response. A

French mine, using the same gallery as their 10 January mine, was fired on 9 February, heralding a month of tit-for-tat small scale actions with no real objective other than harassment and keeping the infantry of both sides in a state of nervous alert. A month later, on 10 March 1915, towards the end of the relief of the Reserve-Infanterie-Regiment Nr, 120 by Reserve-Infanterie-Regiment Nr. 119, a larger mine was detonated by the French in almost exactly the same location. This was followed by yet another infantry assault, once more driven off.

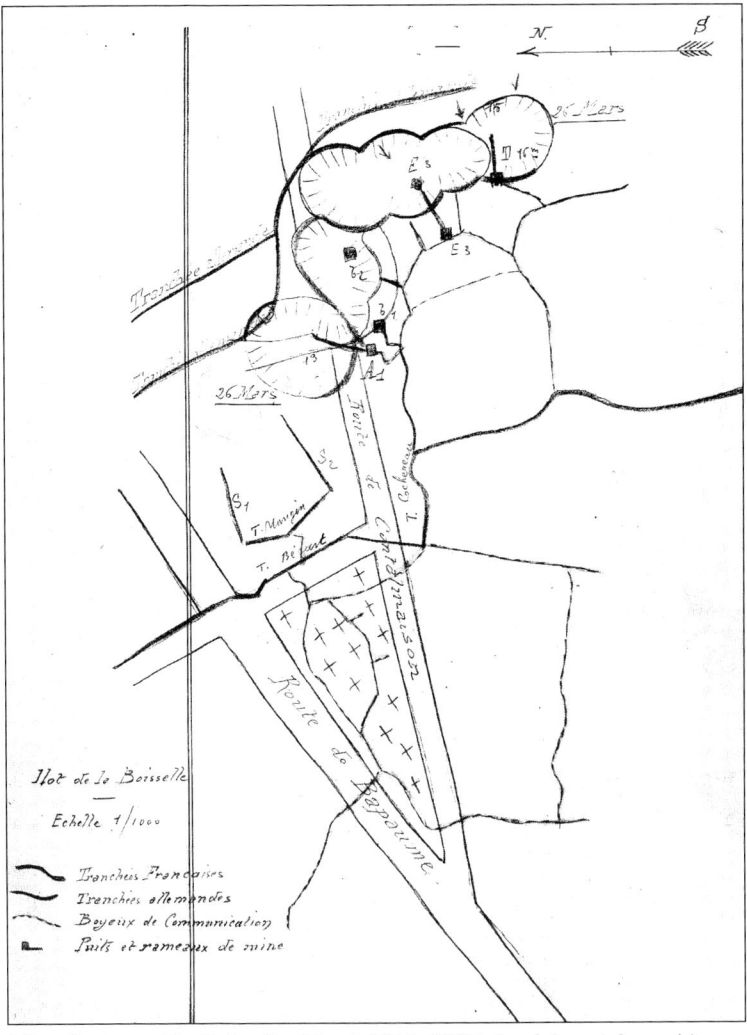

Mine Craters at La Boisselle, March 1915. (JMO *6e régiment du genie*)

The next large scale mine detonation at La Boisselle took place on 26 March; but there was a slight change in tactics by the French in their mine warfare. They first evacuated their positions at the *Îlot*, and then blew a 1000 kg mine at 4.30pm immediately to the south east of this position. Allowing a company from Reserve-Infanterie-Regiment Nr. 119 to break cover for the expected 'race' for the crater, it was followed by another, larger, blast (2,600kg) about a hundred metres distant, on the road into La Boisselle, just four minutes later. This second explosion, as was hoped, caused numerous casualties amongst the Germans who had rushed to occupy the first crater. However, the French attack that followed, as by now seemed *de rigueur*, was driven back by the use of hand grenades.

Though mine warfare and the associated small scale surface actions that inevitably followed lessened somewhat in intensity as 1915 drew on, it did continue up to and beyond the British arrival on 31 July 1915. On that date the 51st (Highland) Division relieved part of the *22e division d'infanterie* in this sector. At La Boisselle the 1/7th Black Watch relieved part of the *19e régiment d'infanterie* and moved into their trenches between La Boisselle and Bécourt. *11/4 compagnie du genie*, however, stayed at La Boisselle until 22 August 1915, remaining behind to instruct and assist the arriving tunnelling companies RE, who would inherit sixty-six major mine shafts between Beaumont-Hamel and Maricourt but did not yet have the personnel to operate them. The Black Watch did not have to wait long for a rude introduction to this sector. Their first days in the line were marked by the Germans with heavy trench mortar fire and the detonation of a mine at 6.50pm on 1 August; whilst the French *génie* retaliated with a mine of 800kg blown at 4.25am on 3 August. During the remaining few weeks of their tenure, the *11/4 compagnie du génie* blew another two mines at La Boisselle (a 2,500kg mine at 10.30am on 13 August and a 3,000 kg mine at 7.23pm on 19 August), both of which provoked heavy German shelling of the line. At 5pm on 22 August 1915, after gradually handing control of the workings to the Royal Engineers, the last 'resident' French soldier left the La Boisselle front line for good. Some French artillery batteries remained in the area as late as July/August 1916, requiring French artillery observers to operate as far forward as the front line (and even beyond!). Between January 1915 and January 1916, approximately seventy mines and camouflets of varying size had been fired over this small section of front line, measuring less than 400 metres in length, making it for a while – especially during the first half of 1915 – one of the most compact and dangerous 'micro-battlefields' on the whole of the Western Front.

Further down the line, east and south of Fricourt, a similar but less intense, though no less dangerous, situation to that at La Boisselle had

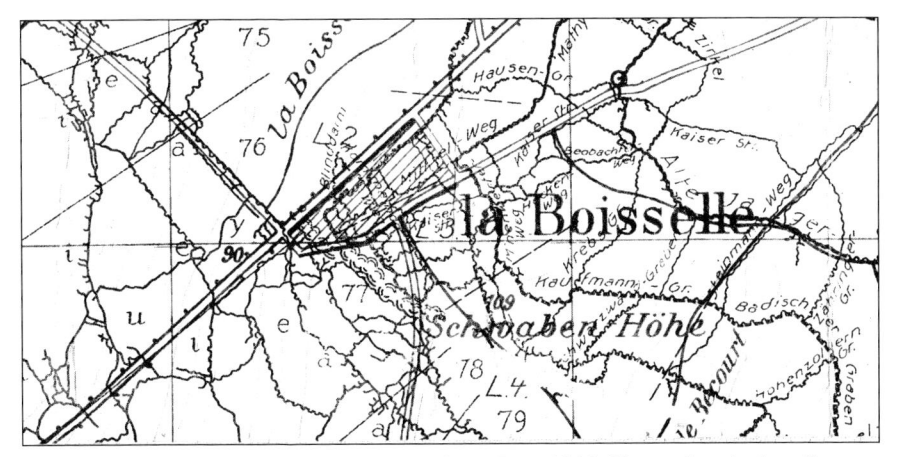

German trench map of La Boisselle from June 1916, illustrating the length of the crater field.

also developed. Between February and May 1915, raids and patrols through No Man's Land were commonplace, some of which were conducted by *11/3* and *11/4 compagnies du génie* taking time from their tunnelling and other digging or construction activities to experiment with using explosives to clear paths through the German wire.

Though both sides were aware of each other's tunnelling activities, at least since December 1914, mine warfare south and south east of La Boisselle was instigated by the Germans north of Carnoy when they detonated a mine on 15 March 1915. This provoked several days of fighting for the crater until the *11/3 compagnie du génie* (by now headquartered at Méaulte) sprung 'their' first mine (they did not dig it as an individual unit) under the German Jägerstellung position near Fricourt. This brought mining attention, if only temporarily, westwards to this sector, leaving the French and Germans to share Carnoy Crater as they dug communication trenches to its southern and northern lips respectively. By the last week of April 1915, two more mines had been detonated at Carnoy – again, equally shared after the inevitable combats that followed the detonations; three were fired on Cote 110 in the area of Bois Français and Bois Allemand; and another three to the west of Fricourt at a location that became known as the Tambour. Within two months, this figure had risen to nine at the Tambour (soon to rise to fourteen); twenty-five along Cote 110 between Bois Français and the south west of Mametz (in three distinct clusters along a length of front line spanning approximately one kilometre); and no less than fourteen at Carnoy along a 140 metres length of front. At the end of April 1915, three were French held and eleven German, creating a No Man's Land in this short length of front with a depth of less than five metres. Ownership of

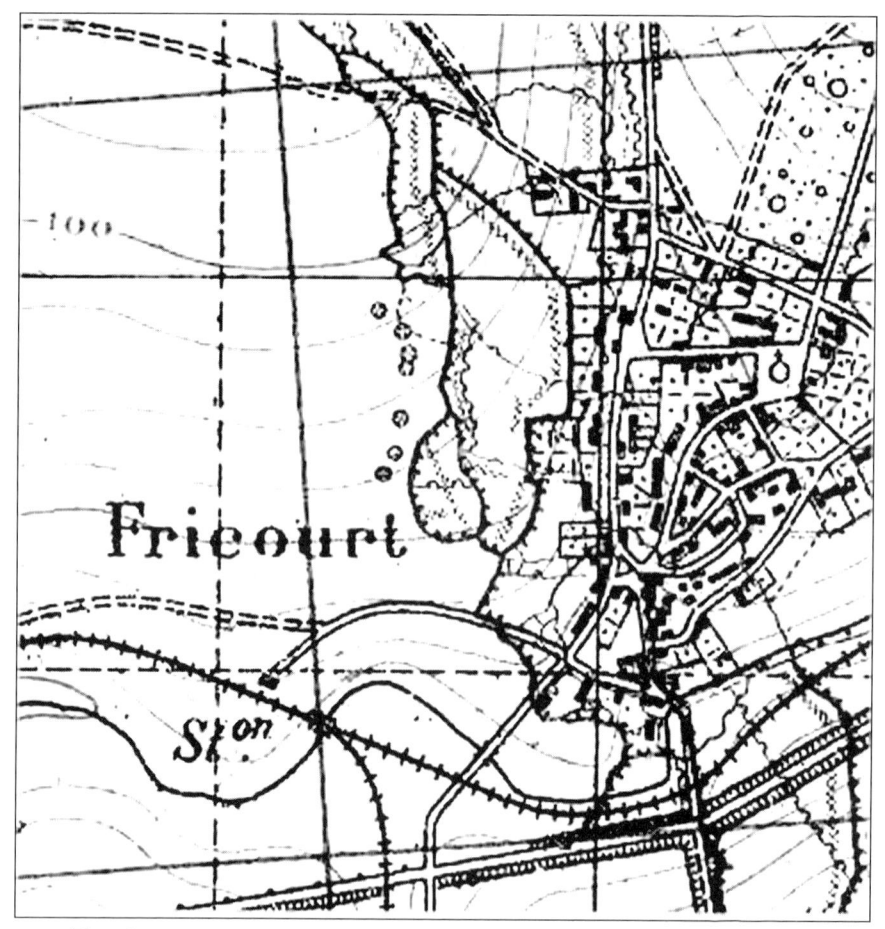

Trench map extract showing the 'Tambour' crater field, May 1915.

these craters would be disputed up to and beyond the British arrival in this sector.

Held by the *53e division d'infanterie* until the end of April 1915, when they were replaced by the *151e division d'infanterie*, and, in part by the *28e division d'infanterie* (who straddled the river between Carnoy and Frise), the sector between Fricourt and the River Somme, other than in the mining sectors, remained static following the intense and costly actions of August to December 1914. As was the case all along much of the French Somme front, the days were marked by sporadically heavy shelling, sniper activity, intense patrolling activity and trench raids. Numerous small scale and local actions also occured throughout the period, such as the attacks between Carnoy and Mametz by the *293e régiment d'infanterie* on 10 July and through the Bois Français and Bois

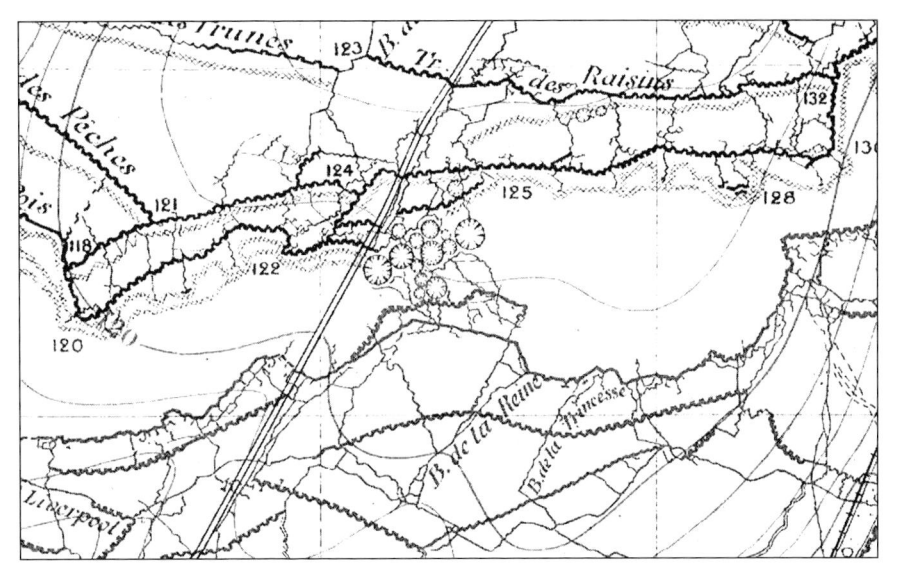

Trench map extract showing the Carnoy crater field, May 1916.

Allemand by the *6e* and *7e companies* of the *403e régiment d'infanterie* on 19 July, both of which were intended to take prisoners and destroy German mine workings. Both were relatively successful enterprises. However, the second of the attacks provoked a hurricane bombardment of the French line and two counter attacks, of which a neighbouring unit, the *10e compagnie* of the *410e régiment d'infanterie,* bore the brunt. Despite heavy losses, they managed to hold their line. Away from the mining sectors, however, such events became more scarce as the summer of 1915 progressed.

Beyond the crater field above Carnoy and along the line as it curved around Maricourt to Moulin de Fargny on the north bank of the Somme river was the one sector of the Somme front that could possibly be described by the cliché 'idyllic' from the spring of 1915 onwards. It was held from 19 April to 10 August by the *22e régiment d'infanterie* and, on the river bank at Fargny, by one company of the *99e régiment d'infanterie*. They had both crossed the river to this sector from a much more active sector that stretched from Fay in the south, through Dompierre and up to the Somme at Frise. The regimental history of the *22e régiment d'infanterie* looked at the stay in their new area with some fondness:

> '…The area is calm, and the trenches are well organized. Everyone remembers the village of Maricourt, the Chapeau de Gendarme and the Moulin de Fargny, where we enjoyed

French trench at La Boisselle in June 1915.

miraculous fishing in the Somme. Every eight days we went to rest, either to Bray or to Suzanne, where we spent pleasant hours...'

At the end of July 1915, as had happened north of the Ancre, the British Third Army began to arrive to take over the French held sectors north of the Somme, freeing the French divisions. These latter shifted to the south east and within two months of being relieved from the Somme were all involved in the Second Battle of Champagne. Many hundreds of these veteran troops, some of whom had been in almost constant action since September 1914, would fall in this battle.

X Corps, comprising (from north to south) the 51st (Highland), 18th (Eastern) and 5th Divisions, gradually took over the areas held by the *22e divison d'infanterie*, *151e division d'infanterie* and a section of the *28e division d'infanterie* between the Ancre and the Somme between 31 July and 10 August. Initially relieving individual companies, the British units served alongside the French until, by the second week of August, all the French infantry was withdrawn from the sector. The *génie,* as elsewhere,

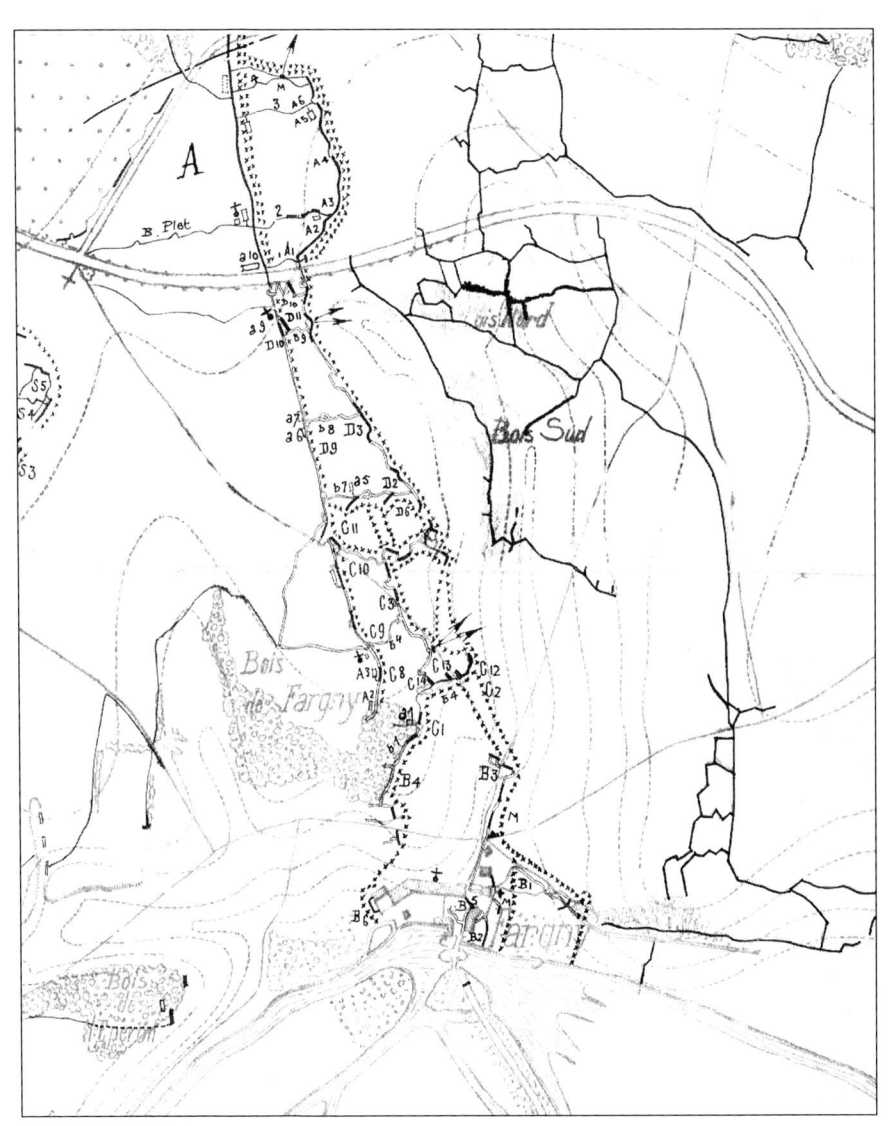

French and German trenches from Fargny on the River Somme to the south of Maricourt Wood, April 1915.

remained for a few weeks to assist the RE tunnelling companies and some French were located behind the front line in the area until the Battle of the Somme the following year. The *22e régiment d'infanterie*'s 'halcyon sector', which included the ruins of the mill at Fargny (destroyed in the battles of September 1914 and further damaged in the December 1914 action), the pleasant pools and streams and the (shell absorbing) marshes

Ruins of the mill at Fargny, with the Chapeau de Gendarme in the background.

that were still rife with wildlife, was reluctantly handed over to 14 Brigade (1/Devonshire Regiment, 1/East Surrey Regiment, 1/ Duke of Cornwall's Light Infantry, 2/Manchester Regiment and [the attached] 1/5 Cheshire Regiment) of the 5th Division. They would be the first British troops able to experience the 'miraculous fishing in the Somme' and bathe in the waters in full and open view of the Germans (who were doing the same). Their introduction to this battlefield was a polar opposite to that of 153 Brigade, 51st (Highland) Division around La Boisselle.

Tour 3

The Ancre to the Somme 1914-15
A Walking and Driving Tour

The tour is forty-five kilometres long, including a 9.4 kilometres walk.

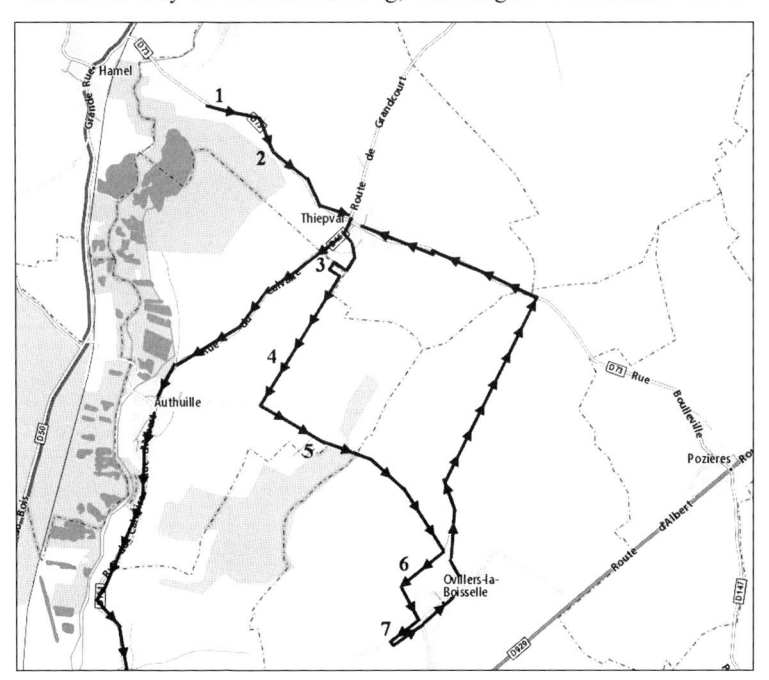

Tour 3: The Ancre to the Somme 1914-15 – Points 1 to 7.

Begin the tour at one of the optional spots for the end of the last tour: **The Ulster Tower (1)**, *to the north west of Thiepval.*

Some excellent views over the Ancre valley and the 17 December 1914 battlefield can be had from the area of the entrance to the Tower. With your back to it and facing Thiepval Wood, a look to the right gives views of the slopes where the left flank of the *19e régiment d'infanterie*, supported by elements of the *64e régiment d'infanterie*, were cut down

View across the Ancre valley from the rear of the Ulster Tower. Ancre British Cemetery, marking the centre of No Man's Land as it climbed the slope towards the Newfoundland Memorial Park, can be seen in the left centre of the view.

by cross fire coming from German positions on the rise to your rear, behind the Tower and, as they emerged into view, from across the Ancre valley. They were attempting to cross the road and advance up the slopes roughly against the line of the farm track leading off the road to your right in an attempt to gain the high ground overlooking the Ancre and to bring pressure on the Germans in Thiepval from the north.

Looking to your left, towards Thiepval, a similar scene developed, though involving fewer men, as the same regiments pushed towards the rise from Thiepval Wood and (just out of sight from this location) towards Thiepval from the south eastern edge of the wood.

Take the D73 towards Thiepval. In 230 metres, stop at **Connaught Cemetery (2).**

To the rear of this cemetery is **Thiepval Wood**. In December 1914 it had become an almost uninhabitable quagmire and was all but impenetrable, due to broken branches, damaged natural drainage channels and wire obstacles. On the other hand, the wood had a major redeeming feature, in that the ground cover was so thick that in the areas where movement was actually possible it was invisible to the enemy. This allowed for the speedy construction of quite a complex system of communication trenches that led to the front line, which ran – more or less – along the eastern and part of the southern perimeter of the wood. In early 1915 drainage was improved and a pumping station, which allowed the faster removal of ground water, was installed.

Continue on the D73 for 750 metres to the crossroads at Thiepval. Turn right onto the D151 for ninety metres then take the road to the left, following the signs for the **Thiepval Memorial**. *Park in the Visitors Centre car park. In front (ie on the western side) of the memorial is* **Thiepval Anglo-French Cemetery (3).**

French graves in the Thiepval Anglo-French Cemetery.

Currently bearing the names of 72,337 British and South African officers and other ranks who died in the Somme sector before 20 March 1918, and whose graves are not known, the construction of the Thiepval Memorial began in 1928 and was unveiled 1932.

During the winter of 1931/32 it was decided that a small mixed cemetery should be made at the memorial's foot to represent the losses of both the French and the British Empire who had fought in roughly equal measures during the 1916 Battle of the Somme. There are 300 graves from each nation, symbolizing this equality. Of the 300 British Empire burials in the cemetery, 239 are unidentified and, of the 300 French, 253. Though the British bodies, found in December 1931 and January-March 1932, originate from as far north as Loos and as far south as Le Quesnel, the majority came from the Somme battlefields of July-November 1916. The French remains were mainly discovered on the 1916 Somme battlefields too, but, as the French had fought on these same fields earlier in the war, the majority of the identified remains date from 1914 and 1915.

Instead of returning to the car park, take the obvious track leading south-west from the memorial and walk down this for 750 metres. Where the track passes through a small copse is the site of a pre-war chalk quarry.

The 1914-16 front line was approximately 170 metres to your right as you walk down this track until just before the copse, which became a front line position and the point of a small, heavily defended salient known to the Germans as the **Granatloch (4)**. Located on (to the French) **Cote 141**, this area was lost by the *44e brigade d'infanterie* during German attacks on 5 October 1914 but, following attacks by the *19e* and *118ᵉ régiments d'infanterie*, which failed to dislodge the Germans from the crest but allowed some movement of the line up the slopes, the French front line had been pushed to about 200 metres west and south of this quarry. In October 1914 and, again, in December 1914, the fields within your line of vision to your front would have been strewn with French corpses.

Continue 170 metres to the minor Authuille to Ovillers road and turn left. After 380 metres, the approach path to **Lonsdale Cemetery (5)** *is reached, behind which can be seen the expanse of* **Bois d'Authuille**.

Completely captured by the Germans in September 1914, Bois d'Authuille became a charnel house for the temporary occupants from Reserve-Infanterie-Regiment Nr. 121 and Infanterie-Regiment Nr. 180 as French artillery specifically targeted the wood, forcing them to withdraw. Partly occupied by the French immediately afterwards, they pushed their front line to the north east corner and to the tree line to the south east during October 1914; and it was one of the few areas where any advance was made during the 17 December attacks – the French

View towards the Thiepval Memorial across Cote 141 with the 'Granatloch' in the middle distance. This area was a blood soaked killing ground in October and December 1914.

managed to advance the front line some 300 to 400 metres closer to Ovillers from the south eastern fringe of the wood.

Continue towards Ovillers for another 1,400 metres.

As the road skirts the north eastern fringe of Bois d'Authuille, it lies on the front line of December 1914 to 1916 before it followed the track to your right at the first cross roads beyond the wood; and then it dropped southwards, cutting across the fields towards Ovillers Military Cemetery. Descending the slope, you are walking through one of the 'hot spots' of the December 1914 (and September 1914) fighting. Looking to the south west as you descend you can see the battlefield of the *19e, 118e, 64e* and *65e régiments d'infanterie*, along with that of the volunteers from the *116e régiment d'infanterie*.

Just as the first buildings of Ovillers are reached (a farm building on the left), take the rather nondescript, farm track to the right (rue des Coquelicots) and follow this for 280 metres until the **Calvaire Breton (6)** *is reached on the left.*

The *Calvaire Breton* at Ovillers.

163

Originally erected in 1924 on behalf of the de Boisanger family and renovated in 2011, this memorial is in homage to the Bretons of the *19e régiment d'infanterie* (from Brest) who fought and died in these fields on 17 December 1914. The memorial stands on land very close to the spot where *lieutenant* Augustin Breart de Boisanger of that regiment was killed in action that day.

Born at Quimperlé, Finistère on 16 January 1874, Augustin embarked upon his compulsory military service with the *19e régiment d'infanterie*, at Brest on 12 November 1895. Rapidly promoted, he was a *caporal* by June 1896 and, service complete, was discharged to the reserve in November 1898, continuing with part time service for the next few years, during which he was promoted to *sergent* in July 1899. A slight brush with the law earned Augustin a month in prison in October 1902, but this did not affect his military career as he transferred, still as a *sergent*, to the territorials in 1908, serving with the *87e régiment d'infanterie territoriale* until gaining a commission in 1910 and transferring to the *86e régiment d'infanterie territoriale* as a *sous-lieutenant*. Mobilised into full time service on 2 August 1914 with the *87e régiment d'infanterie territoriale*, Augustin initially reverted to *sergent* before having his (sub) lieutenancy confirmed by decree for the duration of the war on 13 September 1914 following a transfer to the *219e régiment d'infanterie (réserve)*. He was promoted to *lieutenant* in the *19e régiment d'infanterie* in November 1914.

Augustin Breart de Boisanger 1874 – 1914.

After being hit by a rifle bullet and falling wounded, Augustin refused to be evacuated, exclaiming: *Je n'abandonne pas mes Bretons*! He was killed in action soon afterwards and his words are displayed on this memorial. He is buried in Ovillers Military Cemetery. There is also a useful and informative bilingual information panel located here.

Continue past the memorial, following the track as it takes a ninety degree turn to the left, for another 180 metres to the crossroads and turn right. In 280 metres, **Ovillers Military Cemetery (7)** *is reached.*

Located in the No Man's Land of 1914-1916 and established in 1916, this cemetery contains the remains of 3,559 British and French soldiers. Though the vast majority of burials are British from 1916, there are 119 French burials; thirteen of the identified burials died on 17 December 1914. Of these thirteen, ten are from the *19e régiment d'infanterie* and

The French section of Ovillers Military Cemetery.

French trench near Ovillers, early 1915.

include *lieutenant* Augustin Breart de Boisanger, whose family erected the Breton memorial you have just visited. The French burials cover a broad range of dates, with the earliest from September 1914 and the latest from June 1918.

Return along the same road you have just travelled for 700 metres and into Ovillers village, in due course turning left onto the route d'Authuille. Continue up this road, passing the track to the Breton memorial, for 300 metres and, noticing the sight of the Thiepval Memorial on the horizon, turn right on to the side road you will have reached and continue until it forks into two farm tracks, after 450 metres. Take the right hand track for a further 1,400 metres until it meets the D73.

As you walk along this track, you are travelling in the opposite direction of (but over the same ground) the advances of Württembergisches Reserve-Infanterie-Regiment Nr. 121 during the battles at the end of September 1914 in which Ovillers was originally captured.

At the junction with the D73, the farm to your front is **Mouquet Farm**, *described in an earlier tour.*
Turn left on the D73 and the cross roads in **Thiepval** *leads back to your vehicle in the Visitors Centre car park after 1,700 metres.*

Return to your car and leave the car park, turning left onto the D151 and passing through Authuille after 1,800 metres. After another two kilometres, stop in the small, newly created park area on the left immediately before the junction with the D20. The commune of Aveluy has erected (2016) what at first sight looks a most peculiar memorial with an even stranger title, the La Nymphe d'Aveluy. *This is a replica of a carving, almost certainly done by a French soldier – or soldiers –in Aveluy and which appeared on postcards of 1915. Aveluy at the time was a support area for the troops in the line. There are various figures in the replica, including the eponymous nymphe, who lies seductively at the top. Turn left at the junction onto the D20 towards Ovillers. Continue on this road for 1,100 metres to the junction with the minor road that leads past Ovillers Military Cemetery to the village itself. Do not take this road but, if safe to do so, stop here and study the expansive* **view of the battlefield (8)** *that may be had from here. Be aware that this can be a busy road and the traffic moves at some speed.*

Looking towards the area between Ovillers and La Boisselle, these dangerously exposed fields were the main killing grounds in the area both in September and December 1914. Away from the set piece battles, the

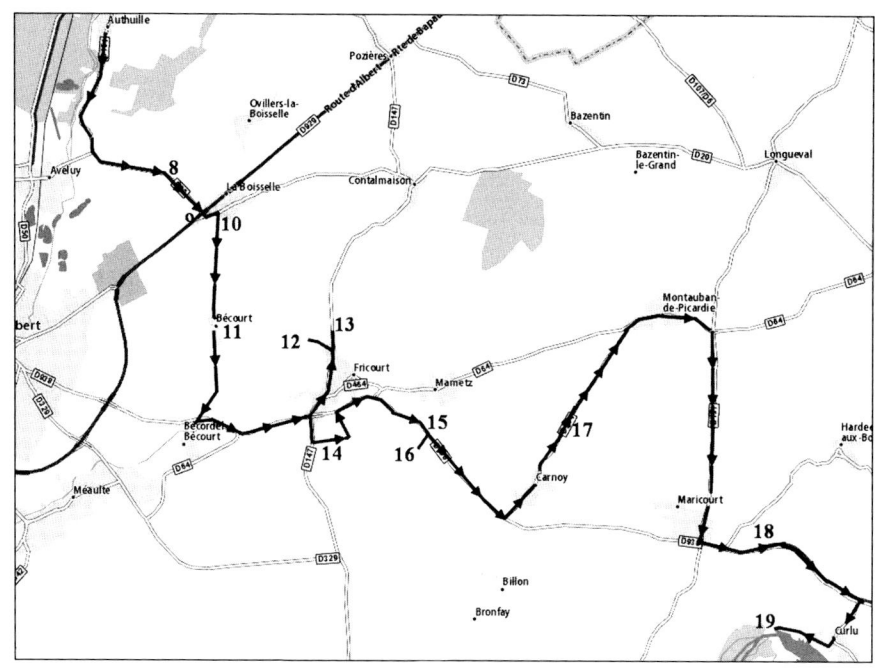

Tour 3: The Ancre to the Somme 1914-15. Walking and Driving Tour – Points 8 to 19.

View from the French front line near the Ovillers road towards La Boisselle illustrating the dominant position of this latter village over the lower lying No Man's Land in front of Ovillers.

width of the No Man's Land here (approximately from the road upon which you are currently situated to just before Ovillers, about a kilometre distant), was one of the widest on the Somme and encouraged heavy and prolonged patrol activity from both sides throughout 1915.

Continue along the D20 for 780 metres to where it crosses the major D929 Albert to Bapaume road. Carefully cross this road and stop as soon as you safely can. The grass triangle to your right is the site of **La Boisselle Cemetery (9)**.

For a time, one of the 'hottest' spots on the Western Front: the entrance to La Boisselle.

An intensely concentrated micro-battlefield, you have just travelled from one of the widest sections of No Man's Land to one of the narrowest – the French front line located at the eastern wall of the cemetery (the right hand side of the road upon which you are stood/parked) and the German front line, located in the vicinity of the houses on the left. The scene of innumerable actions (some of which are illustrated in the narrative), the area between here and the next stop was one of the most dangerously active spots on the whole Somme front from late 1914 and throughout 1915.

Continue on the D20 as it bends left into La Boisselle. After a hundred metres or so, the **site of the Îlot (10)** *farm buildings and the remains of* **several 1915 mine craters** *can be seen on the right. At the time of writing public access to this most interesting, privately owned site has become considerably easier. There is a small association that helps to maintain it and they have a website, http://ilotdelaboisselle.com. Visits (which can last thirty minutes or as much as ninety minutes) are arranged by reservation (which is usually done by internet) and there is a small entry fee.*

Remaining 1915 mine craters on site of *l'Îlot* (some of these have now been cleared of foliage).

Known to the Germans as the 'Granathof' or 'Granatenhof', and to the British as 'The Glory Hole', the actions at the *Îlot* are described in some detail in the narrative. This was, perhaps, the most dangerous sector on the Somme in 1915. Constantly fought over both on the surface and underground and with, at one point, a No Man's Land of just three metres, nearly seventy mine detonations occurred in this miniscule area between 1915 and 1916. The undulating ground, which was too disturbed to even contemplate attacking across it on 1 July 1916, still bears witness to this violence.

Turn right at the junction after another 120 metres, then take the right fork onto the C9 towards Bécourt, noticing the continued crater field to your right. After 1,500 metres, after passing the surrounding woodland, the hamlet of Bécourt is reached. **Bécourt Château (11)** *can be seen on the left.*

Bécourt Château as it appeared later in the war.

The scene of the disastrous 28. Reserve-Division attack on 7 October 1914, the hamlet and woods were defended by the *160e régiment d'infanterie*, reinforced by the *26e régiment d'infanterie*. After pushing through to the château, the German survivors reorganised in the grounds before attempting (and failing) to capture Cote 106. After the 17 December actions, this area was some distance behind the French line and remained so for the remainder of the French occupation.

Follow the road to the left (past the entrance to the château) and continue for 1,500 metres towards Bécordel-Bécourt, passing **Norfolk Cemetery** *en route. Just before Bécordel-Bécourt, the road passes underneath the D938. Turn left once through the underpass and join the D938 in the direction of Fricourt. After 1,400 metres, turn left onto the D147 into Fricourt and continue through the village for one kilometre (in the direction of Fricourt German Cemetery). Turn left onto rue de La Boisselle (signposted with a green CWGC sign for Fricourt New Military Cemetery) and continue for 250 metres to where a track forks from this road (also signposted to Fricourt New Military Cemetery). It is possible to park here and walk the 350 metres to* **Fricourt New Military Cemetery (12).**

View of the Tambour crater field from Fricourt New Military Cemetery.

Containing 210 burials, of which twenty-six are of unidentified soldiers, Fricourt New Military Cemetery was established by the 17th (Northern) Division following the capture of Fricourt. The cemetery is constructed around four mass graves made by the 10/West Yorkshire Regiment in July 1916, with a few individual graves from September 1916. 159 of the graves are of soldiers from the 10/West Yorkshire Regiment. Situated in the No Man's Land of October 1914 to July 1916, the eastern wall gives good views of the **Tambour crater field** (note that, though there are numerous mine craters still clearly visible, approximately nine of which are quite easily discernable in the winter or early spring, this area is on private

A closer view of the crater field, with Fricourt village in the background.

property and should, under no circumstances, be entered without prior permission). The scene of two mine explosions (and a third that failed to detonate) on 1 July 1916, the Tambour was already a warren of tunnels and small craters when the British took over the sector. At least fourteen small mines were blown in this sector between March and July 1915.

Return to the junction with the D147 and turn left. After 330 metres, **Fricourt deutscher Soldatenfriedhof (13)** *is found on the right.*

Established by the French in 1920, this cemetery contains German remains from seventy-nine different communes around the Somme. Though over half of the burials are of German soldiers who fell during the Battle of the Somme in 1916, about a thousand date from 1914 and 1915, the remainder from the Somme battles of 1918. Currently, there are 17,031 German soldiers interred here, of whom 6,477 are unknowns. 11,986 of the burials are in one of the four kameradengräbern mass graves and the cemetery. For a while the famous German fighter ace, Manfred von Richthofen, was buried in this cemetery.

Return through Fricourt, staying on the D147 to the crossroads with the D938. Continue across the crossroads in the direction of Bray-sur-Somme, past the village cemetery (following the line of the French front line, which was located in the field sixty-five metres to your left) *for 330 metres and a crossroads with two farm tracks is reached. Take the left track,* still following the French front line as it swept east towards the crest of Cote 110 *(if the conditions are poor, or you feel safer walking*

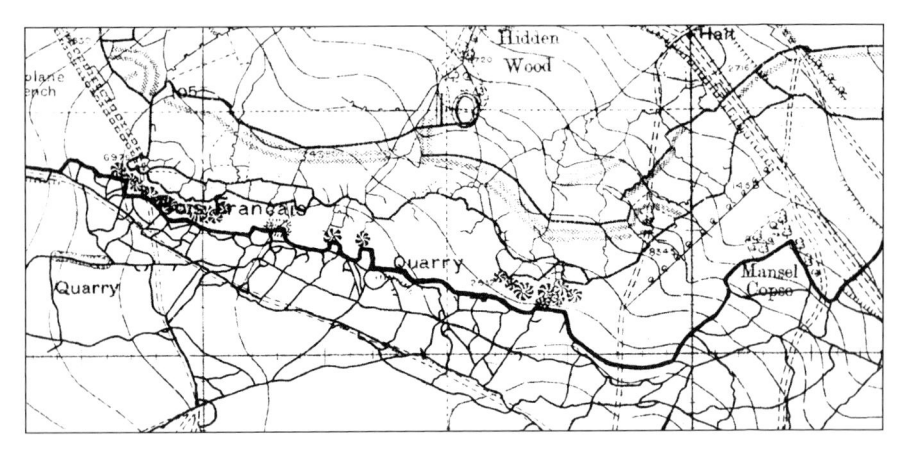

Cote 110 to Mametz crater field - 1916 trench map extract.

1915 mine craters on Cote 110.

this track, which is fairly rutted, there is room for parking on the right just after making this turn) and continue for 600 metres to **Bois Français, Bois Allemand and Cote 110 (14)**.

Visited in an earlier tour (along with the **private memorial to H. Thomassin** in Bois Français), it is worthwhile revisiting this spot to consider the work of *11/3 compagnie du génie* and their German opponents. By August 1915, twenty-five mine craters marked the hill top

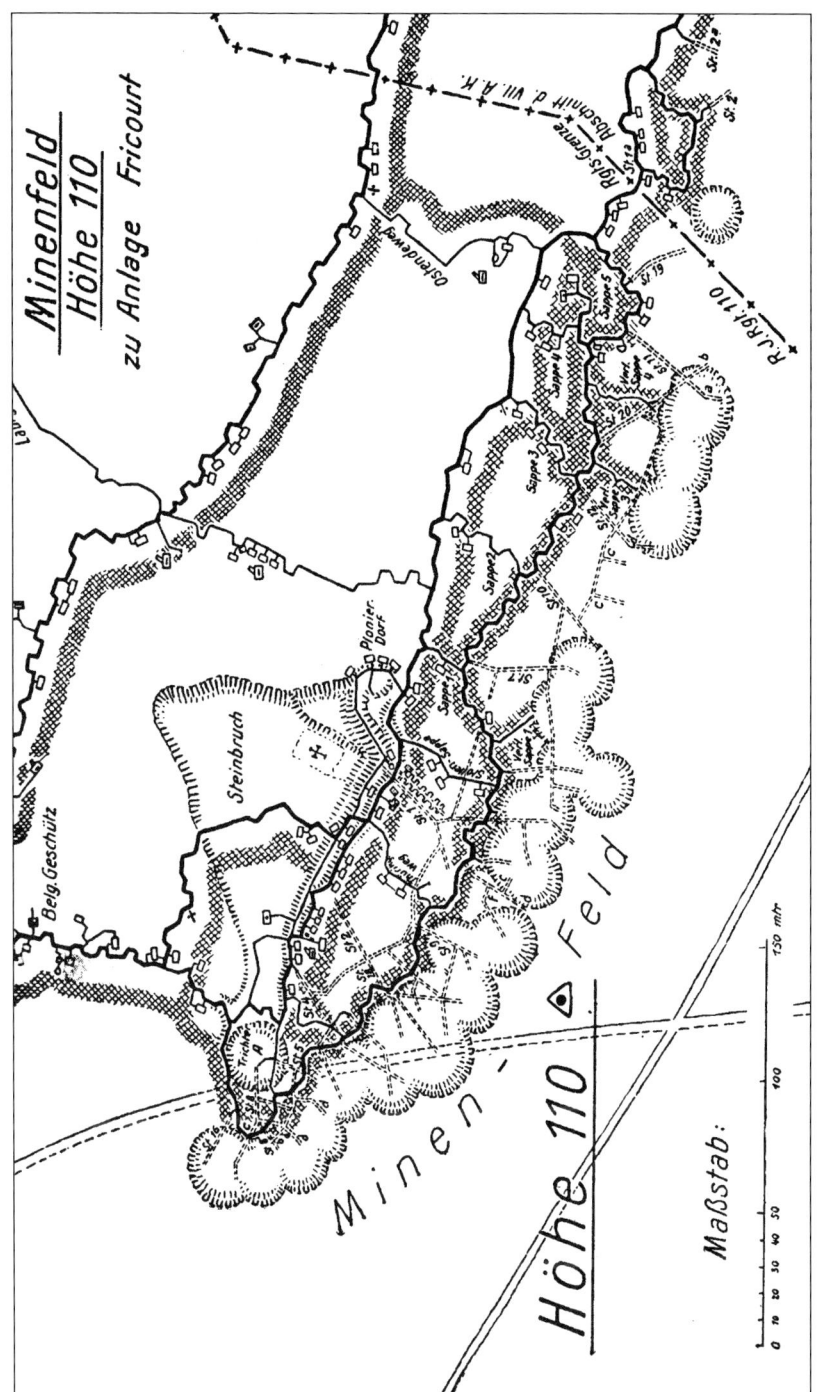

Cote 110 and the crater field, German sketch map.

east of Bois Français, with some, along with the remains of trenches and shell holes, still visible within the (private property) woodland.

Take the narrow road between the woods (or, if your vehicle was left at the start of the track near the D147, return to it, turn right towards Fricourt, then another right onto the D938 where, after 350 metres, the tour trail will be rejoined) down to the junction with the D938 after 600 metres.

As you travel down this track, the German front line lay a few metres in the field to your right and the French line was 540 metres to you left. About mid way between the woods and the road is the location of the 1914 'Christmas Truce' involving the *205e régiment d'infanterie*.

Turn right onto the D938 and continue for 1.8 kilometres until the turn off for Devonshire Cemetery; there is a parking area to the left soon after you start up this road.

From the parking area there is an interesting **view of the battlefield (15)**. The location illustrates how important the higher ground in the area was and how observation was restricted for the soldiers holding the lower ground. While here, a stroll of 350 metres up the hill, past the copse containing Devonshire Cemetery, is worthwhile. Looking to your right as you climb affords a good **appreciation of the whole of the Cote 110 battlefield (16)**, the crater fields and the hill's dominant position. Indeed an excellent view of much of what was to be the southern half of the British Somme battlefield, from the Albert-Bapaume road (with the radio mast at Pozières, for example, clearly visible on a good day) and around to the area of Carnoy is to be had when you reach the track junction towards the crest of the hill.

Return to the D938, turn right and continue for 1,400 metres towards Carnoy. Turn left onto the D254 into, and through, Carnoy in the direction of Montauban. After travelling 1.73 kilometres from the D938 junction, a farm track leads to the left, followed almost immediately by another track leading to the right. These indicate the French and British (left track) and German (right track) front lines of 1914 to 1916; the area to the right of the road at this point is the site of the **Carnoy crater field (17)**, *marked today only by slight undulations in the ground. Some of the craters have only been filled in within the last thirty years.*

The first mine was detonated at this spot by the Germans on 15 March

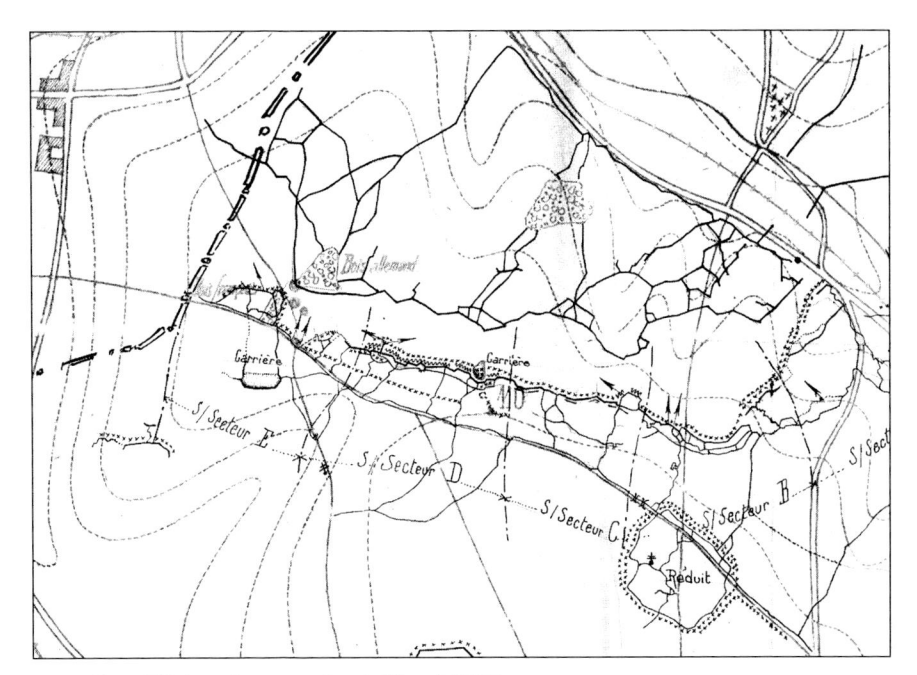

Cote 110 trench map extract, March 1915.

1915, which sparked a bitter and prolonged struggle for the crater and the onset of a deadly underground war that would result in fourteen craters along a 140 metre length of front before the British took over the sector.

Support positions near Carnoy, December 1914.

Continue 1.6 kilometres to Montauban and turn right onto the D64 through the village for 1.3 kilometres. At the cross roads near Bernafay Wood, turn right onto the D917 towards Maricourt and continue for three kilometres to the junction with the D938. Turn left and, in 900 metres, a **monument to** *lieutenant* **Brodu (18)** *will be seen on the left – the monument used to be completely obscured by surrounding trees, but these have been reduced substantially in size. It is usually possible to park on the verge of the road in the direction of travel; but be aware that this is a fast road with plenty of traffic (for the Somme, at least).*

Memorial to *lieutenant* **Robert Brodu and the** *224e régiment d'infanterie***, who died near here during their assault on Hardecourt on 17 December 1914.**

The memorial is dedicated to the *224e régiment d'infanterie* and their unsuccessful attack on Hardecourt aux Bois at 7.05am on 17 December 1914 in which, after coming under heavy fire almost instantly after leaving their positions in front of Maricourt, three officers and fifty-eight men were killed and 263 wounded.

Specifically, it commemorates *lieutenant* **Robert Brodu**, who was one of the officers killed that day. Born in Paris on 30 March 1881, Marie Joseph Jules Robert Brodu was the commanding officer of the *20e* *compagnie, 5e bataillon, 224e régiment d'infanterie.* He was killed, along with his second in command and all of the section commanders, near this spot within minutes of the start of the attack on 17 December 1914. The memorial translates as:

> 'To the memory of Lt Robert Brodu
> Légion d'honneur, Croix de Guerre
> Commanding the 20th Company of the 224th Infantry Regiment
> and the officers, NCOs and soldiers who fell with him
> during the attack of 17 December 1914.'
> *Lieutenant* Brodu is buried in the *Nécropole Nationale* at Albert.

Continue along the D938 for 1.7 kilometres, then turn right onto the rue de Maurepas, leading into Curlu, for 800 metres and the T junction nearest to the river is reached. Turn right onto the rue du Four and travel along here for 900 metres. When the road forks, take the left (narrower) fork for 150 metres. Turning left here takes us to the river, the site of the **Moulin de Fargny (19)** *and the 22e régiment d'infanterie's 'little piece of heaven', making this haven an ideal location to end the tour after studying and visiting the sites of some horrendously violent actions from the first twelve months of the war.*

The Somme at Fargny, with a view towards the German lines. The Chapeau de Gendarme is on the left bank.

The scene of a small skirmish between French infantry controlling a Somme crossing point and German cavalry in December 1870, this was a front line position from September 1914 to July 1916. It last witnessed any major action on 17 December 1914. This was one of the few places where a bizarre, but genuine, state of 'live and let live' developed and existed into 1916 (as noted by various diarists [and not only from the pens of the 'official' scribes of the *22e régiment d'infanterie*], the 'fishing was good' here). Soldiers from both sides took the opportunity to bathe in the waters of the Somme, wash clothes and embark on fishing expeditions, often in full view of each other. This would all change, however, in the run up to the Battle of the Somme, when the Moulin de Fargny would become the advanced jumping off point for the *37e Régiment d'infanterie* in their assault on the village of Curlu.

To return to Albert or Péronne, the easiest way from here is to retrace your steps through Curlu back to the D938 and turning either left or right. However, the route through Vaux and Suzanne, before heading back towards Maricourt, is more picturesque. At the far end of Vaux a sharp turning to the right will bring you, within several hundred metres, to the Belvedere de Vaux, complete with adequate parking. From the viewpoint you can appreciate the scale of the loop in the Somme and the extensive waterways and marshes associated with it.

End of Tour

GPS Waypoints, The Ancre to the Somme 1914-16 Walking and Driving Tour

1 – 50° 3'38.52"N, 2°40'47.17"E   2 – 50° 3'32.27"N, 2°40'50.40"E
3 – 50° 3'1.82"N, 2°41'5.19"E   4 – 50° 2'39.53"N, 2°40'51.85"E
5 – 50° 2'27.92"N, 2°41'4.66"E   6 – 50° 1'54.36"N, 2°41'42.56"E
7 – 50° 1'42.41"N, 2°41'31.13"E   8 – 50° 1'26.67"N, 2°40'50.15"E
9 – 50° 1'7.81"N, 2°41'17.65"E   10 – 50° 1'7.83"N, 2°41'23.46"E
11 – 50° 0'19.07"N, 2°41'27.73"E   12 – 50° 0'3.66"N, 2°42'28.85"E
13 – 50° 0'15.18"N, 2°42'52.01"E   14 – 49°59'20.84"N, 2°43'5.23"E
15 – 49°59'19.62"N, 2°44'9.52"E   16 – 49°59'6.63"N, 2°44'3.78"E
17 – 49°59'33.96"N, 2°45'45.36"E   18 – 49°58'36.65"N, 2°48'5.27"E
19 – 49°58'1.65"N, 2°48'13.01"E

Epilogue

1916 and the Return of the French Army to the Northern Sector

By 25 August 1915, X Corps and VII Corps of the British Third Army held the Somme front from Frise (14 Brigade straddled the river at this point) on the south bank of the river to Monchy-au-Bois, four kilometres north of Gommecourt. Apart from numerous artillery batteries located as far north as Aveluy, there were no longer any French troops near the front line on the Somme battlefield north of the River Somme. Nearly a month later, on the night of 21/22 September 1915, XII Corps (26th, 22nd and 27th Divisions), also of Third Army, arrived and relieved the *154e division d'infanterie* south of the river, meaning that, for a month, the British held the entire Somme front as far south as Foucaucourt on the Amiens to St Quentin road. This Corps was in turn relieved by the *6e division d'infanterie* from 22 October 1915, as it and its divisions began to embark for service in Salonika; the *5e division d'infanterie* arrived to allow the units of 14 Brigade at Frise to join their compatriots north of the river.

Following the discussions at the Second Chantilly Conference, held at *Généralissimo* Joseph Joffre's *Grand Quartier Général* at the Hôtel du Grand Condé, Chantilly, between 8 and 12 December 1915, where the common Allied strategy for 1916 was discussed, a follow up meeting was called on 29 December 1915. This was attended by Joffre, the French President, Raymond Poincaré, Prime Minister Aristide Briand, Minister of War *général* Gallieni and *généraux* Dubail, de Langle de Cary and Foch; the British were represented by the newly appointed Commander in Chief of the BEF, General Sir Douglas Haig. Here Joffre persuaded Haig to order the replacement of the French *Tenth Army* between Arras and the Somme by the BEF and suggested an examination of the possibilities of a combined Franco-British offensive over a sixty mile front either side of the River Somme. He had ordered Foch to prepare an offensive from the River Somme southwards to Lassigny, informing Haig that a French offensive would be greatly aided by a simultaneous offensive of the British forces between the Somme and Arras, arguing that it would be advantageous to attack an enemy on a front where minimal activity had taken place for quite a while.

By 20 January 1916, Joffre revealed that he would have five offensives prepared by the end of April 1916: three in Alsace-Lorraine, one on the Champagne Front and the previously discussed offensive, on the Oise-Somme front. Whichever was selected would depend on the specific situation at that particular time but, in the meantime, it would be important to wear the Germans down as much as possible. Consequently, Joffre suggested that the British should attack to the north of the River Somme on a minimum of a seven mile length of front on around 20 April 1916. With no strategic importance, this was to part of Joffre's *bataille d'usure* – intended simply to cause damage and soften up the enemy prior to a major, French led, offensive.

Haig, however, could not agree to this plan as, other than being politically unacceptable, sufficient forces would not be ready by April and he therefore considered alternative plans for the remainder of the month. Joffre abandoned this plan on 14 February 1916 after further discussions and it was agreed that a combined Franco-British offensive should be carried out on the Somme towards the end of June, with a smaller, solely British, attack being simultaneously launched between La Bassée and Ypres. A *corps d'armée* from the French *Sixth Army* would also be placed immediately north of the River Somme to act as flank protection to the larger French forces attacking to the south. These attacks were to be launched in conjunction with the allies, notably Italy and Russia, undertaking major offensives on their own fronts at about the same time.

However, on 21 February 1916 the Germans struck first. Launching their own huge offensive at Verdun on this date – their biggest on the Western Front since the opening phases of the war ended in the winter of 1914, it soon became clear that this battle was to become a long, drawn out battle of attrition in which much of the French Army on the Western Front would become committed. Joffre pressed Haig to continue with the relief of the *Tenth Armée*, enabling the release of French reserves and, in March, requested that he do all that he could to harass the enemy and to prevent German reserves from reinforcing the Verdun front. He also asked that the preparations for the attack on the Somme should continue unabated. The plan was now for a combined attack between Hébuterne in the north and Lassigny in the south but, possibly, commencing at an earlier date than that originally considered.

By the end of April 1916, due to the French situation at Verdun, it was beginning to look like the proposed Somme operation would have to be cancelled and that all offensive operations for the year might have to be undertaken by the British. In May it seemed that any Somme offensive might would to be made without any French assistance at all; it was now apparent that simultaneous Allied attacks employing maximum available force in a war-winning move were no longer possible.

However, following a meeting at Saleux on 31 May 1916, attended by Haig, Joffre, Briand, Foch, Poincaré, *général* de Castelnau and the new French Minister for War, *général* Pierre Roques, Haig stated that all he needed was a date to begin offensive operations on the Somme. It was originally fixed for 1 July 1916, but switched to 25 June, then 29 June before fate and the weather brought it back to 1 July. Joffre then gave an assurance that, no matter what the situation at Verdun, Haig would have the French army's assistance. The planned French role at this stage, besides assisting the British in their task, was simply to guard the right flank of the main British attack and follow their advance on either side of the River Somme as the line moved eastwards over a broad front, drawing in as many German reserves as possible.

For the forthcoming offensive, General Haig committed the newly formed (March 1916) Fourth Army, Lieutenant General Henry Rawlinson, to the offensive, with the Reserve Army (Lieutenant General Hubert Gough) in reserve. Elements of Third Army (Lieutenant General Edmund Allenby) would take part in a diversionary action in the Gommecourt salient immediately to the north of the planned northern boundary of the offensive. The French committed much of *général* Ferdinand Foch's *groupe d'armées Nord*: the *Sixth Army*, under the command of *général de division* Marie Émile Fayolle, straddling the River Somme, with the *Tenth Army*, under the command of *général de division* Joseph Alfred Micheler, in reserve and holding the line to their south.

Fayolle deployed the *XX corps d'armée* (the highly reputable *corps de fer*, the Iron Corps) under *général de division* Maurice Balfourier on the north bank of the river, giving protection to both the right flank of the British attack and the left flank of the French. To the south was the *I corps d'armée coloniale* (*général de division* Pierre Berdoulat) and *XXXV corps d'armée* (*général de division* Charles Jacquot). A fourth corps, *II corps d'armée* (*général de division* Denis Auguste Duchêne) was to be held in reserve.

On the north bank of the Somme, the British XIII Corps (at that time comprising just the 30th and 18th (Eastern) Divisions; the 9th Division would not join until 14 June) was shifted along the line to the north west as the *XX corps d'armée* began to arrive between 1 and 2 June 1916. Along with the two highly experienced veteran divisions of this latter corps (the *39e division d'infanterie* took over the front line from Fargny to Maricourt Wood; the *11e division d'infanterie* taking the line from Maricourt Wood to the Maricourt to Bernafay Wood road sector), masses of similarly battle-experienced artillery batteries arrived via Corbie and Albert to the rear. These reinforced the French batteries that had stayed in this sector in support of the British army after August 1915. By 24 June there were over 150 French batteries of various calibres located north of the River Somme, with the highest concentrations being around and forward of Albert and on the north bank between Suzanne and Maricourt; they had over eight million shells at their disposal. The *génie* was also hard at work alongside British pioneer troops and Royal Engineers, improving the road networks, constructing and operating light railways to assist in the forward movement of troops and supplies, constructing, strengthening and repairing bridges, improving accommodation and building supply depots and stores dumps. They worked constantly and tirelessly up to and beyond (and under) the front lines in the weeks running up to the offensive.

On 24 June 1916, the artillery preparation began. Like their infantry counterparts, the French gunners in the *XX corps d'armée sector* were almost all, to a man, veterans of one of the most intense artillery battles in history – Verdun. Many were also veterans of the Battles of Artois and Champagne, whilst some had even fought here before, in September 1914. This experience, combined with the high quality and quantities of ammunition that was made available to them, made the French preliminary bombardment highly effective. The concentrated bombardment of high explosives, shrapnel and gas rained down on the German defences, smashing trenches and dugouts, clearing barbed wire obstacles and destroying specifically targeted strong points. In addition, the German defending forces south of the river had been weakened by the move of a regiment to the north, in the Thiepval-Serre area: because of Verdun, German intelligence was not at all convinced that the French army had the remaining capability of launching an offensive of any great consequence. At the front line, nightly patrols assessed the amount of damage that the bombardment was causing, and intelligence reports were written – and acted upon – informing the artillery of their effectiveness and advising any alteration that could or should be made to the fire plan. Patrols even approached the German wire during bombardments to increase the accuracy of these reports. During any lull in the bombardment fighting patrols roved No Man's Land in an attempt to prevent any repairs being made on the German positions. These often returned with further intelligence and they were only infrequently prevented from completing their tasks.

By midnight on 30 June (from south to north) the *37e, 79e, 69e, 26e, 156e, 146e* and *153e régiments d'infanterie* were all in position and fully prepared. Trusting in the effectiveness of their artillery over the previous week and in its planned role and tactics over the coming days, the attackers had also been made fully aware and knowledgable of their own tasks ahead. As they waited for the order to *aller le feu!* at 7.30am on 1 July (in conjunction with the British attack; the French attack south of the river was scheduled to begin two hours later), the *corps de fer* was fully confident of the success of this meticulously planned operation. What could possibly go wrong?

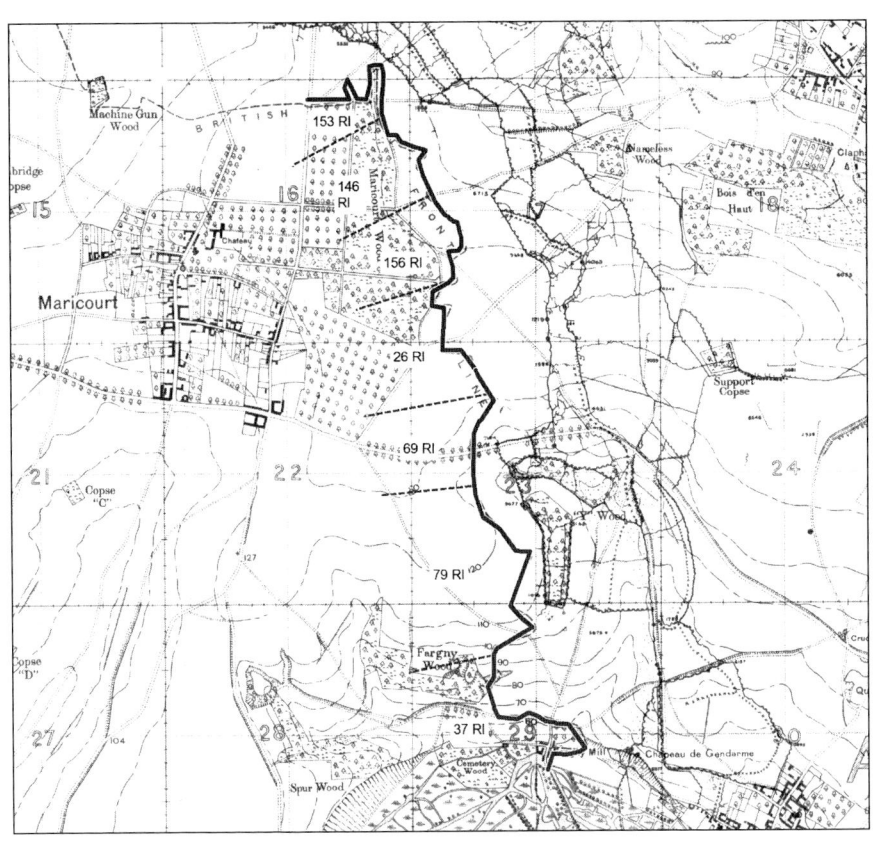

Regimental order of *XX corps d'armée*, 1 July 1916.

Appendix 1
Advice to Tourers

The Tours
Covering practically the whole of the French area of combat during the 1914-15 actions on the Somme north of the river (either physically or within view), the tours within this book have been designed to be practicable by minibus, car, motorbike and bicycle (and, of course, foot for the more hardy traveller!). Larger vehicles may have problems in a few locations as several of the roads are quite narrow though, generally, rather open with passing places; there are a couple of sharp turns and two low bridges to negotiate, thus, for anyone planning to use a larger vehicle or bus/coach, a pre-tour reconnaisance is strongly recommended.

Note that a particular location may appear in more than one tour. This is intentional as each tour is designed around a certain theme and will only look at the relevant points for that specific theme when visiting; for example, Cote 110 near Fricourt appears in two tours: one specifically looking at the September 1914 actions and the other looking at the events of late 1914 into 1915.

GPS References. Note that at the end of each tour section there is a list of GPS references for each of the numbered stop points within that tour.

Maps
Recommended mapping for the area are the topographical 1:25,000 scale IGN Blue Series or 'Top 25' *cartes de randonée*. To completely cover the French sector of 1914-1916 for, not just north of the river but for the entire area covered by this series of books, the following maps from this series would be needed: 2408 E (Bray-sur-Somme), 2508 O (Péronne), 2409 E (Roye), 2407 O (Acheux-en-Amiénois), 2407 E (Bapaume) and 2509 O Nesle. The 1:100,000 scale IGN 'Top 100' Yellow Series tourism road map number 103 (Amiens/Arras) also covers the area in lesser detail. There is also now a new '*départementale*' 1:150 000 series: in this case, D80 Somme. For historical interest, the IGN have also produced a centennial edition map of the 1916 Somme battle area in 1: 75,000 scale entitled '*Grande Guerre: Bataille de la Somme 1916*' which, though not error-free, details divisional locations for 1 July, the battle lines and certain

movements along with (some) cemeteries, memorials and visitable vestiges of the battle, etc. This is one of a special series of maps produced by the IGN, others being maps for the Battle of Verdun 1916, the Chemin des Dames 1917 and, generically, the Western Front 1914-18.

British trench maps for the area are readily viewable from a variety of online sources and, in DVD format, from the Western Front Association and from the Naval and Military Press in conjunction with the Imperial War Museum. However, the Great War Digital offering of the 'Linesman' package is most highly recommended which, with the aid of a compatable portable GPS device, enables the visited area to be viewed using period trench maps. Recently, the company has released a preloaded selection of trench maps on a tablet that makes a more user-friendly option available for the less computer literate. Bear in mind, however, that with all available maps for this package currently being British, this is less useful for coverage of earlier (French) battles and actions and the French actions south of the river prior to the late autumn of 1916 (with the exception of when the British held the line south of the Somme for a few months in the autumn of 1915). Though the areas fought over in 1914 and 1915 are still covered by maps of various dates within this package (and on online sources), they all, as would be expected, depict the lines as they were after these actions had finished. Early French or German trench maps are ideally needed for these areas, but these are far more difficult to source, though several extracts can be found on the pages of this book and many more French trench map extracts can be found online on my own website which can be found at **https://some-disputed-barricade.weebly.com**.

Driving

As many of the people who will be reading this volume will have some experience or knowledge of continental driving, I will not waste any valuable print space detailing the 'do's and do nots' of this subject. However, at the time of printing, we do appear to be going through a transitional period regarding regulations, speed limits, what must be carried, emissions etc., so I will just mention that it would be wise to be aware of any changes. For updated information, before travelling, it is recommended to take a look at websites such as:

https://www.eurotunnel.com,
https://about-france.com/highway-code.htm,
https://www.rac.co.uk
https://www.theaa.com/european-breakdown-cover

Accommodation
Plentiful hotel accommodation can be found in the area of the battlefields with Albert, Péronne and Bapaume the most suitable major towns for visits to the sectors of the French Somme battlefield covered by this book; a number of well known hotel chains operate in these areas. Bed and breakfast accommodation is also plentiful and can be found in many of the villages of the northern sectors (i.e. the 'British' sectors) of the battlefield. Highly recommended is Dave and Anita Platt's 'Beaumont Hamel View' located at 15 Rue Delattre, Auchonvillers (http://www.beaumonthamelview.com). Away from the 'British' sector, similar accommodation is scarcer, but a small number do exist, as do a few 'Gîtes de France' self-catering cottages that can be located and booked from their English language website: https://en.gites-de-france.com.

For camping, I have used the three star Camping du Port de Plaisance at Péronne (http://www.camping-plaisance.com), which is within easy strolling distance from the town centre or Biaches and centrally placed for visits to both the northern and southern French Somme battlefield – especially those of August and September 1914 and of July to December 1916. It has a small shop, bar, take-away and swimming pool and is also near to a petrol station and supermarket. This camp site also happens to be built on the site of the *ouvrage du faubourg de Paris,* which was a small defensive fort that played a role in the siege of Péronne in 1870-71 and served as (German) soldiers accommodation during 1914-1917. Though nothing is visible of this *ouvrage* today, watch out when hammering in those tent-pegs!

With the northern sector specifically in mind, the more basic Camping Bellevue at Authuille or Camping du Velodrome at Albert are both ideally located (possibly more so than that at Péronne, depending on which sites are being visited), though Authuille can be a little laborious to get to if you are on foot or reliant on public transport. The site at Albert is within easy walking distance from the town centre and its associated facilities (including the train station), which is another favourable point for anyone who happens to be hiking the battlefields. A number of other, smaller camp sites also exist further afield, especially, along the Somme River (often geared to fishing), including one at the infamous Grenouillére position near Frise.

Refreshments
Apart from the ubiquitous (but not as many as there once were) *boulangeries* and some local village cafés and bars, refreshment stops are a rare commodity in the French sectors of the Somme. Though they are far easier to find north of the river than in the southern sectors, it is,

however, advisable to stock up with any necessary supplies from the more considerable towns in the area (Péronne, Albert or Bapaume), one of which will always be within eleven or twelve kilometres from your location on these tours. All are well served by supermarkets, cafés, bars and restaurants, with the larger supermarkets in these towns containing all of these, plus petrol stations, in one location. All of the facilities (other than the petrol station) at the motorway service station at Assevillers can also be accessed on foot from the car park located at the end of the side road immediately east of the motorway. This is often open when the others are closed, so can be quite a handy stop. The sectors covered by this book also have the benefit of being near to a number of refreshment stops that seem particularly geared to the battlefield visitor such as 'Le Tommy' bar and restaurant at Pozières and the Ulster Tower near Thiepval. Even the visitor centre at the Thiepval Memorial has vending machines for light snacks and drinks. Finally, the *Historial de la Grande Guerre* at Péronne has a café and, should the need arise, McDonald's restaurants can be found at Albert, Bapaume, Péronne, Roye, Montdidier and Amiens (which has four!).

Museums

The French 1914-1916 Somme battlefield has two main museums, the *Musée Somme 1916* at Albert and the *Historial de la Grande Guerre* at Péronne.

The *Historial de la Grande Guerre* (http://www.historial.org) attracts over 80,000 visitors per year and has tri-lingual displays and exhibitions aiming to illustrate the experiences of the major combattants and the impact of the Great War in general on the 20th century as well as the experiences of those involved in the Battles of the Somme, including the civilian population. There are usually several temporary exhibitions at any one time, alongside the more permanent features, film shows, and display cases, art and technology also feature prominently. Artefacts and information panels explain the course of the war from its origins to the post-war reconstructions; an original display educates the visitor on the uniforms and equipment of the protaganists.

Built within the remains of the heavily repaired walls of the old 13th century Château de Péronne (look for the memorial plaque above the entrance to the *120e* and *320e régiments d'infanterie* and the *16e régiment d'infanterie territoriale* – who had their depot here in August 1914), there is a Documentation Centre in the museum; accessible by appointment only, it aims to provide an international approach to the study of the military, political and cultural history of the Great War and has an archive of photographs, postcards, leaflets and other documents on the Great War, along with a library of over 4,000 books and periodicals. A café with terrace that can cater for groups and a variably stocked shop selling books in numerous languages, DVDs, maps, posters and other souvenirs can also be found at the museum (although the Thiepval Visitor Centre, also run by the Historial, has a better and more extensive selection of books, certainly in English).

In Albert, the *Musée Somme 1916* is located in a 250 metres long underground passageway that stretches between the basilica and the public garden some ten metres under the town centre of Albert that dates from the ninth century and was reinforced to be used as a public air raid shelter just prior to the outbreak of World War II. Along the length of this passageway can be seen many artefacts, images, uniforms, weapons and some excellent dioramas that depict life in and out of the trenches of this area from the whole war and not just the 1916 battle as the title of the museum would suggest (though, as would be expected, the 1916 battle does get most emphasis). A well-stocked souvenir shop ends the visit to this museum and a selection of light snacks and refreshments is usually available for purchase.

Other displays can be found at the Thiepval Visitor Centre (which now has an extended museum area), the Ulster Tower, the Beaumont-Hamel Newfoundland Memorial Park, 'Le Tommy' café at Pozières and at the *Nécropole Nationale* at Rancourt. However, Rancourt aside, these mainly focus on the British and Dominion efforts during the 1916 battle.

In the French rear area can be found another museum. Though it is not a museum of the battles as such, it is a very interesting diversion anyway. Located at Froissy, on the opposite river bank from Bray-sur-Somme, the *P'tit Train de la Haute Somme* houses a narrow-gauge railway museum displaying several engines of Great War vintage. The highlight of a visit here, however, is a ride on a fourteen kilometre stretch of narrow-gauge railway line that was originally built in 1916 to move ammunition and supplies to the artillery and forward areas south of the River Somme (post-war it was used by the sucrerie at Dompierre, hence its survival). Travelling up onto the Santerre plateau as far as Dompierre, it is an interesting ride with some beautiful views.

Toilet Facilities

Toilets can be located at most of the places mentioned in the refreshments and museums section (though it is usually regarded as courteous to actually buy something first if using the facilities in a local bar/café). Additional to these, there are also facilities to be found in the visitor centre at the *Nécropole Nationale* at Rancourt.

Clothing and Footwear
None of the ground covered in the tours is particularly difficult, but several locations will require walking over rough ground in order to appreciate the location fully. The Somme is not particularly extreme for weather conditions, but common sense (and, perhaps, a look at the local weather forecast) should dictate clothing and footwear. One point to bear in mind, however, is that in a number of locations, such as near Toutvent or on Redan Ridge, the tours visit areas that are open, exposed and with not much shelter. For this reason it may be advisable to pack some sort of sun protection, carry a bottle of water and cover up on hot summer days. Likewise, keep water-proof and wind-proof clothing handy for days that are less clement (sage advice from someone who was once caught in a howling thunder storm in the middle of a field on the Flaucourt Plateau, south of the river, wearing a T-shirt, shorts and sandals!). In all cases, especially if you anticipate doing some walking, it is a good idea to have some stout boots handy. Even if they are not needed at the outset of a tour, the changeable weather and topography of the Somme could make them necessary by the end. A further tip would be to keep a plastic bag in which to put your boots before getting back into a vehicle, saving you from cleaning out considerable quantities of Somme mud from it in due course.

Appendix 2

Organisation of
The Metropolitan Infantry 1914–1916

The Infantry Regiment (*régiment d'infanterie*)
1914
There were 173 active regiments of line infantry (numbered 1 to 173) in August 1914, each comprising three *bataillons* (apart from the *69e, 157e, 159e, 163e, 164e,165e, 166e, 170e* and the *173e régiments d'infanterie*, which were all made up of four *bataillons*). Each *bataillon* had four *compagnies* that were correspondingly numbered (the *1e bataillon* comprising the *1e* to *4e compagnie*, the *2e bataillon* the *5e* to the *8e compagnie*, and the *3e bataillon* the *9e* to the *12e compagnie*), plus one machine gun section. There were also, within the *régiment*, additional units, such as the regimental general staff, the battalion staff, the headquarters company and regimental supply train, bringing the full strength of a *régiment* up to approximately 3,250 officers and other ranks.

All of these active regiments were supplemented with a corresponding reserve regiment, consisting of two battalions. These reserve regiments were numbered accordingly with their parent regiment by taking their parent unit's number and adding 200. For example, the reserve regiment of the *70e régiment d'infanterie* was the *270e régiment d'infanterie*, the reserve regiment of the *141e régiment d'infanterie* was the *341e régiment d'infanterie*, etc. In total, therefore, there were 346 *régiments d'infanterie* in 1914. Within the reserve regiments, *bataillons* were numbered *5e (17e* to *20e compagnies)* and *6e (21e* to *24e compagnies)*.

Totally separate from their parent units, these reserve regiments did not serve alongside and, generally, served in reserve divisions; but two regiments were placed as reserve regiments for each active *corps d'armée*.

The final type of *régiment d'infanterie* in 1914 was the *régiment d'infanterie territoriale*. In 1914, there were 145 (numbered 1 to 145) territorial regiments, made up of 35 to 41 year old men and 148 reserve territorial regiments (numbered 201 to 347, 500 and 501), made up of 42 to 47 year olds (the latter age group only being called into full time service if they possessed a particular skill or who had been engaged in a

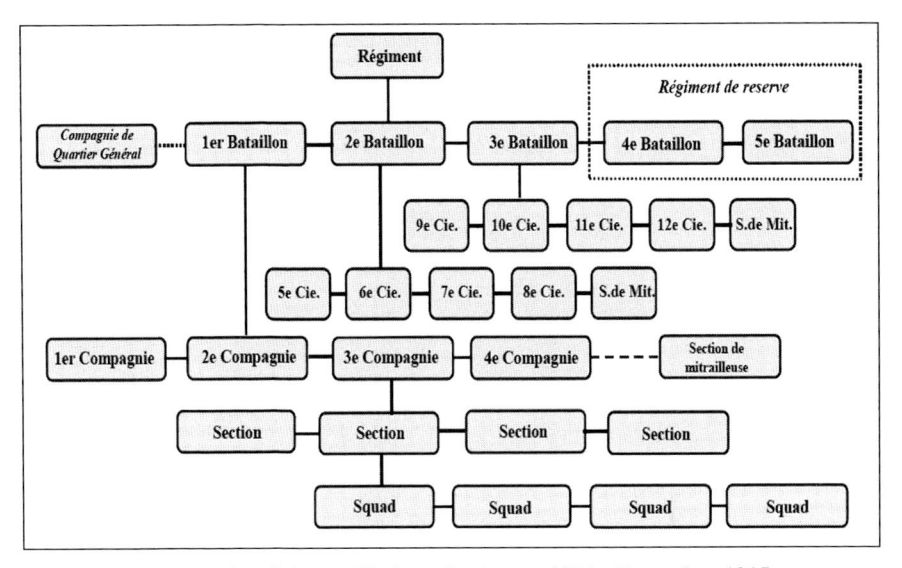

Organisation of a *régiment d'infanterie*, August 1914 – December 1915.

specific trade). *Régiments d'infanterie territoriale* were composed of three or four battalions, one for each subdivision of the region from which they originated; but some consisted of as many as seven or as few as two.

1915
Three new regiments (the *174e, 175e* and *176e régiments d'infanterie*) were formed at the start of 1915, two of which were destined for service at Gallipoli and Salonika, and a further twenty (numbered 401 to 421) were formed within a few weeks of these. With the exception of the 419e *régiment d'infanterie*, the numerical designation was decided by adding 400 to the army corps region number from where the regiment originated. These new regiments were composed almost entirely of new recruits (*classe de 1915* and *1916*) and bolstered by a number of veteran soldiers and non-commissioned officers transferred from other regiments (plus recovered soldiers returning to service from wounds or injuries).

Due to the massive number of casualties sustained in 1914 and 1915, alterations to the regimental structure had to be made. *Compagnie* size was reduced from 250 to 200 men and *bataillons* were reduced to three *compagnies* (reducing the effective strength of a bataillon from 1000 men to 750). Reserve regiments were completely separated from their parent units and became independent units (though the two battalion organization of reserve regiments would still remain in place for the time

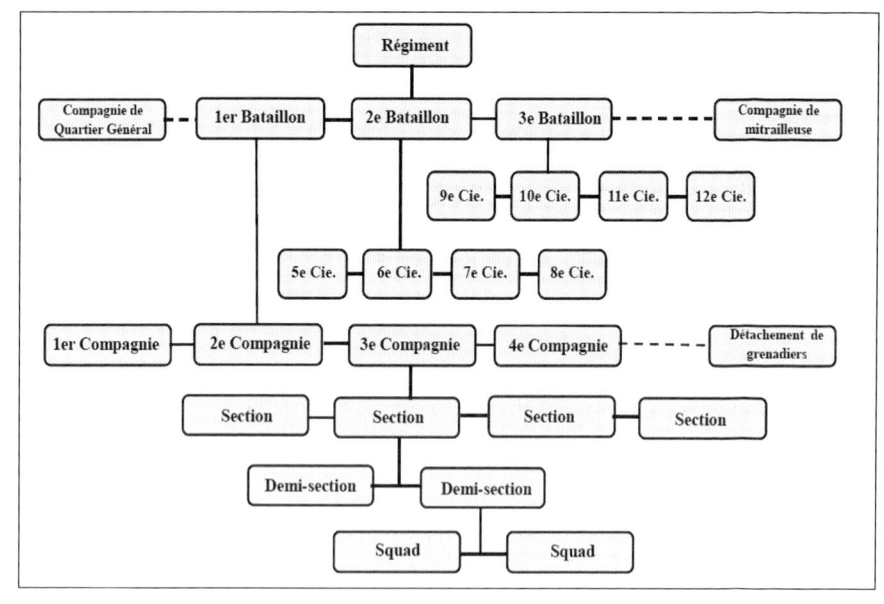

Organisation of a *régiment d'infanterie*, December 1915 – April 1916.

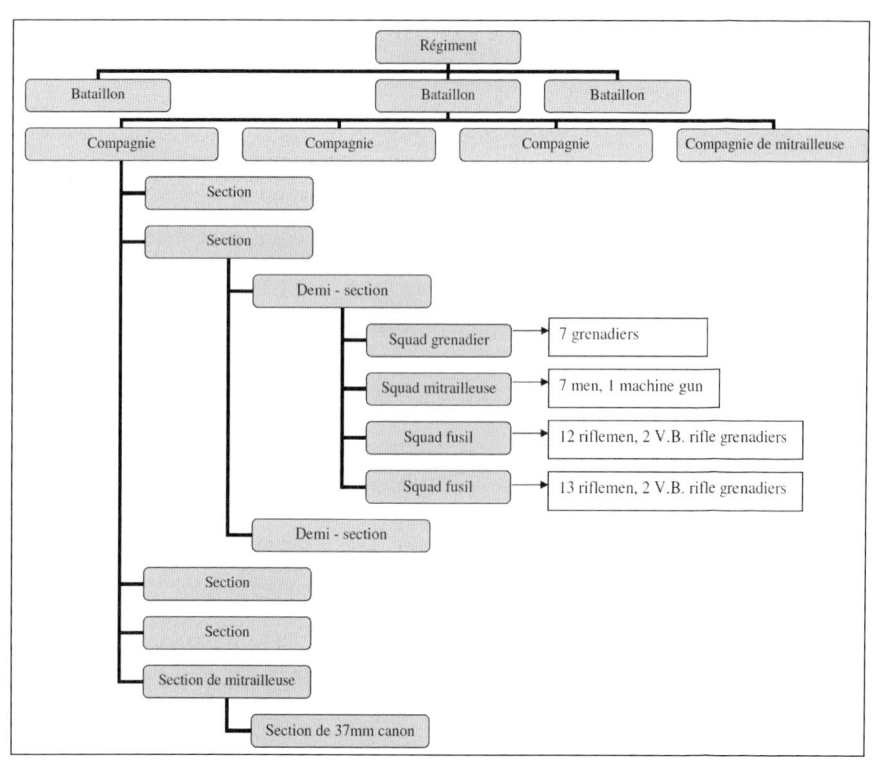

Organisation of a *régiment d'infanterie*, April 1916 – October 1917.

being). Detachments of grenadiers were also created at company level. Consisting of sixteen men led by a non-commissioned officer, eight of these (led by a corporal) were trained as bombardiers, becoming familiar with the operation of a number af varied light trench weapons, such as catapults and light mortars, along with training in the use of hand grenades. The number of machine gun sections within a regiment was also increased to four and they were reorganised into an autonomous machine gun company.

The Infantry Division (*division d'infanterie*)
1914
When France mobilised for war on 1 August 1914, the 'metropolitan' French Army consisted of forty-four active divisions. Forty-one of these were 'line' infantry divisions (numbered 1 to 36 and 39 to 43) and three were colonial (*1e, 2e,* and *3e divisions d'infanterie coloniale*). Upon mobilisation, a further three divisions were formed: the *44e* (composed of four Alpine Infantry regiments) and the *37e* and the *38e* – bringing the total number of active divisions at the war's start to forty-seven.

Within three weeks, the *45e division d'infanterie* and the *division Marocaine* were formed in North Africa but, on 5 September 1914, the *44e division d'infanterie* was dissolved. This same date, however, saw the formation of the *76e* and *77e divisions d'infanterie,* boosting the numbers of active infantry divisions to forty-nine (plus the 'non-metropolitan' *division Marocaine*) by the end of of 1914.

In 1914, an infantry division was composed of two *brigades d'infanterie,* each comprising two *regiments d'infanterie* and each consisting of 3,000 soldiers, split between three *bataillons*. Three *goupes d'artillerie* (each consisting of three *batteries de tir* of four 75mm guns), a cavalry squadron (*escadron de cavalerie*) and a company of engineers (*compagnie de génie*) were also part of the divisional make-up, along with ancilliary services, such as the divisional Provost company (*compagnie de gendarmes*), a Medical Section (*section de service de santé*), a Transport Squadron (*escadron de Train des équipages*) and the Administration Section (*section d'intendance*). Some infantry divisions also had an attachment of one or two *bataillons de chasseurs*. When at full strength, a *division d'infanterie* would consist of approximately 16,000 soldiers, of whom over 85% would be infantrymen.

It was planned that two regiments of reserve infantry would be attached to each division but, upon mobilisation on 1 August, the majority of these were brought together and formed into twenty-five independent reserve infantry divisions (the *51e* to the *75e divisions d'infanterie*). Four of these reserve divisions were assigned to the defence of fortified regions: the 57e *division d'infanterie* was assigned to Belfort, the *71e* to Epinal, the *72e* to Verdun and the *73e* to Toul. The remaining twenty-one became field formations. In September 1914, the *54e* and *75e* were dissolved, leaving twenty-three reserve divisions by the end of the year.

The composition of a reserve infantry division differed to that of an 'active' infantry division in that it consisted of two *brigades,* each made up of three *régiments*. A reserve infantry regiment was smaller than an active infantry regiment, however, having only two *bataillons* (2,000 soldiers). Active and reserve infantry divisions were, therefore, both made up of twelve battalions each but, due to a lesser number of ancilliary troops, a reserve infantry division was slightly smaller overall in size, consisting of approximately 14,000 soldiers when at full strength.

1915

During 1915 reorganisations of divisions and inter-divisional regimental transfers removed the lack of uniformity between active and reserve infantry divisions. All active divisions began to remove their attached reserve regiments (the few that had retained them) and all reserve divisions became active. Extra ancilliary troops were added to each division and the *génie* were allocated to, and fell under the jurisdiction of, each *bataillon* as opposed to being under divisional control, as was the previous situation.

An increase in the size of the army due to the incorporation of the *classe de 1915* in December 1914 and the *Classe de 1916* in April 1915, along with the incorporation of several unafilliated regiments, allowed for the formation of twenty-six new divisions, including a further four *divisions d'infanterie coloniale,* throughout the year. By the end of 1915, the French Army consisted of ninety eight active army *divisions d'infanterie.*

The Territorial Division (*division d'infanterie territoriale*)
1914

Numbered *81e* to *92e*, *94e, 96e* and *97e,* there were fifteen *divisions d'infanterie territoriale* in existence at the time of the August 1914 mobilisation. Mainly assigned to coastal defence, Alpine border guard duties and the garrison of Paris, the *90e* and *94e divisions* (amalgamated into the *94e* in September) were both disbanded by October, with their regiments being distributed amongst the other divisions. Territorial divisions were independent of any particular *corps d'armée* though, at various times, some divisions were brought together to form a divisional reserve group within a *corps*.

A *division d'infanterie territoriale* was composed of two *brigades* of two *régiments d'infanterie territoriale*, but the number of *bataillons* in a territorial regiment varied depending on the size of the population local to the area where the regiment was raised. The usual size of a regiment was three or four *bataillons* but, due to the variable nature of these units, there could be as many as seven or even as few as two. For this reason, a *division d'infanterie territoriale*, though its component parts were similar, was generally far smaller than an active or reserve division. At full strength, a *division d'infanterie territoriale* varied in size between 8,000 and 12,000 soldiers.

1915

Following on from the increase in the size of the army, the incorporation of non-allocated formations, and the call up into full time service of the *classes* of 1892 in December 1914, 1891 in March 1915 and of 1890 and 1889 in April 1915 (all of whom were part of the *réserve de l'armée territoriale* and nearing the end of their compulsory service commitments), it was possible to form a further six territorial divisions during 1915: the *99e* to the *101e* in February, the *102e* in May, and the *103e* to the *105e* in August. In June and July, however, seven territorial divisions (*82e, 84e, 85e, 86e, 91e, 92e* and the *96e*) were disbanded, with all of the regiments of the *85e* and *86e divisions d'infanterie territoriale* being transferred to active army *divisions d'infanterie*.

Appendix 3

Organisation of the *corps du génie* 1914-1916

Within metropolitan France at the outbreak of war, the Engineers of the French Army – the *corps du génie* -consisted of seventy-one field companies, fifteen fortress companies, twenty-one searchlight sections, ten detachments of cyclists, twelve detachments of Alpine engineers, sixteen railway companies, twelve telegraph companies, two wireless companies, twelve companies of drivers and thrirteen staff and 'non-combattant' sections. Twenty-four companies of the previously mentioned types of unit (except cyclists and Alpine engineers) were serving in North Africa. These units, following a reorganisation of 15 April 1914, made up nine regiments and five battalions that formed the **corps de sapeurs-mineurs**, with one railroad regiment (the *5ᵉ régiment du génie*) and one regiment of telegraph troops (*8ᵉ régiment du génie*). Each battalion consisted of between three and five companies (of varying role) and it was within the *bataillons de sapeurs-mineurs de campagne*, perhaps as their name suggests, where the tunnelling companies of the *génie* would be located.

Tunnelling in the Somme sector of 1914-15 would be covered by companies from two *régiments du génie* – the *14ᵉ bataillon de sapeurs-mineurs de campagne* from the *4e régiment du génie* and the *11ᵉ bataillon de sapeurs-mineurs de campagne* from the *6e régiment du génie*. The *11ᵉ bataillon* (specifically the *1e, 3e* and *4e compagnies*) had control north of the Somme as far as Hébuterne, and the *14ᵉ bataillon* (*1e, 2e 3e,* and *6e compagnies*) had the south as far as Lihons.

Composition of the regiments and battalions of the *génie* by early 1916:

1ᵉʳ régiment du génie – Versailles
4ᵉ bataillon de sapeurs-mineurs de campagne
5ᵉ bataillon de sapeurs-mineurs de campagne
22ᵉ bataillon (attached to the *corps d'armée coloniale*): Flame and gas companies
31ᵉ bataillon: (*compagnies de gaz*)

A *génie télégraphistes* post in a (near) front line trench near Hébuterne, February 1915.

32e bataillon: (*compagnies de gaz*)
33e bataillon: (*compagnies de gaz*)
34e bataillon: (*compagnies de gaz*)
40e bataillon: (*compagnies lance-flammes*)

2e régiment du génie – Montpellier:
16e bataillon de sapeurs-mineurs de campagne
17e bataillon de sapeurs-mineurs de campagne
18e bataillon de sapeurs-mineurs de campagne
Five companies from Morocco
Six other (unattached) companies

3e régiment du génie – Arras:
1er bataillon de sapeurs-mineurs de campagne
2e bataillon de sapeurs-mineurs de campagne
3e bataillon de sapeurs-mineurs de campagne

4e régiment du génie – Grenoble and Dode:
8e bataillon de sapeurs-mineurs de campagne
13e bataillon de sapeurs-mineurs de campagne
14e bataillon de sapeurs-mineurs de campagne

5e régiment du génie – Versailles
1er bataillon du chemin de fer
2e bataillon du chemin de fer
3e bataillon du chemin de fer
4e bataillon du chemin de fer

6e régiment du génie -Angers and Eblé:
9e bataillon de sapeurs-mineurs de campagne
10e bataillon de sapeurs-mineurs de campagne
11e bataillon de sapeurs-mineurs de campagne
12e bataillon de sapeurs-mineurs de campagne

7e régiment du génie – Avignon and Hautpoul:
15e bataillon de sapeurs-mineurs de campagne
23e bataillon (*Pontonniers*)
24e bataillon (*Pontonniers*)

8e régiment du génie – Rueil, Mont Valérien:
1er bataillon télégraphistes
2e bataillon télégraphistes

3e bataillon télégraphistes
4e bataillon télégraphistes

9ᵉ régiment du génie – Verdun:
6ᵉ bataillon de sapeurs-mineurs de campagne
25ᵉ bataillon de sapeurs-mineurs de campagne (Place de Verdun)
(plus seven other [unattached] companies)

10ᵉ régiment du génie – Toul:
20ᵉ bataillon de sapeurs-mineurs de campagne
26ᵉ bataillon de sapeurs-mineurs de campagne (Place de Toul)

11ᵉ régiment du génie – Épinal:
21ᵉ bataillon de sapeurs-mineurs de campagne
27ᵉ bataillon de sapeurs-mineurs de campagne (Place de Thornal)

Unattached battalions:
7ᵉ bataillon (Supplementary) in Besançon
19ᵉ bataillon (Supplementary) at Hussein-Dey (Algeria)
28ᵉ bataillon (Supplementary) in Belfort
29ᵉ battalion (Supplementary) in Bizerte (Tunisia)
34ᵉ bataillon (Supplementary)

(In April 1917, a *21ᵉ régiment du génie* was (temporarily) formed from the *1ᵉʳ régiment du génie* with the intention of distributing the units of this regiment into two groups. Later amendments, however, caused some companies to be counted on the strength of both regiments, resulting in difficulty in differentiating the two regiments. The *21e* was disbanded in 1919.)

Appendix 4

French Army Rank (*grade*) Structures, 1914-1918

	French	British
Honourary	Maréchal de France	
General Officers	Général de groupe d'armées *	
	Général d'armée *	
	Général de corps d'armée *	Lieutenant General
	Général de division	Major General
	Général de brigade	Brigadier General
Officers	Colonel	
	Lieutenant-colonel	Colonel
	Commandant/Chef de bataillon/Chef d'escadron	Lieutenant Colonel / Major
	Capitaine	Captain
	Lieutenant	Lieutenant
	Sous-lieutenant	2nd Lieutenant
Officer trainees	Aspirant	Officer candidate
	Élève-officier	Officer cadet
Warrant Officers	Adjudant-chef	Warrant Officer Class I
	Adjudant	Warrant Officer Class II
N.C.O.s	Sergent-chef/Sergent-major/Maréchal des logis chef	Staff Sergeant
	Sergent-fourier	**
	Sergent/Maréchal des logis	Sergeant
Other Ranks	Caporal-fourier	**
	Caporal/Brigadier	Corporal
	Soldat 1er classe	Lance Corporal
	Soldat 2e classe	Private

Role-specific	Chasseur	Conducteur	Hussard	Lancier
private	Marsouin	Chacal	Dragon	Cuirassier
soldier titles	Légionnaire	Brancardier	Cavalier	Canonier

* As opposed to being an actual 'rank', these were titles of *appointement* issued to officers holding the rank of *général de division*. These appointments indicated seniority over others holding the same rank and were not officially recognised as ranks until 1936.

** No real British Army equivalent, but they would be a Quartermaster Corporal and a Quartermaster Sergeant.

Medical Service Ranks
(*Service de Santé* [officers] & *Sections d'infirmiers militaires* [ORs])

	French	British
General Officers	Médecin général des armées	Lieutenant General
	Médecin inspecteur général	Major General
	Médecin inspecteur	Brigadier General
Officers	Médecin principal de 1ère classe	Colonel
	Médecin principal de 2ème classe	Lieutenant Colonel
	Médecin-major de 1ère classe	Major
	Médecin-major de 2ème classe	Captain
	Médecin-aide-major de 1ère classe	Lieutenant
	Médecin-aide-major de 2ème classe	2nd Lieutenant
Officer trainees	Aspirant médecin	Officer candidate
	Élève officier médecin	Officer cadet
Warrant Officers	Sous-aide major	Warrant Officer Class I
	Médecin auxiliaire	Warrant Officer Class II
N.C.O.s	Infirmier-chef/ Sergent	Sergeant
Other Ranks	Infirmier principle / Caporal	Corporal
	Infirmier 1er classe / Soldat 1er Cl.	Lance Corporal
	Infirmier 2e classe / Soldat 2e Cl.	Private

Appendix 5
French War Graves on the Somme

In the earlier companion volume to this book (*The Somme 1916: Touring the French Sector*), a chapter was dedicated to the care of dead within the French *Nécropoles Nationales* accompanied by a listing, with details, of all eighteen of these cemeteries that are in the area of the 1916 Somme battlefield (out of a total of twenty-two within the *département*, one of which contains the dead from the Second World War). Within the chapter, reference was made to other *cimetières* and *carrés militaires* that are not designated as *Nécropoles Nationales*, such as the French cemetery at Éclusier-Vaux, which contains 126 French graves from the 1914 to 1917 period and the *carré Breton* at Albert, with its 115 graves from 1914 and 1915. Also mentioned, but not detailed, were those French soldiers who are interred in Commonwealth War Graves Commission cemeteries. To make amends for that omission, below are listed details of the CWGC cemeteries of the Somme battlefields that contain French war graves. Following it is the listing of *Nécropoles Nationales*:

A familiar scene into 1915 on the Somme front. One of the thousands of unburied French dead from September 1914.

CWGC cemeteries containing French war graves

Cemetery Name	Number of French Graves	Date Range
A.I.F. BURIAL GROUND, FLERS	168	1914-16
ASSEVILLERS NEW BRITISH CEMETERY	1	1914
BLANGY-TRONVILLE COMMUNAL CEMETERY	1	1918
BOVES WEST COMMUNAL CEMETERY	10	1918
CHIPILLY COMMUNAL CEMETERY	4	1916
CROUY BRITISH CEMETERY, CROUY-SUR-SOMME	6	1918
CRUCIFIX CORNER CEMETERY, VILLERS-BRETONNEUX	137	1916-18
DOULLENS COMMUNAL CEMETERY EXTENSION NO.1	8	1915-18
FOLIES COMMUNAL CEMETERY	3	3 Unknowns
FRICOURT BRITISH CEMETERY	1	1 Unknown
HANGARD WOOD BRITISH CEMETERY	20	1918
HERISSART COMMUNAL CEMETERY	1	1915
LONDON CEMETERY AND EXTENSION, LONGUEVAL	2	2 Unknowns
LONGPRE-LES-CORPS SAINTS BRITISH CEMETERY	1	1918
LONSDALE CEMETERY, AUTHUILLE	1	1914
LOUVENCOURT MILITARY CEMETERY	76	1915
NAMPS-AU-VAL BRITISH CEMETERY	15	1918
OVILLERS MILITARY CEMETERY	120	1914-15
PICQUIGNY BRITISH CEMETERY	1	1918
RAILWAY HOLLOW CEMETERY, HEBUTERNE	2	1915
QUARRY CEMETERY, MONTAUBAN	1	1916
QUEENS CEMETERY, BUCQUOY	5	1915
THIEPVAL ANGLO-FRENCH CEMETERY	300	1914-17
VILLE-SUR-ANCRE COMMUNAL CEMETERY	1	1915
WARLENCOURT BRITISH CEMETERY	2	2 Unknowns
WARLOY-BAILLON COMMUNAL CEMETERY	158	1914-16

French *Nécropoles Nationales* on the Somme Battlefield

Albert:
Creation date: 1923
6,293 French burials, including 2,879 buried within four ossuaries
3 British burials
Contains the remains of soldiers who died throughout the actions on the Somme from 1914-18 and is a concentration of small cemeteries from across the entire Somme *département*.

Amiens *'Saint Acheul'*:
Creation date: Wartime Cemetery. Exact date not known (1914-18)
2,739 French burials, 10 Belgian, 12 British and 1 Russian from the Battles of the Somme 1914-18
12 French burials from 1939-45
Extended in 1921 and 1935 with exhumations from cemeteries in the areas of Conty, Thoix, Boves and Cagny.

Amiens *'Saint Pierre'*:
Creation date: Wartime Cemetery. Exact date not known (1914-18)
1,347 French and 25 Belgian burials from 1914-18
Extended in 1921 and 1934 with exhumations from around Amiens, Dury and La Madeleine

Beaumont-Hamel *'Cimetière de Serre-Hébuterne'*:
Creation date: 1919. Constructed by the Imperial War Graves Commission and maintained by them into the 1930s
834 French burials including 240 in the ossuary. Mainly from the combats at Hébuterne of June 1915.
Extended between 1919 and 1923 with the concentration of graves from the *243e* and *327e Régiments d'infanterie*

Beuvraignes *'nécropole nationale du bois des Loges'*:
Creation date: Wartime Cemetery. Exact date not known (1914-15 combats of the bois des Loges)
1,854 French burials, including 654 within four ossuaries, from 1914-18 and three French burials from 1939-45.
Extended in 1921, 1929 and 1936 with the reburial of remains exhumed around Beuvraignes and Popincourt.

Biaches:
Creation date: Wartime cemetery. 1916-18
1,362 French burials from the Battles of the Somme, including 322 within two ossuaries.
Extended in 1920 and 1936 with the concentration of smaller cemeteries from across the entire Somme *department*. Closed for further burials in 1974

Bray-sur-Somme:
Creation date: Wartime Cemetery. Exact date not known (1914-18)
1,044 French burials including 102 in an ossuary
1 British burial.
Extended in 1923 and 1935 with concentrations from cemeteries in front of Bray and Suzanne. Closed for further burials in 1990.

Cerisy:
Creation date: Wartime cemetery. 1916
990 French burials.
Extended in 1923 with the concentration of bodies from the *carré militaire* of the communal cemetery at Cerisy. Closed for further burials during 1979-80.

Clery-sur-Somme *'Le Bois des Ouvrages'*:
Creation date: 1920
2,332 French burials including 1,129 buried in two ossuaries.
Extended in 1920 and 1936 with burials exhumed from the sectors of Monacu Farm, Fargny Mill, bois de Berlingots and *carrés militaires* at Morlancourt and Vaires-sous-Corbie.

Condé – Folie
Creation date: Wartime cemetery, exact date unknown (Battle of the Somme, June 1940)
3,311 French burials, including 878 in an ossuary, from 1939-45, and one Soviet soldier.
Extended between 1953 and 1957 with the reinhumation of remains from communal cemeteries throughout the Somme department. Also contains the remains of numerous members of the resistance.

Dompierre-Becquincourt:
Creation date: 1920
7,032 French burials, including 1,671 buried in four ossuaries.
1 German burial from 1914-18 and 1 French from 1939-45
Extended in 1920, 1935 and 1936 with the concentration of various cemeteries from across the Somme. Individual graves and remains discovered between 1948 and 1985 were also buried here.

Etinehem *'La Côte 80'*:
Creation date: Wartime Cemetery. Exact date not known (1914-18)
955 French burials, 49 British
Extended in 1923 with the concentration of remains from the cemeteries between Etinehem and Méricourt-sur-Somme. Contains the personal headsone marking the grave of *l'abbé* Thibaut, regimental chaplain (*aumonier*) of the *1e Régiment d'infanterie*, who was killed in action on 26 September 1916.

Hattencourt:
Creation date: 1920
1,942 French burials including 667 buried in four ossuaries
2 Russians from 1914-18 and 5 French from 1939-45
Extended in 1920, 1934 and 1936 with the concentration of various cemeteries from across the Somme, in 1951 with the addition of the Second World War graves and in 1960-61 with the discovery of several isolated remains. Closed for further burials in 1974.

Lihons:
Creation date: Wartime Cemetery. 1915
6,581 French burials, including 1,638 within four ossuaries.
6 British burials from 1914-18
Extended in 1919, 1935 and 1936 with the concentration of various cemeteries from across the Somme. Closed for further burials in 1988. Contains the remains of the American poet Alan Seeger of the RMLE who was killed in action at Belloy on 4 July 1916.

Marcelcave *'Les Buttes'*:
Creation date: Wartime Cemetery. 1916
1,610 French burials
Extended in 1932 and 1936 with the concentration of various cemeteries from across the Somme. Closed for further burials in 1980.

Maucourt:
Creation date: 1920
5,272 French burials, including 1,534 buried in six ossuaries
24 French and 6 British burials from 1939-45
Extended in 1920, 1935 and 1936 with the concentration of various cemeteries from across the Somme and in 1949-53 with the addition of the Second World War graves.

Maurepas:
Creation date: Wartime Cemetery. 1916
3,657 French burials, including 1,588 within two ossuaries.
1 French civilian, 1 Roumanian and 19 Russians from 1914-18
Extended in 1921 and 1936 with the concentration of various cemeteries from the areas of Maurepas, Suzanne and Albert.

Moislains *'Cimetière de la Charente'*:
Creation date: Wartime Cemetery. 1914
465 French dead, including 366 buried within an ossuary.
Extended in 1923 and 1924. Originally established and maintained by the German Army for the French dead of 28 August 1914.

Montdidier *'L'Egalité'*:
Creation date: Wartime Cemetery. Exact date not known (Battle of the Somme 1916)
745 French burials.
Extended in 1933 to 1934. Closed for further burials in 1982.

Montdidier:
Creation date: 1924
7,406 French burials, including 1,617 buried within two ossuaries, one Belgian and one Italian from 1914-1918. Twenty-Four French burials from 1939-45
Extended in 1935 and 1936 and now contains the remains of soldiers who died throughout the actions on the Somme from 1914-18. This cemetery is a concentration of small cemeteries from across the entire Somme *département*.

Rancourt:
Creation date: 1921
8,563 French burials, including 3,240 within four ossuaries.
3 French civilian burials from 1914-18 and 1 French burial from 1939-45
Concentration cemetery formed by the concentration of smaller cemeteries around Combles, Cléry and Curlu. Open for burials of individual remains located on the battlefields between 1945 and 1973. Extended in 1980 with the concentration of isolated graves and *carrés militaires* around Flixécourt and Bus-la-Mesière. Closed for burials between 1987 and 1988.

Villers-Carbonnel:
Creation date: 1920
2,285 French burials, including 1,295 within two ossuaries.
18 French burials from 1940
Concentration cemetery formed by the concentration of smaller cemeteries around Barleux and Flaucourt. Extended by the German Army in 1941 with the burials of the French soldiers from 1940.

Hébuterne Communal Cemetery, illustrative of the many hundreds of *carrés militaires* across France.

Appendix 6

French Army Abbreviations 1914–1918

A.	*Armée*	Army
A.C.	*Artillerie de Corps*	Corps Artillery
A.C.A.	*Artillerie de Corps d'Armée*	Corps Artillery
A.C.D.	*Artillerie de Campagne Divisionnaire*	Divisional Field Artillery
A.C.D.A.	*Artillerie de Corps d'Armée*	Corps Artillery
A.D.	*Artillerie Divisionnaire*	Divisional Artillery
A.L.	*Artillerie Lourde*	Heavy Artillery
A.L.C	*Artillerie Légère de Campagne*	Light Field Artillery
A.L.C.A.	*Artillerie Lourde de Corps d'Armée*	Corps Heavy Artillery
A.L.D.	*Artillerie Lourde Divisionnaire*	Divisional Heavy Artillery
A.L.G.P.	*Artillerie Lourde à Grande Portée*	Long Range Heavy Artillery
A.L.V.F.	*Artillerie Lourde sur Voie Ferrée*	Heavy Railway Artillery
A.M.	*Auto-Mitrailleuse*	Armoured Car
Amb.	*Ambulance*	Ambulance
A.M.C.	*Auto-Mitrailleuse de Cavalerie*	Cavalry Armoured Cars
A.R.S.	*Appareil Respiratoire Spécial*	Respirator (int. 1918)
Art.	*Artillerie*	Artillery
A.S.	*Artillerie Spéciale*	Special Artillery (Tanks)
A.T.	*Artillerie de Tranchées*	Trench Artillery
B.	*Bataillon*	Battalion
Bat.	*Bataillon*	Battalion
B.C.A.	*Bataillon de Chasseurs Alpins*	Mountain Light Infantry Battalion
B.C.P.	*Bataillon de Chasseurs à Pied*	Light Infantry Battalion
Bde.	*Brigade*	Brigade
B.I.	*Bataillon d'Infanterie*	Infantry Battalion
Bie.	*Batterie*	Battery
B.I.LA	*Bataillon d'Infanterie Légère d'Afrique*	African Light Infantry
B.M.	*Bataillon de Mitrailleurs*	Machine Gun Battalion

Abbr.	French	English
Brig.	*Brigade*	Brigade
B.T.C.A.	*Bataillon Territorial de Chasseurs Alpins*	Territorial Mountain Light Infantry
Btn./Baon.	*Bataillon*	Battalion
Btn.M.	*Bataillon de Mitrailleuses*	Machine Gun Battalion
B.T.S.	*Bataillon de Tirailleurs Sénégalais*	Senegalese Riflemen Battalion
C.A.	*Corps d'armée*	Army Corps
C.A.C.	*Corps d'armée coloniale*	Colonial Army Corps
C.A.I.	*Corps d'armée Italien*	Italian Army Corps
C.A.P.	*Corps d'armée Provisoire*	Provisional Army Corps
Cav.	*Cavalerie*	Cavalry
C.C.	*Corps de cavalerie*	Cavalry Corps
C.E.P.	*Corps Expéditionnaire Portugais*	Portuguese Expeditionary Corps
C.E.O.	*Compagnie d'equipages d'ouvrages*	Fortress Garrison Company
Chass.d'Af.	*Chasseurs d'Afrique*	Army of Africa Light Cavalry
C.H.R.	*Compagnie Hors-Rang*	Regimental Administration Company
C.I.D.	*Centre d'Instruction Divisionnaire*	Divisional Training Centre
Cie.	*Compagnie*	Company
Cie.T.	*Compagnie de Télégraphistes*	Telegraphist Company
C.M.	*Compagnie de Mitrailleuses*	Machine Gun Company
Cuir.	*Cuirassiers*	Cuirassiers (Cavalry)
D.C.	*Division de Cavalerie*	Cavalry Division
D.C.A.	*Défense Contre Avions*	Anti-Aircraft Defences
D.C.P.	*Division de Cavalerie à Pied*	Foot Cavalry Division
D.D.	*Dépôt Divisionnaire*	Divisional Depot
Dét.	*Détachement*	Detachment
D.I.	*Division d'Infanterie*	Infantry Division
D.I.C.	*Division d'Infanterie Coloniale*	Colonial Infantry Division
D.I.P.	*Division d'Infanterie Provisoire*	Provisional Infantry Division
D.I.R.	*Division d'Infanterie de Réserve*	Reserve Infantry Division
D.I.T.	*Division d'Infanterie Territoriale*	Territorial Infantry Division
D.M.	*Division Marocaine*	Moroccan Division

D.R.	*Division de Réserve*	Reserve Division
Drag.	*Dragons*	Dragoons (Cavalry)
D.T.	*Division Territoriale*	Territorial Division
D.T.	*Détachement de Télégraphistes*	Telegraph Detachment
E.M.	*État-major*	Staff (or Headquarters)
E.R.D.	*Équipe de Réparation de Division*	Divisional Salvage and Repair
Esc.	*Escadron*	Squadron
Esc.	*Escadrille*	Squadron
E.S.M.	*École Spéciale Militaire (Saint-Cyr)*	Military Academy (Saint-Cyr)
F.A.	*Forces Aériennes*	Aerial Forces
F.M.	*Fusil Mitrailleur*	Light Machine Gun
F.M.	*Fusilier Marin*	Naval Infantry
G.A.	*Groupe d'Armées*	Army Group
G.A.C.	*Groupe d'Armées du Centre*	Army Group Center
G.A.E.	*Groupe d'Armées de l'Est*	Army Group East
G.A.F.	*Groupe d'Armées des Flandres*	Army Group Flanders
G.A.N.	*Groupe d'Armées du Nord*	Army Group North
G.A.P.	*Groupe des Armées de Paris*	Army Group Paris
G.A.R.	*Groupe d'Armées de Réserve*	Reserve Army Group
G.B.C.	*Groupe de Batteries de Corps*	Corps Artillery Battery Group
G.B.C.	*Groupe de Brancardiers de Corps*	Corps Stretcher-Bearer Group
G.B.D.	*Groupe de Brancardiers Divisionnaire*	Divisional Stretcher-Bearer Group
G.D.I.	*Groupe de Divisions d'Infanterie*	Group of Infantry Divisions
G.D.R.	*Groupe de Divisions de Réserve*	Group of Reserve Divisions
G.D.T.	*Groupe de Divisions Territoriales*	Group of Territorial Divisions
G.E.	*Groupe d'Exploitation*	Divisional Operations Group
G.Q.G.	*Grand Quartier Général*	Supreme Head Quarters
G.Q.G.A.	*Grand Quartier Général des Armées Alliées*	Supreme Head Quarters of Allied Armies
Gr.	*Groupe*	Group
I.D.	*Infanterie Divisionnaire*	Divisional Infantry
Inf.	*Infanterie*	Infantry
P.A.	*Parc d'Artillerie*	Artillery Park

P.A.C.A.	Parc d'Artillerie de Corps d'Armée	Army Corps Artiilery Park
P.A.D.	Parc d'Artillerie Divisionnaire	Divisional Artillery Park
P.C.	Poste de Commandement	Command Post
P.O.	Poste d'Observation	Observation Post
P.R.	Point de Résistance	Strong Point
P.S.D.	Poste de Secours Divisionnaire	Divisional Aid Post
P.S.R.	Poste de Secours Régimentaire	Regimental Aid Post
Q.G.	Quartier Général	Head Quarters
R.A.	Régiment d'Artillerie	Artillery Regiment
R.A.C.	Régiment d'Artillerie de Campagne	Field Artillery Regiment
R.A.C.C.	Régiment d'Artillerie de Campagne Coloniale	Colonial Field Artillery Regiment
R.A.D.	Régiment d'Artillerie Divisionnaire	Divisional Artillery Regiment
R.A.L.	Régiment d'Artillerie Lourde	Heavy Artillery Regiment
R.A.P.	Régiment d'Artillerie à Pied	Foot Artillery Regiment
R.C.A.	Régiment de Chasseurs d'Afrique	African Light Cavalry Regiment
R.C.C.	Régiment de Chars de Combat	Tank Regiment
R.D.	Réserve de Division	Divisional Reserve
R.E.	Régiment Étranger	Foreign Regiment (Foreign Legion)
R.G.A.	Réserve Générale d'Artillerie	General Artillery Reserve
R.G.A.L.	Réserve Générale d'Artillerie Lourde	General Heavy Artillery Reserve
Rgt.	Régiment	Regiment
R.I.	Régiment d'Infanterie	Infantry Regiment
R.I.C.	Régiment d'Infanterie Coloniale	Colonial Infantry Regiment
R.I.C.M.	Régiment d'Infanterie Coloniale du Maroc	Moroccan Infantry Regiment
R.I.R.	Régiment d'Infanterie de Réserve	Reserve Infantry Regiment
R.I.T.	Régiment d'Infanterie Territoriale	Territorial Infantry Regiment
R.M.	Régiment de Marche	Provisional Regiment
R.M.A.	Régiment de Marche d'Afrique	African Provisional Regiment
R.M.L.E.	Régiment de Marche de la Légion Étrangère	Foreign Legion Provisional Regiment

R.M.T.	*Régiment de Marche de Tirailleurs*	Provisional Regiment of Tirailleurs
R.M.T.A.	*Régiment de Marche de Tirailleurs Algériens*	Provisional Regiment of Algerian Tirailleurs
R.M.T.I.	*Régiment de Marche de Tirailleurs Indigènes*	Provisional Regiment Indigenous Tirailleurs
R.M.Z.	*Régiment de Marche de Zouaves*	Provisional Regiment of Zouaves
R.M.Z.T.	*Régiment Mixte de Zouaves et Tirailleurs*	Combined Zouave-Tirailleur Regiment
R.S.A.	*Régiment de Spahis Algériens*	Regiment of Algerian Cavalry
R.S.M.	*Régiment de Spahis Marocains*	Regiment of Moroccan Cavalry
R.T.A.	*Régiment de Tirailleurs Algériens*	Regiment of Algerian Riflemen
R.T.I.	*Régiment de Tirailleurs Indigènes*	Regiment of Indigenous Riflemen
R.T.M.	*Régiment de Tirailleurs Marocains*	Regiment of Moroccan Riflemen
R.T.N.A.	*Régiment de Tirailleurs Nord-Africains*	Regiment of North African Riflemen
R.T.S.	*Régiment de Tirailleurs Sénégalais*	Regiment of Senegalese Riflemen
R.T.T.	*Régiment de Tirailleurs Tunisiens*	Regiment of Tunisian Riflemen
S.C.O.A.	*Section de Commis et Ouvriers d'Administration*	Section of Clerks and Administration
Sect.	*Secteur (ou Section)*	Sector or Section
S.O.A.	*Section d'Ouvriers d'Administration*	Administration Section
S.O.A.	*Section d'Ouvriers d'Artillerie*	Artillery Labourer Section
S.M.A.	*Section de Munitions d'Artillerie*	Artillery Ammunition Supply Section
S.M.I.	*Section de Munitions d'Infanterie*	Infantry Ammunition Supply Platoon
S.M.I.	*Section de Mitrailleuses d'Infanterie*	Infantry Machine Gun platoon
S.O.	*Sous-Officier*	Non-commissioned Officer
S.P.	*Section de Projecteurs*	Trench Mortar Platoon
S.R.	*Service de Renseignements*	Intelligence Service

S.R.A.	*Section de Ravitaillement d'Artillerie*	Artillery Supply Section
S.S.	*Service de Santé*	Medical Service
S.S.A,	*Section Sanitaire Automobile*	Motor-Ambulance Section
S.S.A.A.	*Section Sanitaire Automobile Anglaise*	English (volunteer) Motor-Ambulance
S.S.U.	*Section Sanitaire automobile américaine*	American (volunteer) Motor-Ambulance
S.T.A.	*Section de Transport Automobile*	Motor transport section
S.T.D.I.	*Section Topographique de Division d'Infanterie*	Divisional Topographical section
T.R	*Train Régimentaire*	Regimental Supply Train
T.S.F	*Télégraphie Sans Fil*	Wireless Telegraphy
V.B	*Vivien Bessière*	Rifle Grenade
V.F.	*Voie Ferrée*	Rail Track

Appendix 7

French Orders of Battle Somme 1914–15

Bataille de Pèronne (North), August 1914.

61e division d'infanterie:
    121 brigade d'infanterie
        264e régiment d'infanterie
        265e régiment d'infanterie
        316e régiment d'infanterie

    122 brigade d'infanterie
        262e régiment d'infanterie
        219e régiment d'infanterie
        318e régiment d'infanterie

62e division d'infanterie:
    123 brigade d'infanterie
        278e régiment d'infanterie
        263e régiment d'infanterie
        338e régiment d'infanterie

    124 brigade d'infanterie
        308e régiment d'infanterie
        307e régiment d'infanterie
        250e régiment d'infanterie

84e division d'infanterie territoriale:
    28e régiment d'infanterie territoriale

Cavalry:
    5e & 6e escadron, 20e régiment de dragons
    2e escadrons, 1er régiment de dragons

Artillery:
    28e régiment d'artillerie de campagne
    35e régiment d'artillerie de campagne
    51e régiment d'artillerie de campagne
    21e régiment d'artillerie de campagne
    34e régiment d'artillerie de campagne
    52e régiment d'artillerie de campagne

***Bataille d'Albert*, September 1914.**

11e division d'infanterie
    21e brigade d'infanterie
        26e régiment d'infanterie
        69e régiment d'infanterie
        2e bataillon de chasseurs à pied
    22e brigade d'infanterie
        37e régiment d'infanterie
        79e régiment d'infanterie
        4e bataillon de chasseurs à pied

19e division d'infanterie
    37e brigade d'infanterie
        48e régiment d'infanterie
        71e régiment d'infanterie

    38e brigade d'infanterie
        41e régiment d'infanterie
        70e régiment d'infanterie

21e division d'infanterie
    41e brigade d'infanterie
        64e régiment d'infanterie
        65e régiment d'infanterie
    42e brigade d'infanterie
        93e régiment d'infanterie
        137e régiment d'infanterie

22e division d'infanterie
    43e brigade d'infanterie
        62e régiment d'infanterie
        116e régiment d'infanterie

44e brigade d'infanterie
    19e régiment d'infanterie
    118e régiment d'infanterie

81e division d'infanterie territoriale
    161e brigade d'infanterie
        11e régiment d'infanterie territoriale
        12e régiment d'infanterie territoriale
    162e brigade d'infanterie
        14e régiment d'infanterie territoriale
        16e régiment d'infanterie territoriale

82e division d'infanterie territoriale
    163e brigade d'infanterie
        17e régiment d'infanterie territoriale
        18e régiment d'infanterie territoriale
    164e brigade d'infanterie
        21e régiment d'infanterie territoriale
        22e régiment d'infanterie territoriale

84e division d'infanterie territoriale
    167e brigade d'infanterie
        25e régiment d'infanterie territoriale
        26e régiment d'infanterie territoriale
    168e brigade d'infanterie
        27e régiment d'infanterie territoriale
        28e régiment d'infanterie territoriale

88e division d'infanterie territoriale
    175e brigade d'infanterie
        81e régiment d'infanterie territoriale
        82e régiment d'infanterie territoriale
    176e brigade d'infanterie
        83e régiment d'infanterie territoriale
        84e régiment d'infanterie territoriale

1e division de cavalerie
    6e régiment de dragons
    23e régiment de dragons
    27e régiment de dragons
    32e régiment de dragons
    1e Régiment de Cuirassiers

2e Régiment de Cuirassiers
26e bataillon de chasseurs à pied (cyclists)

5e division de cavalerie
    5e régiment de chasseurs à cheval
    15e régiment de chasseurs à cheval
    16e régiment de dragons
    22e régiment de dragons
    9e régiment de dragons
    29e régiment de dragons
    29e bataillon de chasseurs à pied (cyclists)

10e division de cavalerie
    15e régiment de dragons
    20e régiment de dragons
    10e régiment de dragons
    19e régiment de dragons
    1e bataillon de chasseurs à pied (cyclists)

Artillery:
    8e régiment d'artillerie de campagne
    11e régiment d'artillerie de campagne
    13e régiment d'artillerie de campagne
    14e régiment d'artillerie de campagne
    20e régiment d'artillerie de campagne
    28e régiment d'artillerie de campagne
    29e régiment d'artillerie de campagne
    35e régiment d'artillerie de campagne
    39e régiment d'artillerie de campagne
    44e régiment d'artillerie de campagne
    51e régiment d'artillerie de campagne
    61e régiment d'artillerie de campagne

1er bataille d'Hébuterne, **October 1914.**

22e division d'infanterie
    43e brigade d'infanterie
        62e régiment d'infanterie
        116e régiment d'infanterie
    44e brigade d'infanterie
        19e régiment d'infanterie
        118e régiment d'infanterie

81e division d'infanterie territoriale
   161e brigade d'infanterie
      11e régiment d'infanterie territoriale
      12e régiment d'infanterie territoriale
   162e brigade d'infanterie
      14e régiment d'infanterie territoriale
      16e régiment d'infanterie territoriale

82e division d'infanterie territoriale
   163e brigade d'infanterie
      17e régiment d'infanterie territoriale
      18e régiment d'infanterie territoriale
   164e brigade d'infanterie
      21e régiment d'infanterie territoriale
      22e régiment d'infanterie territoriale

88e division d'infanterie territoriale
   175e brigade d'infanterie
      81e régiment d'infanterie territoriale
      82e régiment d'infanterie territoriale
   176e brigade d'infanterie
      83e régiment d'infanterie territoriale
      84e régiment d'infanterie territoriale

8e division de cavalerie
   12e régiment de hussards
   14e régiment de chasseurs à cheval
   11e régiment de dragons
   17e régiment de dragons
   18e régiment de dragons
   26e régiment de dragons
   15e bataillon de chasseurs à pied (cyclists)

Artillery:
   4e régiment d'artillerie de campagne
   11e régiment d'artillerie de campagne
   13e régiment d'artillerie de campagne
   14e régiment d'artillerie de campagne
   20e régiment d'artillerie de campagne
   28e régiment d'artillerie de campagne
   29e régiment d'artillerie de campagne
   35e régiment d'artillerie de campagne
   61e régiment d'artillerie de campagne

Bataille de Toutvent (2eme bataille d'Hébuterne), June 1915

21e division d'infanterie
    41e brigade d'infanterie
        64e régiment d'infanterie
        65e régiment d'infanterie
    42e brigade d'infanterie
        93e régiment d'infanterie
        137e régiment d'infanterie

27e division d'infanterie
    53e brigade d'infanterie
        75e régiment d'infanterie
        140e régiment d'infanterie

51e division d'infanterie
    101e brigade d'infanterie
        233e régiment d'infanterie
        243e régiment d'infanterie
        327e régiment d'infanterie

56e division d'infanterie
    112e brigade d'infanterie
        361e régiment d'infanterie

Artillery:
    1e régiment d'artillerie de montagne
    2e régiment d'artillerie de montagne
    2e régiment d'artillerie de campagne
    13e régiment d'artillerie à pied
    25e régiment d'artillerie de campagne
    32e régiment d'artillerie de campagne
    40e régiment d'artillerie de campagne
    15e régiment d'artillerie de campagne
    27e régiment d'artillerie de campagne
    41e régiment d'artillerie de campagne
    51e régiment d'artillerie de campagne

Acknowledgements

With this book being about a, possibly, rather niche subject in the English language, it proved difficult to find many people who could possibly assist in the actual subject matter. However, this fact only reinforces the importance of a work such as this in our overall understanding of the Somme battlefield and, indeed, in the more famous battle of 1916. Once again, therefore, the first of my acknowledgements should go to the series editor, Nigel Cave, not only for presenting me with the opportunity of getting some of the fruits of several decades worth of research and file accumulations into print, but also for allowing me to view and use if need be some of his own researches into a similar subject. At this point I also thank Jack Sheldon who, working alongside Nigel on various projects, allowed me to view some of the files he had accessed from the German archives. Many thanks go to Dave and Anita Platt of 'Beaumont Hamel View' guest house, Auchonvillers (http://www.beaumonthamel view.com) for some of the modern photographs that you will see in the pages of this book and for being available to me whenever I might have needed them for any 'on the spot' photographs or advice. I would also like to thank the staff of the Commonwealth War Graves Commission for going 'above and beyond' for their assistance in supplying (very comprehensive) details regarding the graves of French soldiers in the care of the commission.

Heartfelt thanks are due to my family: to my wife, Anita, for all the crucial encouragement in the writing of these books and for her patience, great company and understanding whilst dragging her to yet another battlefield on a regular basis (though it did take a while to convince her of the importance of driving down some dirt track in the middle of nowhere simply to photograph a hole in the ground or a, seemingly, insignificant lump of stone!); to my two boys, Billy and Harrison; and to my dog, *Eric le chien*, for trudging countless miles of battlefield with me over the years – even if Eric tended to prefer to chase things rather than indulge in any serious battlefield study!

An honorable mention is due to Mick 'Pugwash' Blackburn, whose constant nagging for a first edition of my last book encouraged me to write faster just to shut him up – a situation that did not change with the writing of this second book (he must have liked the first one!); and to the members of the East Lancashire Branch of the Western Front Association for all the support and encouragement in various projects and allowing me to indulge my interest by presenting several talks on the subject.

Finally, my thanks to perhaps the most significant people of all involved in the writing of this book, my last book and all my future books: my parents, Brian and Joyce O'Mara. From the massive support and encouragement – including taking me on my first fourteen of fifteen visits to the battlefields and funding the beginnings of my obsession – during the most formative years of my interest to the present day, no-one else could have been more influential.

Sources and Bibliography

French Language Sources:
14-18 Magazine Hors série: 'Guide de la Somme 1914-1918': Soudagne, Jean-Pascal, Éditions 14-18, 2006

28 Août 1914: Les combats de Le Transloy, Rocquigny, Sailly-Saillisel: Pasquet, Maurice, 1972

Atlas des Nécropoles Nationales: Ministère des anciens combattants et victimes de guerre, La documentation Français, 1994

De la Mort à la Mémoire: Yann, Thomas, OREP Editions, 2008

Guide des Cimetiéres Militaires en France: Grive –Santini, Catherine, le cherche midi éditeur, 1999

Guide Michelin Les champs de bataille 1914-1918 – Somme (Amiens, Péronne, Albert): Michelin & Cie./ECPAD, 2014

Journal Militaire officiel: Librairie Militaire R.Chapelot et Cie., Paris (various years 1899-1914)

Les Armées Françaises dans la Grande Guerre, Tome I 'La guerre de mouvement', Vols. 1 to 4: Service Historique, Ministére de la Guerre, 1925-1933

Les Armées Françaises dans la Grande Guerre, Tome II 'La stabilisation du Front – Les attaques locales': Service Historique, Ministére de la Guerre, 1931

Les Armées Françaises dans la Grande Guerre, Tome III 'Les Offensives de 1915-l'Hiver de 1915-1916': Service Historique, Ministére de la Guerre, 1923

Les Armées Françaises dans la Grande Guerre, Tome X, Ordres de bataille des grandes unités Vol.1 & 2: Service Historique, Ministére de la Guerre, 1923-24

La Grande Guerre sur le Front Occidental, Vol V– 'La Retraite sur la Seine': Palat, général Barthelemy-Edmond, Berger-Levrault, 1920

La Grande Guerre sur le Front Occidental, Vol VII – 'La Course à la Mer': Palat, général Barthelemy-Edmond, Berger-Levrault, 1921

La Grande Guerre sur le Front Occidental, Vol IX – 'Les Offensives de 1915': Palat, général Barthelemy-Edmond, Berger-Levrault, 1922

Mort au Combat!: Vauclair, Gilles, Editions-Sutton, 2015

Tranchées Magazine No.3: Ysec Éditions, October/November/December 2010

Regimental Histories:
5ᵉ régiment de dragons; Historique de la campagne 1914-1918: Charles-Lavauzelle, Henri. Paris 1920
8ᵉ régiment de Hussards; Campagne 1914-1918: (undated)
26ᵉ régiment d'infanterie; Historique 1914-1918: Berger-Levrault, Nancy-Paris-Strasbourg (undated)
34ᵉ régiment d'artillerie; Historique du régiment: Charles-Lavauzelle, Henri. Paris 1920
48ᵉ régiment d'infanterie; Historique du régiment Pendant la Campagne du 2 août 1914 au 11 novembre 1918: Oberthur 1920
233ᵉ régiment d'infanterie; Historique pendant la Grande Guerre: Doumoulin, J. Paris 1920
307ᵉ régiment d'artillerie; Historique du régiment pendant la Grande Guerre: Helluy & Cie., Angoulême 1920
'Arraõk – en Avant!' – Historique du 262ᵉ Régiment d'infanterie: Charles Lavauzelle et cie, Paris 1921
Historique des 28ᵉ et 228ᵉ régiments d'artillerie pendant la Guerre 1914-1918: Berger-Levrault, Nancy-Paris-Strasbourg (undated)
Historique des 52ᵉ et 252ᵉ régiments d'artillerie de campagne: Charles-Lavauzelle, Henri. Paris 1920
Historique des 137ᵉ et 337ᵉ régiments d'infanterie et des 84ᵉ et 284ᵉ régiments d'infanterie territoriale: Charles-Lavauzelle, Henri. Paris 1920
Historique du 1ᵉʳ régiment de dragons: Campagne contre l'Allemagne 1914-1919: (regimentally published, undated)
Historique du 2ᵉ bataillon de chasseurs â pied: Berger-Levrault, Paris 1922
Historique du 3ᵉ régiment de Hussards: Strasbourg (undated)
Historique du 4ᵉ bataillon de chasseurs â pied pendant la Guerre 1914-1918: Berger-Levrault, Nancy-Paris-Strasbourg (undated)
Historique du 6ᵉ régiment du génie: Demange, Angers 1920
Historique du 11ᵉ régiment d'infanterie territoriale, Guerre 1914-1918: Picard, Paris 1920
Historique du 12ᵉ régiment territoriale pendant la campagne 1914-1918: Charles-Lavauzelle, Henri. Paris 1920
Historique du 14ᵉ régiment d'infanterie: Privat, Edouard, Toulouse 1920
Historique du 14ᵉ régiment d'infanterie territoriale: Charles-Lavauzelle, Henri. Paris 1920
Historique du 14ᵉ régiment d'infanterie territoriale: Paillard (undated)
Historique du 16ᵉ régiment territoriale d'infanterie pendant la Guerre 1914-1918: Berger-Levrault, Nancy-Paris-Strasbourg (undated)

Historique du 18ᵉ régiment d'infanterie territoriale: Deugnier (*Lieut.*), Aune & cie., Paris 1921

Historique du 20ᵉ régiment de dragons pendant la Guerre 1914-1918: Berger-Levrault, Nancy-Paris-Strasbourg (undated)

Historique du 21ᵉ régiment d'artillerie de campagne: Berger-Levrault, Nancy-Paris-Strasbourg 1920

Historique du 21ᵉ régiment de dragons pendant la Guerre 1914-1918: Berger-Levrault, Nancy-Paris-Strasbourg (undated)

Historique du 21ᵉ régiment territoriale d'infanterie 1914-1919: Defontaine, Henri, Rouen 1920

Historique du 22ᵉ régiment territoriale d'infanterie 1914-1919: Wolf, Rouen (undated)

Historique du 25ᵉ régiment territoriale d'infanterie, Guerre 1914-1919: (Undated)

Historique du 26ᵉ régiment territoriale d'infanterie du 2 août 1914 au 10 août 1918: Protat Frères, Mayenne 1920

Historique du 28ᵉ territoriale d'infanterie: Chapelot, Paris (undated)

Historique du 37ᵉ régiment d'infanterie: Berger-Levrault, Nancy-Paris-Strasbourg (undated)

Historique du 62ᵉ régiment d'infanterie 1914-1918: Charles-Lavauzelle, Henri. Paris 1920

Historique du 65ᵉ régiment d'infanterie: Charles-Lavauzelle, Henri. Paris 1920

Historique du 69ᵉ régiment d'infanterie, Campagne 1914-1918: Chapelot, Paris (undated)

Historique du 70ᵉ régiment d'infanterie: Oberthur, Rennes 1920

Historique du 71ᵉ régiment d'infanterie pendant la Campagne contre l'Allemagne: Guyon, Francisque, St Brieuc, 1920

Historique du 75ᵉ infanterie; Campagne 1914-1918: Berger-Levrault, Nancy-Paris-Strasbourg (undated)

Historique du 83ᵉ régiment d'infanterie territoriale: Hammonet, E. La Roche sur Yon, 1920

Historique du 93ᵉ régiment d'infanterie: Hammonet, E. La Roche sur Yon, 1920

Historique du 116ᵉ régiment d'infanterie pendant la Guerre 1914-1919: Commelin, Vannes (undated)

Historique du 118ᵉ régiment d'infanterie au cours de la Guerre 1914-1918: Fournier, L. Paris 1923

Historique du 120ᵉ régiment d'infanterie pendant la Guerre 1914-1918: Watelet, Paris 1932

Historique du 135ᵉ régiment d'infanterie pendant la campagne du 2 août 1914 au 2 août 1919: (undated)

Historiques du 150ᵉ régiment d'infanterie et du 350ᵉ régiment d'infanterie: Fremont (undated)
Historique du 224ᵉ régiment d'infanterie: Charles-Lavauzelle, Henri. Limoges 1922
Historique du 243ᵉ régiment d'infanterie: (undated)
Historique du 250ᵉ régiment d'infanterie de réserve: Castanet, J. Bergerac 1920
Historique du 263ᵉ régiment d'infanterie: Charles-Lavauzelle, Henri. Paris 1920
Historique du 264ᵉ régiment d'infanterie 1914-1918: Demange, P. Angers 1920
Historique du 278ᵉ régiment d'infanterie: Charles-Lavauzelle, Henri. Paris 1921
Historique du 308ᵉ régiment d'infanterie: Castanet, J. Bergerac 1920
Historique du 316ᵉ régiment d'infanterie: Commelin, Vannes (undated)
Historique du 318ᵉ régiment d'infanterie: Fournier, L. Paris (undated)
Historique du 327ᵉ régiment d'infanterie: Fassiaux-Dufrene, P. St Amand les Eaux, 1920
Historique du 347ᵉ régiment d'infanterie: (undated)
Historique du 354ᵉ régiment d'infanterie: (undated)
Historique du 361ᵉ régiment d'infanterie: Dactylographie, 1918
Historique Sommaire du 41ᵉ régt d'infanterie: Charles-Lavauzelle, Henri. Paris 1920
Historique Sommaire du 64ᵉ régt d'infanterie: Charles-Lavauzelle, Henri. Paris (undated)
Historique Sommaire du 82ᵉ régt d'infanterie territoriale: Demange, P. Angers 1920
Le 4ᵉ Cuirassiers de 1914-1919: Rey.A, Lyon 1920
Le 4ᵉ régiment du génie pendant la Guerre 1914-1918: Nouvelle, Grenoble (undated)
Le 19ᵉ régiment d'infanterie pendant la Guerre 1914-1918: Berger-Levrault, Nancy-Paris-Strasbourg (undated)
Le 27ᵉ régiment territoriale d'infanterie dans la Grande Guerre: Chevalet, Alfred, Mamers 1920
Récits et Faits de Guerre du 9ᵉ régiment de cuirassiers 1914-1918: Société Français, Poitiers 1919
Le 45ᵉ régiment d'infanterie pendant la Guerre 1914-1918: Librairie Chapelot, Paris (undated)
Le 140ᵉ régiment d'infanterie pendant la Guerre 1914-1918: Berger-Levrault, Nancy-Paris-Strasbourg (undated)
Le 219ᵉ régiment d'infanterie pendant la Guerre 1914-1918: Brest 1920

Le 338ᵉ régiment d'infanterie pendant la Guerre 1914-1918: Ussel Fréres, Limoges 1920

Le Régiment Rose – Histoire du 265ᵉ régiment d'infanterie, 1914-1919: du Plessis, Jean. Payot, Paris, 1920.

Un régiment de Lorraine – Le 79ᵉ, Verdun-la Somme: Mangin, E. Payot, Paris, 1934

Journaux des marches et opérations (J.M.O.s) – **French War Diaries**
The vast majority of these are on the *Mémoire des hommes* website, owned and maintained by the *Service historique de la Défense* (a section of the *Ministère de la Défense*). They can be freely accessed at: http://www.memoiredeshommes.sga.defense.gouv.fr

English Language Sources
Before Endeavours Fade: Coombs, Rose E.B., After the Battle, (12th edition) 2006

Bloody Victory – The Sacrifice on the Somme: Philpott, William. Abacus, 2010

Handbook of the French Army 1914: General Staff, War Office, 1914 (reprinted by IWM & Battery Press, 1995)

Major & Mrs. Holt's Definitive Battlefield Guide to the Somme: Holt, Tonie & Valmai, Pen & Sword, 2016

History of the Great War Based on Official Documents – Military Operations: France and Belgium 1914 Vol.1 (revised edition): Edmonds, Brig.Gen. Sir James E, Macmillan & Co. Ltd, 1937

History of the Great War Based on Official Documents – Military Operations: France and Belgium 1915 Vol.2: Edmonds, Brig. Gen. Sir James E, Macmillan & Co. Ltd, 1928

History of the Great War Based on Official Documents – Military Operations: France and Belgium 1916 Vol.1: Edmonds, Brig. Gen. Sir James E, Macmillan & Co. Ltd, 1932

Paths of Glory – The French Army 1914-18: Clayton, Anthony, Cassell, 2003

Pyrrhic Victory: Doughty, Robert A. Harvard University Press, 2008

Serre: Horsfall, Jack & Cave, Nigel, Pen and Sword, 1996

The French Army 1914-18: Sumner, Ian, Osprey (Men at Arms), 1995

The French Army and the First World War: Greenhalgh, Elizabeth, Cambridge University Press, 2014

The German Army on the Somme 1914-1916: Sheldon, Jack, Pen and Sword, 2007

The Germans at Beaumont Hamel: Sheldon, Jack, Pen and Sword, 2006

The Germans at Thiepval: Sheldon, Jack, Pen and Sword, 2006
The Illustrated Michelin Guides to the Battlefields – The Somme Vol.1: Michelin & Cie., 1919
The March to the Marne – The French Army 1871-1914: Porch, Douglas, Cambridge Univesity Press, 1981
The Middlebrook Guide to the Somme Battlefields: Middlebrook, Martin & Mary, Viking 1991
The Other Side of the Wire (Volume 1): Whitehead, Ralph J., Helion & Co, 2010
The Somme 1916: Touring the French Sector: O'Mara, David, Pen and Sword, 2018
Underground Warfare 1914-1918: Jones, Simon, Pen and Sword, 2010
Walking the Somme (Second Edition): Reed, Paul, Pen and Sword, 2011

German Language Sources

Am Rande der Strassen – Frankreich, Belgien, Luxemburg und Niederlande: Volksbund Deutsche Kriegsgräberfürsorge e.V., 1989
Der Weltkrieg 1914 bis 1918: Band 5 -Der Herbst-Feldzug 1914; Im Westen bis zum Stellungskrieg, im Osten bis zum Rückzug: Mittler, Berlin 1929
Der Weltkrieg 1914 bis 1918: Band 6 – Der Herbst-Feldzug 1914; Der Abschluß der Operationen im Westen und Osten: Mittler, Berlin 1929
Der Weltkrieg 1914 bis 1918: Band 7 – Die Operationen des Jahres 1915; Die Ereignisse im Winter und Frühjahr: Mittler, Berlin 1931
Der Weltkrieg 1914 bis 1918: Band 8 – Die Operationen des Jahres 1915; Die Ereignisse im Westen im Frühjahr und Sommer, im Osten vom Frühjahr bis zum Jahresschluß: Mittler, Berlin 1932
Der Weltkrieg 1914 bis 1918: Band 9 – Die Operationen des Jahres 1915; Die Ereignisse im Westen und auf dem Balkan vom Sommer bis zum Jahresschluß: Mittler, Berlin 1933
Der Weltkrieg 1914 bis 1918: Band 10 – Die Operationen des Jahres 1916: bis zum Wechsel in der Obersten Heeresleitung: Mittler, Berlin 1936
Die 26. (Württembergische) Reserve-Division im Weltkrieg 1914–18. 1. Teil: Die Jahre 1914, 1915 und 1916. (Württembergs Heer im Weltkrieg, Band 6): von Soden, Franz, Bergers Literar, Stuttgart 1939
Militärgeschichtlicher Reiseführer zu den Schlachtfeldern des Ersten Weltkrieges in Flandern und Nordfrankreich: Klauer, Markus, 2004
Schlachten des Weltkrieges Band 20, Somme-Nord , I Teil: von Stosch, Albrecht (ed.), Gerhard Stalling, 1927

Index

A

Ablainzevelle, xix
Albert, 25, 35–7, 41–5, 71–2, 85, 115, 177, 186
  Battle of (1914), 26–46, 215–17
Allenby, Lieut Gen Edmund, 181
Auchonvillers, 87, 90, 132–3
Authuille, 33, 35, 41, 44–5, 90, 142–3, 162–3, 166
Aveluy, 33, 35, 41–2, 44, 142, 166, 179
Avesnes, xxi–xxii

B

Baju, *Chef-de-bataillon* Clément, 13
Balfourier, *Gén* Maurice, 181
Bapaume, xvii–xxx, 1, 10–11, 14–15, 28–30, 32–5, 54, 56–7, 60, 85
  Battle of (1871), xviii–xxii
Barastre, 11, 25, 54
Barnekow, Gen Christof von, xx, xxiii
Baumgarten, *Gén* Maurice, 99, 110
Bazaine, *Maréchal* François Achille, xiii–xiv
Bazentin, 35, 37
Beaucourt, 33, 42, 86–9, 136–7
Beaulencourt, 13, 32–3
Beaumont-Hamel, 33, 42, 45, 87–8, 93, 95, 97–9, 126, 140, 142, 152, 188
Becker, Philipp Oskar, xxvii
Bécourt, 63, 91–2, 140, 152, 169
Berdoulat, *Gén* Pierre, 181
Bertincourt, xx, 11, 18
Beugny, 13, 15–17, 20, 33, 54–5
Biefvillers, xix–xxi, xxvii, xxix–xxx, 56
Bihucourt, xx, xxix
Blanchard, *Adj-chef*, 24
Blondeau, *Médecin-maj*, 60
Boblet, *Col*, 17
Boisanger, *Lieut* Augustin Breart de, 164, 166
Bonodeau, *Sous-lieut*, 23
Bouchavesnes, 30, 50
Bourbaki, *Gen* Charles, xvi

British Army:
  Armies:
    Third, 115, 156, 179, 182
    Fourth, 181
  Corps:
    V, 116, 119, 126, 136
    X, 115, 156, 179
    XII, 115, 179
    XIII, 181
  Divisions:
    4th, 129
    5th, 115, 156, 158
    18th (Eastern), 67, 181
    22nd, 179
    26th, 179
    27th, 179
    30th, 181
    31st, 113, 124
    48th (South Midland), 115
    51st (Highland), 115, 152, 156, 158
  Brigades:
    14 Bde, 115, 158, 179
    153 Bde, 158
  Regiments:
    1/Devonshire Regt, 158
    1/DCLI, 158
    1/East Surrey Regt, 158
    1/King's Own (Royal Lancaster) Regt., 118
    1/Lancashire Fusiliers, 128
    1/Somerset Light Infantry, 118
    1/5 Cheshire Regt, 158
    1/6 Royal Warwickshire Regt, 115
    1/7 Black Watch, 152
    2/Manchester Regt, 158
Brodu, *Lt* Robert, 176–7
Brousmiche, *Lieut*, 17
Brunery, *Adj*, 23
Brunet, *Commdt*, 32
Bucquoy, xviii, 86
Bus, 11, 18, 20

228

C

Carnoy, 30, 36–7, 45, 47, 140, 144, 146, 153–5, 174–5
Castelnau, *Gén* Noël Édouard de, 99–102, 146, 181
Cemeteries – British:
 Albert Communal, 72
 Ancre, 136, 160
 Auchonvillers, 132
 Connaught, 160
 Englebelmer Communal, 130
 Fricourt New, 170
 Mailly-Maillet Communal, 129
 Ovillers, 163–6, 203
 Railway Hollow, 123–5, 203
 Redan Ridge No 1, 125–6, 128
 Redan Ridge No 2, 125–6, 128
 Serre Road No 1, 119, 125
 Serre Road No 2, 116, 128
 Sucrerie, 128–9
 Thiepval, 161, 203
Cemeteries – French:
 Albert, 71, 177, 203
 Albert Communal, 72
 Amiens 'Saint Acheul', 203
 Amiens 'Saint Pierre', 204
 Beaumont-Hamel 'Cimetière de Serre-Hébuterne', 115, 119–20, 204
 Biaches, 204
 Bray-sur-Somme, 204
 Cerisy, 204
 Cléry-sur-Somme ' Le Bois des Ouvrages', 205
 Dompierre-Becquincourt, 205
 Éclusier-Vaux, 202
 Etinehem 'La Côte 80', 205
 Hattencourt, 205
 Le Transloy, 57–8
 Lihons, 206
 Maucourt, 206
 Maurepas, 206
 Moislains 'Cimetière de la Charente', 50–1, 206
 Rancourt, 207
 Thiepval Anglo-French, 161, 203
 Villers-Carbonnel, 207
Cemeteries – German:
 Fricourt, 171

Chapeau de Gendarme, 139, 155, 158, 177
Chaulnes, 5, 25, 28, 99
Cléry sur Somme, 11, 30, 81
Collardet, *Chef de bataillon*, 16
Combles, xx, 9–12, 15, 20, 30, 33, 60
Commailleau, *Chef de bataillon* Marcel, 12
Contalmaison, 34–5, 37–40, 63–4
Costebonel, *Col* Paul Léon, 130–2
Cornulier-Luciniere, *Gén,* 11
Courcelette, 35, 40–1, 46, 62, 71
Crouchet, *Capt*, 23
Curlu, 30, 35–7, 146, 177–8

D

Delagrange, *Col*, xix
Delaunay, *Sous-lieut*, 22
Demerville, *Adj*, 23
Dompierre, 76, 155, 188
Douay, *Gén* Abel, xiv
Drapier, *Capt*, 23
Duchêne, *Gén* Denis Auguste, 181
Dubail, *Gén* Augustin, 179

E

Écochard, *Lieut-col* Joseph, 110–11
Ervillers, xix–xx, xxviii

F

Faidherbe, *Gén* Louis, xvi–xx, xxii–xxv, xxx
Fargny, 115, 139, 155–8, 177–8, 181
Farms:
 Beauregard, 42, 46, 68, 70–1, 85–7
 La Signy, 96, 123
 Monacu, 28, 30, 80
 Mouquet, 40, 45, 66–7, 84, 166
 Toutvent, 86, 99–109, 112–13, 121–3
 Waterlot, 12, 33–4, 60–1
Farre, *Gén* Jean Joseph, xvi
Favreuil, xx–xxii, xxvii
Fay, 155
Fayolle, *Gen* Emile, 181
Félix, *Sdt* Pascal François, 71
Feuillères, 28–30, 80–1, 138
Flamini, *Capt*, 24
Flers, 12, 15, 32–3, 59, 62–3
Fockedey, *Capt* Maurice Hippolyte

Marie Joseph, 61
Foncquevillers, 95
Fontenay, *Capt* Aimé Edouard de, 130–2
French Army:
  Armies:
    Armée de Châlons (1870-71), xiv–xv
    Armée de la Loire (1870-71), xvi, xxiii
    Armée de l'Est (1870-71), xvi, xxiii
    Armée de Paris (1870-71), 4
    Armée des Vosges (1870-71), xvi
    Armée du Rhin (1870-71), xiii–xiv
    Armée du Nord (1870-71), xvi–xxx
    Second, 99, 102–103, 146
    Fifth, 9
  Corps:
    I CA (1870), xiv–xv
    I CAC, 181
    II CA (1870), xiii
    II CA, 181
    III CA (1870), xiii
    IV CA, 28
    V CA (1870), xv
    XI CA, 98–9, 101–102, 109–10, 141
    XIV CA (1870), 4
    XX CA, 181–3
    XXII CA (1871), xviii, xx
    XXIII CA (1871), xix–xx, 4
    XXXV CA, 181
  Divisions:
    1 DC, 28, 216
    2 DI (1870-71), xiv
    3 DC, 10
    4 DI, 5
    5 DC, 28, 217
    5 DI, 179
    6 DI, 179
    8 DC, 87, 218
    8 DI, 141
    10 DC, 28–30, 81, 217
    11 DI, 28–30, 35–6, 80, 82, 181, 215
    19 DI, 42, 215
    21 DI, 35, 96, 100, 102, 114–15, 128, 136, 141, 215, 219
    22 DI, 35, 45, 95, 115, 139–41, 152, 215, 217
    27 DI, 100, 219
    28 DI, 115, 154, 156
    39 DI, 139, 181
    51 DI, 101, 112, 219
    53 DI, 139–42, 154
    56 DI, 96, 101, 115, 219
    59 DLI (1940), 7
    61 DI, 10–12, 16–17, 25, 60, 214
    62 DI, 10–11, 17–18, 25, 32, 54, 56–7, 214
    71 DI (1939), 7
    81 DIT, 28, 86, 95, 216, 218
    82 DIT, 28, 32–4, 45–6, 62, 69–70, 86–7, 141, 216, 218
    84 DIT, 9, 12, 28, 33, 214, 216
    88 DIT, 28, 32–3, 44–5, 56, 86–7, 216, 218
    151 DI, 115, 154, 156
    154 DI, 115, 179
    Division Derroja (1871), xviii–xxii
    Division du Bessol (1871), xix–xxii, xxv, xxvii, xxix–xxx
    Division Payen (1871), xxix–xxii, xxvii–xxviii
    Division Robin (1871), xix–xxiii
  Brigades:
    10 Bde, 121
    16 Bde, 141
    21 Bde, 37, 215
    22 Bde, 215
    37 Bde, 215
    38 Bde, 215
    41 Bde, 39, 43, 141, 215, 219
    42 Bde, 215, 219
    43 Bde, 131–2, 215, 217
    44 Bde, 89, 162, 216–17
    53 Bde, 100, 109–10, 219
    78 Bde, 139
    101 Bde, 112–13, 118, 124, 219
    105 Bde, 144
    112 Bde, 219
    121 Bde, 60, 214
    122 Bde, 13, 15, 53, 214
    123 Bde, 20, 57, 214
    124 Bde, 17–20, 214
    161 Bde, 216, 218
    162 Bde, 216, 218
    163 Bde, 62, 216, 218
    164 Bde, 216, 218
    167 Bde, 32, 216
    168 Bde, 216
    175 Bde, 216, 218

176 Bde, 44, 68, 216, 218
Regiments:
1 RD, 214
1 RC, 216
1 BCP, 217
1 RAM, 219
2 BCP, 43, 74, 215
2 RAC, 219
2 RC, 217
2 RAM, 219
4 *Régt du Génie,* 97, 198
4 BCP, 215
4 RAC, 218
5 *régt de chass. à ch.*, 217
6 *Régt du Génie,* 97–8, 128–9, 140, 148–53, 198
6 RD, 216
8 RAC, 37, 217
9 RD, 217
10 RD, 217
11 RIT, 216, 218
11 RAC, 217–18
11 RD, 218
12 RIT, 216, 218
12 RH, 218
13 RAC, 217–18
13 RAP, 219
14 RIT, 216, 218
14 RAC, 217–18
14 *régt. de chass. à ch.*, 218
15 *régt. de chass. à ch.*, 217
15 RD, 217
15 BCP, 218
15 RAC, 219
16 RIT, 216, 218
16 RD, 217
17 RIT, 63, 216, 218
17 RD, 218
18 BCP, 41
18 RIT, 32–3, 59, 63, 85, 216, 218
18 RD, 218
19 RI, 35, 142–3, 146, 150, 152, 159, 163–4, 216–17
19 RD, 217
20 RD, 18, 214, 217
20 RAC, 217–18
21 RAC, 215, 218
21 RIT, 32–3, 46, 70–1, 86, 216
22 RD, 217

22 RI, 155, 157, 216
22 RIT, 32–3, 35, 86, 122, 218
23 RD, 216
25 RIT, 216
25 RAC, 219
26 RI, 75, 82, 92–3, 170, 215
26 RIT, 32, 54, 216
26 BCP, 217
26 RD, 218
27 RAC, 219
27 RIT, 32, 216
27 RD, 216
28 RAC, 217–18
28 RIT, 12, 54, 71, 214, 216
28 RAC, 215
29 RAC, 217–18
29 RD, 217
29 BCP, 217
29 RAC, 217
32 RD, 216
32 RAC, 219
34 RAC, 18–19, 52, 215
35 RAC, 215, 217–18
37 RI, 43, 74, 178, 215
39 RAC, 91, 217
40 RAC, 219
41 RAC, 219
41 RI, 215
44 RAC, 217
45 RI, 30, 144–6
48 RI, 215
51 RAC, 39, 64, 215, 217, 219
52 RAC, 215
61 RAC, 217–18
62 RI, 35, 131–2, 142, 147, 215, 217
64 RI, 35, 38, 40, 64, 66, 104, 107–108, 123–4, 141, 147–8, 159, 163, 215, 219
65 RI, 35, 43, 63, 73, 82, 96, 136, 141, 148–50, 163, 215, 219
69 RI, 30, 36, 76–9, 215
70 RI, 215
71 RI, 42, 215
75 RI, 110–12, 219
79 RI, 215
81 RIT, 216, 218
82 RIT, 32–3, 38, 42, 64, 67–8, 216, 218
83 RIT, 32–3, 42, 136, 216, 218

231

84 RIT, 33, 42, 56, 87, 136, 216, 218
92 RI, 115
93 RI, 35, 38, 40, 64, 66, 103–104, 106, 122–3, 215, 219
99 RI, 155
115 RI, 141, 144–5
116 RI, 35, 88, 90, 136, 143, 163, 215, 217
117 RI, 141, 144
118 RI, 35, 144, 147–9, 163, 216, 217
120 RI, 1–7, 48, 187
137 RI, 35, 38, 63–4, 66, 98, 103–104, 106–107, 110–11, 114, 122, 126, 215, 219
140 RI, 111–12, 219
156 RI, 91
160 RI, 90, 92–3, 139, 170
205 RI, 140, 144, 146, 174
219 RI, 13, 15, 53, 214
224 RI, 144–6, 176–7
228 RI, 144–5
233 RI, 101, 113, 219
236 RI, 144–5
243 RI, 101, 112–13, 119–20, 219
250 RI, 20, 214
262 RI, 12–14, 53–4, 214
263 RI, 17–18, 20, 25, 54, 57, 214
264 RI, 11, 214
265 RI, 11–12, 60–1, 214
278 RI, 17, 20–1, 24, 54, 214
293 RI, 154
307 RI, 18–19, 214
308 RI, 17–19, 214
316 RI, 12, 15, 214
318 RI, 13, 15–17, 53, 214
319 RI, 144
327 RI, 101, 113, 219
329 RI, 139, 144
338 RI, 17, 20–5, 53–4, 57, 214
361 RI, 219
403 RI, 155
410 RI, 155
Frossard, *Gen* Charles August, xiii
Fricourt, 35, 39–40, 42–3, 47, 73–4, 76, 82, 84, 90–2, 138–40, 146, 152–4, 170–1
Foch, *Gen* Ferdinand, 179, 181
Foncquevillers, 95
Frise, 28, 97, 115, 154–5, 179

G
Gaborit, *Capt*, 22–3
Gallieni, *Gén* Joseph, 179
Gambetta, Léon, xvi
Garibaldi, Guiseppe, xvi
Germain, *Chef de bataillon*, 15–16
German Army:
Armies:
First (1870-71), xiv, xvii, xxiii
First (1914), 9
Third (1870-71), xiv–xv
Fourth (1870-71), xv
Sixth, 32
Corps:
I Kgl Bay AK (1870-71), xv
I Kgl Bay AK, 28, 30, 80
II AK, 9, 25
II Kgl Bay AK (1870-71), xiv
II Kgl Bay AK, 28, 30, 35–7
III AK, 10
IV AK (1870-71), xv
IV AK, 10, 85
IV RK, 25
V AK (1870-71), xiv
VIII AK (1870-71), xxvii
XI AK (1870-71), xiv–xv
XIV RK, 32–3, 35–6, 85, 41, 85
XVIII AK, 28
XXI AK, 28
Garde, 85
Divisions:
1 Garde ID, 85, 87, 95
3 Kgl Bay ID, 30, 35, 88
4 Kgl Bay ID, 30, 35, 88
15 ID (1871), xx
16 ID (1871), xx
26 RID, 35, 38, 56, 71, 84
28 RID, 33, 35, 37, 54, 91, 170
Brigades:
8 Art (1870-71), xxvii
15 Kav (1870-71), xxvii
26 Kav, 33
32 Inf (1870-71), xiii
51 Res-Inf, 40, 44–5, 66, 68, 84, 89
52 Res-Inf, 38–9
55 Res-Inf, 37
Regiments:
F.R.40 (1870-71), xiii, xxii
IR 170, 114

232

IR 180, 41–2, 44, 67–8, 84, 143, 162
Kgl Bay IR 5, 39, 82, 88
Kgl Bay IR 17–18
Kgl Bay RIR 1, 119
RIR 40, 39, 42–3, 74, 76, 82, 92, 145
RIR 99, 41–2, 45, 68–70, 87–90, 98, 136
RIR 109, 38–9, 42–3, 59, 63, 139, 146
RIR 110, 87–8, 96, 140
RIR 111, 39, 43, 74, 92–3, 144
RIR 119, 38, 40, 45, 66, 89, 98, 125, 143, 149, 151–2
RIR 120, 38, 63–4, 92–3, 139, 143, 147–51
RIR 121, 41, 44, 90, 118, 143, 162, 166
Ginchy, 10–12, 32–3, 58-62
Glory Hole (*see* Îlot de la Boisselle)
Goeben, Gen August Karl Friedrich von, xx, xxiii
Gommecourt, 42, 86, 179
Gough, Lieut Gen Hubert, 181
Granathof/Granatenhof (*see* Îlot de la Boisselle)
Granatloch (*see* Cote 141)
Grandcourt, 41–2, 46–7, 68–9
Grévillers, xix–xxii
Guérin, *Capt* Raoul, 111
Guillemont, 33–4, 60–1

H

Haig, Gen Douglas, 179–80
Hamel, 33, 41–2, 44, 68, 90, 96, 131, 136
Haplincourt, 11, 17, 20, 54
Hardecourt-aux-Bois, 30, 33, 144–5, 176
Hawthorn Ridge, 87, 90, 136
Hébuterne, 86–7, 95–8, 115
 First Battle of, 85–7, 122, 217–18
 Second Battle of, 99–114
Heidenkopf Redoubt, 118
Heights:
 Cote 106, 91–3, 170
 Cote 110, 39, 43, 74, 76, 82, 91, 138–40, 144, 146, 153, 171–5
 Cote 123, 20, 24, 54
 Cote 125, 144
 Cote 128, 18

Cote 129, 24
Cote 137, 33
Cote 141, 89–90, 162
Cote 143, 87–8, 93, 95–8, 126–8
Cote 150, 44
Cote 151 (Auchonvillers), 131
Hem, 30

I

Îlot de la Boisselle, xxiii, 39, 64, 160, 144, 147–52, 168–9
Imbert-Laboiseille, *Capt*, 24

J

Jacquot, *Gén* Charles, 181
Joffre, *Gén* Joseph, 8–9, 99–100, 112, 179–81

L

La Boisselle, xxiii, 35, 38–40, 45, 47, 63–4, 84, 89, 139–58, 166–9
Lalauze, *Sergt-maj*, 12
Langle de Cary, *Gén* Fernand de, 179
Lebucquière, 17–18
Lecointe, *Gén* Alphonse- Théodore, xviii
Le Forest, 11, 30
Leipzig Redoubt (*see* Cote 141)
Leipzig Salient (*see* Cote 141)
Lejoindre, *Sdt 2Cl* Pierre Georges, 59
Le Sars, 46
Lesboeufs, 12, 15, 32–4, 54, 62
Lespignal, *Sergt-maj*, 23
Le Transloy, 14–17, 20–2, 24, 32–3, 54, 57–8
Ligny-Thilloy, xxx
Longueval, 11, 25, 32–5, 61

M

Mailly-Maillet, 97, 128–30
Mametz, 30, 36–8, 45, 47, 76, 84, 90, 139, 144–5
Manteuffel, Gen Hans Edwin von, xvii
Margueritte, *Gén* Jean Auguste, xv
Maricourt, 30, 36–7, 80, 144–6
Martinpuich, 15, 84
Maurepas, 30
Méaulte, 74, 153
Merzaux, *Lieut*, 24

233

Mesnil-Martinsart, 35, 41, 44, 90
Micheler, *Gen* Joseph, 181
Michelet, *Col* Hippolyte, xix, xxviii
Miraumont, 41–2, 45–7, 68–71
Moislains, 18–20, 26, 50–2
Moltke, Field Marshal Helmuth von, xv
Monacu Farm, 28, 30, 80
Monclin, *Capt* Henri Thiéron de, 76–8
Mont St Quentin, 50
Morval, 12, 14–15, 18, 20–4, 54

N
Nigot, *Capt*, 22

O
Oden, Lieut Siegmund, xxv–xxvii
O'Kelly, *Capt* Conor, 4
O'Neill, *Col* Armand, 4–5
Ovillers, 36, 38, 40–1, 45, 64–6, 72, 84, 89, 138–43, 146–7, 163–8

P
Péronne, xvii–xviii, xx, 1–5, 9–11
  Siege of (1870-71), xviii, xxiii, 1
  Battle of (1914), 9–25
Pfister, *Sergt* Georges, 59
Pichon, *Sous-Lieut*, 143
Pittié, *Col*, xxii
Point 110 (*see* Cote 110)
Point 323, 118
Poitou-Deplessy, *Capt*, 107
Pozières, xxiii, 35, 38, 63–4, 84
Puisieux, xviii, 45, 86–7, 95

R
Rabache, *Sous-lieut*, 24
Rancourt, 15, 188
Rawlinson, Lieut Gen Henry, 181
Redan Ridge (*see* Cote 143)
Robert, *Lieut-col*, 20, 23–4
Rocquigny, 18–20, 24, 32, 54
Roy, *Adj*, 22

S
Sailly-au-Bois, 86
Sailly-Saillisel, xx, 11, 13–18, 20–5, 32, 51–4

Sapignies, xix–xxi, 15–16
Schmitz, *Col*, 15–16
Serre, 32, 45, 86, 95–6, 98–101, 109–13, 116–21
Soden, Gen Franz Ludwig von, 56, 84
Souabaut, *Lieut* Alexandre, 13
Stuhl, *Lieut-col*, 15
Suzanne, 156, 178, 182

T
Tambour, 153–4, 170–1
Testelin, Achille, xvi
Therade, *Sous-lieut*, 22
Thiepval, 33, 35, 40–1, 45–7, 66–8, 84–5, 89–90, 142–3, 160–1
Thomassin, *Sdt* François Henri, 75, 172
Toutvent/Touvent, 86, 98–109, 121–3
Trochu, *Gén* Louis-Jules, xvi

V
Vaulx-Vraucourt, 16, 85
Vaux, 178, 202
Vélu, 17
Verdun, xiv, 6–8, 180–2
Villers-au-Flos, 17, 24, 32

W
Woods:
  Bois d'Authuille (Authuille Wood), 44–5, 68, 90, 138, 143, 162–3
  Bois d'Authuille (Thiepval Wood), 41, 68, 90, 143, 159–60
  Bois d'Aveluy, 41
  Bois de Bernafay, 35, 145, 176, 181
  Bois de Maricourt, 17, 80, 157, 181
  Bois des Trônes, 60
  Bois des Vaux, 18–19, 51
  Bois Favière, 145
  Bois St Pierre Vaast, 18–19, 51
  Wunderwerk [Wundwerk] (*see* Cote 141)

Y
Ypres, 47, 83, 180